Learning from the Enemy

An Intellectual History of
Antifascism in Interwar Europe

Marco Bresciani

VERSO

London • New York

This volume was published with a contribution from the Department of Political and Social Sciences of the University of Florence as part of the project 'The Inglorious Thirties?' and realized with funds from the European Union Next Generation-EU, MUR DM 737/2021, and co-financing from the Fondazione Cassa di Risparmio di Firenze.

This revised English-language edition first published by Verso 2024
Translation © Marco Bresciani 2024
First published as *Quale antifascismo? Storia di Giustizia e Libertà*
© Carocci 2017

1 3 5 7 9 10 8 6 4 2

Verso
UK: 6 Meard Street, London W1F 0EG
US: 388 Atlantic Avenue, Brooklyn, NY 11217
versobooks.com

Verso is the imprint of New Left Books

ISBN-13: 978-1-80429-227-3
ISBN-13: 978-1-80429-228-0 (UK EBK)
ISBN-13: 978-1-80429-229-7 (US EBK)

British Library Cataloguing in Publication Data
A catalogue record for this book is available from the British Library

Library of Congress Cataloging-in-Publication Data

Names: Bresciani, Marco, author.
Title: Learning from the enemy : an intellectual history of Antifascism in
   interwar Europe / Marco Bresciani.
Description: London ; New York : Verso, 2024. | Includes bibliographical
   references and index.
Identifiers: LCCN 2023055168 (print) | LCCN 2023055169 (ebook) | ISBN
   9781804292273 (trade paperback) | ISBN 9781804292297 (ebook)
Subjects: LCSH: Giustizia e Libertà (Antifascist group) | Anti-fascist
   movements—Europe—History—20th century. | Europe—Politics and
   government—20th century.
Classification: LCC D726.5 .B74 2024 (print) | LCC D726.5 (ebook) | DDC
   320.53/3094—dc23/eng/20240208
LC record available at https://lccn.loc.gov/2023055168
LC ebook record available at https://lccn.loc.gov/2023055169

FSC
www.fsc.org
MIX
Paper | Supporting
responsible forestry
FSC® C171272

Typeset in Minion by Hewer Text UK Ltd, Edinburgh
Printed and bound by CPI Group (UK) Ltd, Croydon CR0 4YY

A Brechtian maxim:

'Don't start from the good old things, but the bad new ones.'

Walter Benjamin, *Conversations with Brecht*
25 August 1938, Svendborg, Denmark

Contents

Acknowledgements

I first started working on the themes that this book deals with in the mid-1990s. It was during the thrilling period marked by the aftermaths of the 1989/1993 transitions and the subsequent challenges in East Central Europe as well as in Italy, by the European integration and by the heated debates on the legacies left by World War II and the Cold War, and by the twentieth century in general, that I decided to focus on the complex relations between communism and antifascism in the 1930s. My approach aimed to reframe these themes within a European perspective, with a special emphasis on the Italian–French connections within that sphere, and on the circulation of political cultures through the experience of exile in Paris. My early research and publications were devoted to the life of the Russian-born revolutionary and intellectual Andrea Caffi, and to his relationship with his friend and interlocutor Nicola Chiaromonte. I then broadened my field of interest to the entire revolutionary antifascist group founded by Carlo Rosselli – 'Giustizia e Libertà' (GL) – and its cultural networks in France (with special attention to the French historian Élie Halévy), as well as among international émigrés in the 1930s. Over the course of my research, new questions arose as a result of changes witnessed in the initial years of the twenty-first century, in the form of economic crisis, illiberal and antidemocratic threats, and international instability, which have increased from 2008 up until now. My interests extended to include the combinations of, and differences between, antifascism and anti-totalitarianism, Cold War liberalism and socialism, and the relation-ship between East Central European dissidents and Western political cultures.

My focus on the experiences of political émigrés led me to search for sources in different countries, collecting a large amount of rare or unpub-lished documents from libraries and archives in Italy and elsewhere. In this regard, I want to warmly thank all the archivists and librarians who offered their kind help during my research work.

Over time, friends and colleagues generously encouraged and discussed my research work and stimulated different areas of interest related to this book. Among others, I would like especially to thank: Aldo Agosti, Giulia Albanese, Ersilia Alessandrone Perona, Michele Battini, Antonio Bechelloni, David Bidussa, Francesco Capello, Francesco Cassata, Paola Cattani, Ettore Cinnella, Giovanni De Luna, Diego Dilettoso, Patrizia Dogliani, Marcello Flores, Guido Franzinetti, Carlo Ginzburg, Piero Graglia, Andrea Graziosi, Patrice Gueniffey, Mario Isnenghi, Tony Judt, Giovanni Levi, Simon Levis Sullam, Sergio Luzzatto, Cesare Panizza, Matteo Pasetti, Claudio Pavone, Gianni Perona, Stéfanie Prezioso, Christophe Prochasson, Andrea Ricciardi, Mariuccia Salvati, Domenico Scarpa, Guri Schwarz, Simone Neri Serneri, Pasquale Terracciano, Nicola Tranfaglia, Gabriele Turi, Nadia Urbinati, Cesare Vagge, Antonello Venturi, and Roberto Vivarelli.

This book is a revised and adapted version of *Quale antifascismo? Storia di Giustizia e Libertà*, Rome: Carocci, 2017. That work was awarded the Giorgio Agosti Prize by the Istituto Piemontese per la Storia della Resistenza e della Società Contemporanea (2017) and the Giacomo Matteotti Prize by the Presidenza del Consiglio dei Ministri (2018). I want to thank the publishing house, Carocci, and its editor Gianluca Mori, for permitting the republication of this work in a new English edition by Verso Books. Additionally, I want to thank Sebastian Budgen for consider-ing publishing it. Finally, I thank the translator Patrick Barr for his careful revision of my English.

I am especially grateful to the following colleagues and friends for care-fully and patiently reading earlier drafts of this volume: Michele Battini, Guido Franzinetti, Joseph Fronczak, Hugo Garcia, Carlo Ginzburg, Andrea Graziosi, Michael Seidman, Guri Schwarz, Iain Stewart, Nadia Urbinati, and Antonello Venturi. Their critical comments and helpful suggestions have undoubtedly improved the manuscript, although the responsibility for any flaws and errors remains exclusively mine.

A great deal of gratitude goes to my parents, Saveria and Renato, and my sister Sara, who never cease to follow my stubborn passion for history and to help me in the face of several professional uncertainties. I hope that the fruits of this effort will be taken as a small reward.

My special thanks to Mila for the time she has given and continues to give me, and I apologize for the time I have had to take from her in writing this book. For our many conversations about history and politics, this book, which she was the first to read, is as much her work as it is mine. Most importantly, without her I would not have realized how good it can be to share a lifetime of affection and ideas. I dedicate this book to Mila and to our son Niko, who cultivated a love of turtles from an early age.

Archives and Libraries

Italy

Archivio Centrale dello Stato, Rome
Archivio di Stato, Florence (C. Rosselli Papers)
Archivio di Stato, Turin (L. Ginzburg Papers)
Associazione Nazionale per gli Interessi del Mezzogiorno d'Italia, Rome
  (A. Caffi Papers)
Fondazione Alfred Lewin, Biblioteca Gino Bianco, Forlì (A. Caffi Papers;
  M. Levi Papers)
Biblioteca Nazionale Centrale, Florence (C. Rosselli Papers)
Centro Studi Piero Gobetti, Turin (U. Calosso Papers; S. Trentin Papers)
Centro Documentazione e Ricerca Trentin, Venice (S. Trentin Papers)
Fondazione Giangiacomo Feltrinelli, Milan (A. Tasca Papers)
Istituto Storico Toscano della Resistenza e dell'Età Contemporanea,
  Florence (Giustizia e Libertà Papers; C. Rosselli Papers; F. Schiavetti
  Papers)
Istituto Piemontese per la Storia della Resistenza e della Società
  Contemporanea, Turin (A. Garosci Papers; U. Calosso Papers)

France

Archives Nationales de France, Fontainebleau
Bibliothèque de Lettres et Sciences Humaines, École Normale
  Supérieure-rue d'Ulm, Paris (É. Halévy Papers)
Bibliothèque de Documentation Internationale Contemporaine (now La
  Contemporaine), Nanterre, Paris

Switzerland

Biblioteca cantonale, Lugano (G. Prezzolini Papers)

Netherlands

International Institute for Social History, Amsterdam (V. Voitinsky
  Papers)

United States

Beinecke Library, New Haven (N. Chiaromonte Papers)
Columbia University Library, New York (M. Osorgin Papers)

Abbreviations

CGT	Confédération Générale du Travail
CSAR	Comité Secret d'Action Révolutionnaire
GL	Giustizia e Libertà
GL	*Giustizia e Libertà. Movimento unitario di azione per l'autonomia operaia, la repubblica socialista, un nuovo umanesimo* (weekly magazine)
Pd'A	Partito d'Azione
PCd'I	Partito Comunista d'Italia
POB	Parti Ouvrier Belge
POUM	Partido Obrero de Unificación Marxista
SFIO	Section Française de l'International Ouvrière

List of Plates

1. The editorial board of *Non mollare*, 1925. Istituto Storico Toscano per la Storia della Resistenza e dell'Età Contemporanea, Florence. Archivio Giustizia e Libertà/Carlo Rosselli 11/2.4.5, photo 139.

2. The flight of Carlo Rosselli, Emilio Lussu, and Francesco Fausto Nitti from the island of Lipari. Istituto Storico Toscano per la Storia della Resistenza e dell'Età Contemporanea, Florence. Archivio Giustizia e Libertà/Carlo Rosselli 11/2.4.2., photo 18.

3. Arrival of Carlo Rosselli, Emilio Lussu, Francesco Fausto Nitti, Oxilia, at Cap Bon, in southern France, 1929. Istituto Storico Toscano per la Storia della Resistenza e dell'Età Contemporanea, Florence. Archivio Giustizia e Libertà/Carlo Rosselli 11/2.4.4., photo 33.

4. Marion Cave with Nello and Carlo Rosselli on the sea front of Ostenda, 1930. Istituto Storico Toscano per la Storia della Resistenza e dell'Età Contemporanea, Florence. Archivio Giustizia e Libertà/Carlo Rosselli 11/2.4.4., photo 138.

5. Carlo Rosselli walking at the Bois de Boulogne with his son John, 1930. State Archive of Florence, Rosselli R-16395, Carlo37. Courtesy of the Ministry of Culture/State Archive of Florence.

6. Carlo and Nello Rosselli in France, 1934. State Archive of Florence, Rosselli R-16402, Carlo44. Courtesy of the Ministry of Culture/State Archive of Florence.

7. French historian Elie Halévy, close friend of Carlo Rosselli. Istituto Storico

Introduction

Which Antifascism?

More than a century after the March on Rome, which marked the coming to power of Fascism in Italy in October 1922, public and scholarly debate about antifascism remains as popular and lively as ever. On the global scale, antifascism presents itself as a kaleidoscope of public languages and images, social experiences and memories, political cultures and practices. More recently, the rise of nationalist and populist movements and governments in Europe and elsewhere, together with the political, social, and cultural unrest caused by the Covid-19 pandemic, the widespread, often ambiguous debates about the 'crisis of democracy', and, last but not least, the war waged by Russia on Ukraine, all have contributed towards the resurgence of antifascist sentiments and movements opposed to illiberal, authoritarian threats, real or potential (often described as new forms of 'fascism' or even 'Nazism'). In this respect, antifascism is one of the most pervasive, divisive, ambivalent, and yet persistent legacies of the twentieth century, taking shape in different ways and at different paces between the two world wars, and going well beyond its original premises after 1945. Therefore, despite appearances, the meanings, forms, and implications of antifascism cannot be taken for granted.

What, then, is meant by the term 'antifascism', and how does it relate to the transformations of that radically new political phenomenon that was

Fascism, which took political power in Italy between 1919 and 1926? What does antifascism reveal about the political, social, and intellectual history of the interwar years during a time of Italian, European, and global crisis? How did the cultures and practices opposed to Mussolini's Italy and Hitler's Germany change between the 1920s and 1930s?[1]

Public narratives and historiographical reconstructions regarding antifascism remained within a national framework at least until 1989. Subsequently, several new approaches emerged that found theoretical and methodological form in transnational, European, and world history.[2] To speak of a transnational history of antifascism, or to see antifascism as a transnational phenomenon, undoubtedly challenges, not to say dismisses, any exclusively national approach to the theme. Research within a transnational framework includes new antifascist subjects from a truly global perspective; their paths and networks of relations in the non-European and colonial worlds are reconstructed, and questions are asked about antifascism's relationship with anti-colonialism and anti-imperialism, and with the labour and feminist movements.[3] The Italian war in Ethiopia (1935–36), and in particular the Spanish Civil War (1936–39), have recently taken on key significance as the makers of a 'global Left' attempting to overcome the former, nationally-embedded Left and to mobilize communists, socialists, anarchists, trade unionists, liberal democrats, and republicans all over the world in the name of antifascism.[4] In many ways this historiographical rethinking, despite its

---

1   'Fascism' with a capital *F* is used for Italian Fascism, while 'fascism' is used to indicate the broader generic phenomenon.

2   For a European take on antifascism, see Alberto De Bernardi and Paolo Ferrari (eds), *Antifascismo e identità europea*, Rome: Carocci, 2004.

3   See Hugo Garcia, Mercedes Yusta, Xavier Tabet, and Cristina Clìmaco (eds), *Rethinking Antifascism: History, Memory and Politics, 1922 to the Present*, New York: Berghahn, 2016; Hugo Garcia, 'Transnational History: A New Paradigm for Anti-Fascist Studies?', *European Contemporary History* 4, 2016, 563–72; Kasper Braskén, Nigel Copsey and David J. Featherstone (eds), *Anti-Fascism in Global Perspective: Transnational Networks, Exile Communities, Radical Internationalism*, London: Routledge, 2020.

4   Joseph Fronczak, 'Local People's Global Politics: A Transnational History of the "Hands Off Ethiopia Movement of 1935" ', *Diplomatic History* 39, no. 2, 2015, 245–74, but especially Fronczak, *Everything Is Possible: Antifascism and the Left in the Age of Fascism*, New Haven, CT: Yale University Press, 2023 (I thank the author for

multifaceted ideas and approaches, assumes the existence of 'a new, anti-fascist minimum' rooted in the Enlightenment and in democratic and universalist cultures, or 'a tripartite minimum' based on the desire to work against or fight fascism without adopting an uncompromising anti-totalitarian or anti-capitalist approach, to reject conspiratorial views based on antisemitism and anti-Bolshevism, and to embrace war rather than appeasement.[5] Accordingly, a distinction has been suggested between 'revolutionary antifascism' and 'conservative or even counter-revolutionary antifascism', with the former fighting both fascism and capitalism, while the latter aimed to restore the liberal democratic pre-fascist regimes.[6]

However, in order to adopt new approaches to 1930s antifascism, consolidated and layered forms of teleology need to be removed. The vantage point of 1945, the year in which the antifascist alliance saw victory over the Axis powers, still tends to subtly but decisively condition our understanding of the interwar period. In particular, it empha-sizes the asserted unity of national opposition or resistance to fascism, based on the coherent and consistent actions of individuals and groups prepared to fight against Mussolini's Italy and Hitler's Germany (at least in Europe). In the decades after World War II, autobiographical memoirs and historical works tended to reflect this pattern, endlessly reiterating mutually exclusive visions of fascism and antifascism, one-dimensional self-representations and militant perspectives revolving around the anti-fascist ideas of people, democracy, and nation. However, the experiences of individuals, movements, parties, and governments seeking to combat Italian Fascism in the interwar years were characterized by a series of

---

sending the manuscript, although I could not fully incorporate and discuss his theses in my own work); for insightful remarks see Hugo Garcia, ' "World Capital of Antifascism?" The Making – and Breaking – of a Global Left in Spain, 1936–1939', in Braskén, Copsey, and Featherstone, *Anti-Fascism in Global Perspective*, 234–53.

5   Nigel Copsey, 'Preface: Towards a New Antifascist "Minimum"?', in Nigel Copsey and Andrzej Olechnowicz (eds), *Varieties of Anti-Fascism: Britain in the Interwar Period*, Basingstoke: Palgrave Macmillan 2010, XIV–XXI. For a different, insightful reflection, see Tom Buchanan, 'Anti-Fascism and Democracy in the 1930s', *European History Quarterly* 32, no. 1, 2002, 39–57.

6   Michael Seidman, *Transatlantic Antifascisms: From the Spanish Civil War to the End of World War II*, Cambridge: Cambridge University Press, 2017.

uncertainties and ambiguities, ambivalences and contradictions.[7] The very notion that fascism was the 'enemy' was part of a convoluted, non-linear historical process comprising different understandings of Fascism as a movement and regime in flux, and of its relations with other European movements and regimes. Accordingly, this book aims to highlight the key role of political decisions and situations, the contingent, open-ended nature of national, transnational, and international political dynamics, the broad range of alternatives and expectations in the presence of fascism, and the multiple, often contradictory, social, intellectual, and political strategies and practices deployed to combat the Fascist and Nazi regimes.[8]

This book focuses on the revolutionary antifascist group Giustizia e Libertà (GL), founded by Carlo Rosselli in Paris in 1929. Unlike popular forms of antifascist resistance, GL represented a unique case of political and intellectual elites clearly embracing antifascism.[9] However, having neglected the case of GL for the first three postwar decades, Italian historiography has since examined the Resistance and the role that mass political parties, first and foremost the Communist Party of Italy (PCd'I), played in the 1943–45 struggle. Historians then broadened their focus to include the phenomenon of antifascism between the wars – but continued to underscore the role played by Italy's communists and socialists, and their relationship with democracy as such. Until the late 1970s, the historical analysis of GL reflected the memories of its former members and focused largely on Rosselli's biography, with the emphasis on his unwavering, uncompromising antifascism.[10] From the late 1970s on, scholarship began to investigate the political and cultural legacy that GL

---

7   For a broader approach, see Marco Bresciani, 'Becoming Antifascist: Uncertainties, Dilemmas and Contradictions vis-à-vis Italian Fascism', in Giulia Albanese (ed.), *Rethinking the History of Italian Fascism*, London: Routledge, 2022, 269–93.

8   A still useful reminder of the critical importance of contingency is Gerd-Rainer Horn, *European Socialists Respond to Fascism: Ideology, Activism, Contingency in the 1930s*, New York: Oxford University Press, 1996.

9   Tim Kirk and Anthony McElligott (eds), *Opposing Fascism: Community, Authority and Resistance in Europe*, Cambridge: Cambridge University Press, 1999.

10   Aldo Garosci, a former GL member and historian, wrote Rosselli's first comprehensive biography during his exile in the US (1942–43): Aldo Garosci, *Vita di Carlo Rosselli*, 2 vols, Florence: Vallecchi, 1973 (1945).

was to bequeath to the Partito d'Azione (Pd'A) and that was developed in the Resistance movement during the 1943–45 civil war in central-northern Italy.[11]

A constellation of processes and events dating back to the mid-1980s – including European integration, the slow decline of the Soviet Communist model and its sudden demise, the waning of mass political parties, and the crisis of the welfare state in Western democracies – catalysed interest in the political and intellectual debates within GL. From the early 1990s to the early 2000s, scholarly research focused on Rosselli's search for a 'third way' between socialism and liberalism, with particular attention paid to his relationship with Europe and the multifaceted hybridization of 'liberal socialism'.[12] At a time of serious instability in Italy's antifascist Republic, there was increasing historical work on the political and intellectual biographies of the members of Rosselli's group as part of a new interest in democratic, socialist and yet non-Marxist, traditions.[13] The end of the Cold War and the collapse of Soviet Communism also encouraged a critical reassessment of GL with regard to its quest for an antifascist, anti-totalitarian form of socialism and its limits or contradictions in terms of the evaluation and representation of the Russian Revolutions, Soviet Communism, and Stalin's dictatorship.[14]

GL thus represents an exceptional case study, an opportunity to reconsider the issues traditionally associated with antifascism and to grasp the

---

11 John Wilkinson, *The Intellectual Resistance in Europe*, Cambridge, MA: Harvard University Press, 1982, 195–260, and especially Claudio Pavone, *A Civil War: A History of Italian Resistance*, London: Verso, 2014 (1991). For the context of the most recent discussions, see Marco Bresciani, 'Fascism, Anti-Fascism, and the Idea of Nation: Historiography and Public Debate in Italy since the 1980s', *Contemporary European History* 30, no. 1, 2021, 111–23.

12 Nadia Urbinati, 'Introduction to Another Socialism', in Carlo Rosselli, *Liberal Socialism*, Princeton, NJ: Princeton University Press, 1994.

13 Stanislao Pugliese, *Carlo Rosselli: Socialist Heretic and Antifascist Exile*, Cambridge, MA: Harvard University Press, 1999.

14 See, for instance, Luciano Guerci and Giuseppe Ricuperati (eds), *Il coraggio della ragione. Franco Venturi intellettuale e storico cosmopolita*, Turin: Fondazione Einaudi, 1998; Antonio Bechelloni (ed.), *Carlo e Nello Rosselli e l'antifascismo europeo*, Milan: Franco Angeli, 2001; Alessandro Giacone and Eric Vial (eds), *I fratelli Rosselli: l'antifascismo e l'esilio*, Rome: Carocci, 2011.

latter's ambivalences and turns, its dilemmas and contradictions, while accounting for its multi-layered temporalities. It allows us to observe the different, contingent orientations that determined strategies and languages, relations between politics and culture, organizational forms of political struggle and visions of the future, within Italy and Europe (and beyond). However, the question of a comprehensive analysis of the GL group, its networks and cultures (not only of the political variety) within a European, transnational context, has until now remained open.[15] The present work takes on this challenge by analysing: a) the biographical trajectories of GL's activists; b) the political-intellectual networks of emigration and conspiracy within the context of the 1930s; and c) the long-term premises, developments, and legacies of interwar political cultures. Therefore, this book is at once something more and something less than a comprehensive history of the organized group of GL.

A European, transnational approach is indispensable in the case of a group like GL, the existence of which was only conceivable in exile. Until recently, historians had largely ignored this question of exile. The psychological and existential disorientation and deracination caused by exile have two important cognitive implications. On the one hand, exile offers a privileged view of the deeper social and political dynamics transcending national borders. On the other, it enables a critical perspective on one's political and emotional connections with national tradition, which is either overcome or recouped within a cosmopolitan, European framework.[16] Recent interest in the question of exile has been encouraged by

---

15   Mark Mazower, 'Fascism and Democracy Today: What Use Is the Study of History in the Current Crisis?', *European Law Journal* 3, May 2016, 384.

16   See Edward Said, *Reflections on Exile and Other Essays*, Cambridge, MA: Harvard University Press, 2000; Carlo Ginzburg, 'Straniamento. Preistoria di un procedimento letterario', in *Occhiacci di legno. Nove riflessioni sulla distanza*, Milan: Feltrinelli, 1998, 15–39; Carlo Ginzburg, 'Particolari, primi piani, microanalisi. In margine a un libro di Sigfried Kracauer', in *Il filo e le tracce. Vero falso finto*, Milan: Feltrinelli, 2006, 225–40; Enzo Traverso, *Cosmopoli. Figure dell'esilio ebraico-tedesco*, Verona: Ombre corte, 2004, 7–14; Enzo Traverso, 'Esilio ebraico e Atlantico nero. Sull'ermeneutica della distanza', in *Il secolo armato. Interpretare le violenze del Novecento*, Milan: Feltrinelli, 2012, 142–67; Tony Judt, *Reappraisals: Reflections on the Forgotten Twentieth Century*, New York: Penguin, 2008, 14–16; Renato Camurri, 'Exile: An Acceleration Towards Modernity', *Annals of the Fondazione Luigi Einaudi* LIV, December 2020, 21–8. More broadly and recently, see Peter Burke, *Exiles and*

the process of globalization, a true metamorphosis of state territoriality, which has undoubtedly quickened since the late 1980s. Interwar Europe's exiles have been depicted as figures overwhelmed by political persecution and burdened by an uncertain existential condition, and nevertheless as bearers of ethical integrity and clarity of mind. Such retrospective considerations represent the attempt to situate exile in a dimension that is both heroic and idyllic, and thus meta-historical. However, if we address the historical problem of exile through the GL experience, this allows us better to grasp its political, intellectual, and existential complexities.[17] Despite being investigated through various biographies and specific debates (in particular, the debate concerning totalitarianism), exile has yet to be included in the broader historical narratives of twentieth-century Europe. This book contributes to addressing that imbalance.

Of course, not all members of GL were forced into exile: some never left Italy, but remained in the country where they participated in clandestine operations before being arrested, imprisoned, or deported; others went into exile for varying lengths of time. France, Switzerland, Argentina, the United States, Great Britain, and Egypt were the chosen destinations of those who left Italy and established an extensive network of international relations, coming into contact as they did with other political émigrés and intellectuals. In exile, they participated in the most fascinating and innovative debates of their time. They explored new historical, philosophical, literary, and sociological horizons and broadened their vision of politics. At the same time, exile was a difficult and painful experience in which collective and personal tragedies often intermingled. Emigrant groups such as GL formed a small community often threatened by two-faced spies who monitored antifascist activities abroad and reported them to the authorities in Rome. Fascist propaganda used to call antifascist exiles, and members of GL among them, 'outsiders' (*fuoriusciti*): this derogatory labelling was intended to blame them for 'betrayal' of the national

---

Expatriates in the History of Knowledge, 1500–2000, Waltham, MA: Brandeis University Press, 2017, and Catherine Brice, *Exile and the Circulation of Political Practices*, Cambridge: Cambridge Scholars Publishing, 2020.

17 For another example, see Jean-Michel Palmier, *Weimar in Exile: The Antifascist Emigration in Europe and America*, London: Verso, 2006 (1987).

community, and was not infrequently internalized by the antifascists themselves. The possibility of adopting an 'outsider mentality' that carried with it the risk of forgetting the real reasons for fighting in Italy created fierce controversy among the exiles themselves. Within GL, Andrea Caffi and Leone Ginzburg, both born in the Russian Empire, respectively on the shores of the Baltic Sea (St Petersburg) and of the Black Sea (Odesa), represented two different ways of combining cosmopolitan attitude, European culture, and sense of national belonging. Caffi, with an early, deeply Russian cultural and political background, embodied the model of the bewildered and uprooted exile, although he followed a tortuous path that made him more French than Italian. Conversely, Ginzburg started on a gradual process of nationalization (Italianization) in order to justify his political commitment against the Fascist regime, even as he kept on strengthening his ties with Russian culture.[18]

The principal development of the GL group revolved around Paris, which became the hub of international political emigration in the 1920s and 1930s. The French capital is, in every way, the best possible observatory for historians interested in antifascist culture. Its centrality stemmed from the universalist intellectual tradition that first emerged in the eighteenth century and subsequently spanned the 'long nineteenth century', inspiring and polarizing the debate between revolutionaries and counter-revolutionaries. Nevertheless, the French capital's role became somewhat paradoxical during the interwar years. The intellectual force of Paris was now inversely proportional to the political fragility of France, with its cultural centrality asserted in a world in which French political power had increasingly weakened during the course of the nineteenth century, and especially after the Great War.[19]

---

18   For some comparative considerations concerning Andrea Caffi and Leone Ginzburg, see Marco Bresciani, 'L'étrange silence de Franco Venturi: Andrea Caffi et l'émigration russe en Italie aux premières années vingt', in Stéfanie Prezioso and David Chevrolet (eds), L'Heure des brasiers. Violence et révolution au XXe siècle, Lausanne: Éditions d'en bas, 2011, 203–19.

19   François Furet, The Passing of an Illusion: The Idea of Communism in the Twentieth Century, Chicago: University of Chicago Press, 1999; Tony Judt, The Burden of Responsibility: Blum, Camus, Aron and the French Twentieth Century, Chicago: University of Chicago Press, 1998, 3–27; Anson Rabinbach, 'Paris, Capital of Anti-Fascism', in Warren Breckman et al. (eds), Modernist Imagination: Intellectual

Interpretations of Europe's history between the two world wars have long been shaped – and not infrequently distorted – by the Cold War and its legacies. Since 1945, the idea of 'democracy' has been interpreted and adopted in a variety of different, yet not necessarily alternative understandings (antifascist, anti-communist, anti-totalitarian). On the one hand, antifascism has tended to distinguish the discourse on Fascism, as well as Nazism, from the discourse on Stalinist Communism, and to challenge or reject anti-communism and anti-totalitarianism. On the other hand, anti-communism has been a particular manifestation of anti-totalitarianism, often disregarding antifascism and resulting in the identification between Nazism and Soviet Communism. Two outstanding historians, Eric J. Hobsbawm and François Furet, offered sound arguments for these opposing positions. Hobsbawm attributed the 'alliance' between Western liberalism and Soviet Communism, which had enabled capitalism to overcome its crisis, to the common cause of antifascism.[20] Whereas Furet saw antifascism as a 'mask' for Stalinist Communism, which had itself monopolized revolutionary passions and in this way extended its totalitarian rule.[21] These contrary positions reflect the intellectual mood during the Cold War (and its long, uncertain farewell in the 1990s). Over the last quarter of a century, a new body of research has emerged that has deconstructed and reconstructed the public memory and legacy of World War II, the ambivalence and contradictions of communist antifascism, the diversity of antifascist political cultures and their links to anti-totalitarianism, the forms of total violence witnessed during Europe's civil wars and world wars in the twentieth century, and their own long-standing legacies.[22]

History and Critical Theory. Essays in Honor of Martin Jay, New York: Berghahn Books, 2009, 183–209.

20   Eric J. Hobsbawm, 'In the Era of Anti-fascism, 1929–1945', in *How to Change the World: Reflections on Marx and Marxism*, New Haven, CT: Yale University Press, 2011, 261–313.

21   See Furet, *The Passing of an Illusion*, 209–314. For a critical assessment, see *New German Critique* 67, Winter 1996: Anson Rabinbach, 'Introduction: Legacies of Antifascism', 3–17; Geoff Eley, 'Constructing Democracy in Postwar Europe', 73–100; Dan Diner, 'On the Ideology of Antifascism', 123–32.

22   See Tony Judt, 'The Past Is Another Country: Myth and Memory in Postwar Europe', *Daedalus* 121, Fall 1992, 83–118, in Jan-Werner Müller (ed.), *Memory and Power in Post-war Europe: Studies in the Presence of the Past*, Cambridge: Cambridge

Recent scholarship has chiefly emphasized liberal positions towards the tragedies and catastrophes of twentieth-century Europe, while overlooking the various socialist contributions to this reflection.[23] This book offers a different case: that of a both liberal and socialist group, created on uncompromisingly antifascist foundations, at a time when 'democracy' was still broadly contested and criticized.[24] The challenges of the 1930s offered GL the opportunity to reassess the theoretical and historical heritage of both liberalism and socialism, to redefine the meaning and the political and social scope of 'democracy', to rethink the relationships and connections between the national and European spheres, to test the feasibility of a socialism or communism 'different' from that of the Soviet Union, and to deal with the internal ambiguities of revolution. From this point of view, GL allows us to rethink twentieth-century Italian and European intellectual history, and, in doing so, to move beyond the dualism of the Cold War period and its legacy, in terms of:

a) the relations between antifascism, communism, and anti-totalitarianism, seen through the tangle of hybridization and contamination of liberal and anti-liberal thought;

b) the nature of tyrannies (or totalitarian regimes) within the context of the debate over the contradictions and antinomies of European socialisms.

University Press, 2002, 157–83. For an approach relating the Soviet conceptions of fascism and communist antifascist positions, see also S. G. Payne, 'Soviet Anti-Fascism: Theory and Practice, 1921–45', *Totalitarian Movements and Political Religions* 4, no. 2, 2003, 1–62. For a recent take on Europe's civil wars, see Martin Conway, Robert Gerwarth, 'Europe's Age of Civil Wars? An Introduction', in 'Civil Wars in 20th-Century Europe: Comparative Perspectives', special issue, *Journal of Modern European History* 20, no. 4, 2022, 442–51.

23 See, for instance, the interesting work on liberalism and the 'problem of ruthlessness' by Joshua L. Cherniss, *Liberalism in Dark Times: The Liberal Ethos in the Twentieth Century*, Princeton, NJ: Princeton University Press, 2021.

24 Karl Newman, *European Democracy between the Wars*, Notre Dame, IN: University of Notre Dame Press, 1970; Karl D. Bracher, *The Age of Ideologies: A History of Political Thought in the Twentieth Century*, New York: St. Martin's Press, 1984; Mark Mazower, *Dark Continent: Europe's Twentieth Century*, London: Allen Lane, 1998; Jan-Werner Müller, *Contesting Democracy: Political Ideas in Twentieth-Century Europe*, New Haven, CT: Yale University Press, 2011.

The case of GL thus shows that any clear-cut divide between 'counterrevolutionary antifascism' and 'revolutionary antifascism' is less significant than the hybridization of different cultures and strategies opposed to (and in favour of) Fascism. In questioning the very meaning of politics and its implications in a context of turmoil, the GL members were ready to explore the terrain of a-politics or even anti-politics, without ever severing their ties with antifascism.

In a famous and controversial book entitled *Neither Right nor Left*, Zeev Sternhell argues that one cannot understand fascism without tracing the various stages of socialism's crisis, going back to the revisionism of the early twentieth century, while recognizing its variety of forms: that of Eduard Bernstein and Jean Jaurès, which led to reformist socialism, and that of Georges Sorel, Hendrik de Man and Marcel Déat, which resulted in 'fascism'. The paradoxical case of Rosselli – who was certainly closer to this second form of revisionism, without ever yielding to fascism – demonstrates how other paths were possible. In his analysis of French *ni droite ni gauche* culture, Sternhell evokes 'the atmosphere of openness, of readiness for new ideas, characteristic of the 1930s'. However, by identifying 'the ambiguity and vagueness of thought prevalent in the interwar period' with 'the penetration of the fascist ideology in France', he falls back on an unambiguous and consistent definition of fascism.[25] This definition ends up coinciding with the self-representation of fascists as spiritual, anti-materialist revolutionaries, who in their pursuit of a new national and European order rejected the very meaning of politics as understood at that time. Yet, as Philippe Burrin argues, the various forms of fascism created a powerful 'magnetic field' that increasingly polarized Europe in the mid-1930s, and catalysed the entire range of political and intellectual forces through dynamics of attraction or repulsion.[26] In remaining anchored to a revolutionary antifascist stance, while critically assessing these *ni droite ni gauche* currents, GL thus contributed towards a new way of opposing fascism's 'magnetic field', and towards a new meaning of being on the 'Left'.

---

25 Zeev Sternhell, *Neither Right nor Left: Fascist Ideology in France*, Princeton, NJ: Princeton University Press, 1986, 21, 213, 154, 302, 221.

26 Philippe Burrin, *Le champ magnétique des fascismes*, in *Fascisme, nazisme, autoritarisme*, Paris: Éditions du Seuil, 2000, 211–46.

More recently, against a backdrop of crisis and conflict – which began with the financial and economic slump of 2007–09 and was followed by the attendant political and geopolitical backlash undermining the Western post-Cold War settlement and paving the way for new forms of national-populism and authoritarianism – a new attention has been paid to the instability and uncertainty of the political arrangements of interwar Europe.[27] Certainly, it was the need to meet the fascist challenges to the existing European order that conditioned – and sometimes stimulated and shaped – GL's political and intellectual pursuits of a new order. But what did these challenges consist in? On the one hand, Mussolini and Hitler's dictatorial experiments stemming from the Great War triggered the dynamics of opposition, competition, and collaboration among various conservative and radical right-wingers, which fuelled 'fascist interactions' across the European continent and, through their radicalization and hybridization, led to a new wartime catastrophe.[28] On the other hand, fascism was inscribed in the register of various 'non-conformist' cultures (or 'third ways') which, following the sense of a general crisis of the pre-1914 order, were characterized by a 'search for stability', based on new ways in which social conflicts and economic interests were to be addressed and organized.[29] To understand the novelty and originality of GL, it is therefore necessary to take into account two essential aspects:

a) its compelling link with Italian Fascism and the consequent polarization of the political conflict in Europe between 1929 and 1940;
b) its unprejudiced, open-minded confrontation with the pursuit of a

---

27   For an insightful overview of the recent literature, see Shelley Baranowski, 'Authoritarianism and Fascism in Interwar Europe: Approaches and Legacies', *Journal of Modern History* 94, no. 3, September 2022, 648–72.

28   Among many works, see Robert Paxton, *The Anatomy of Fascism*, New York: Alfred A. Knopf, 2004; António Costa Pinto (ed.), *Rethinking the Nature of Fascism: Comparative Perspectives*, Basingstoke: Palgrave Macmillan, 2011; António Costa Pinto and Aristotle Kallis (eds), *Rethinking Fascism and Dictatorship in Europe*, Basingstoke: Palgrave Macmillan, 2014; David Roberts, *Fascist Interactions: Proposals for a New Approach to Fascism and Its Era, 1919–1945*, New York: Berghahn Books, 2016; Marco Bresciani (ed.), *Conservatives and Right Radicals in Interwar Europe*, London: Routledge, 2021.

29   Charles Maier, *In Search of Stability: Explorations in Historical Political Economy*, Cambridge: Cambridge University Press, 1987.

completely new political, social, economic, and cultural order than the one existing to Europe before 1914 (which, after 1945, was to find expression in the West in mixed economic systems, anti-cyclical policies, and the democratic welfare state in particular).

In both cases, GL's antifascism is to be understood in the light of its deep-rooted links with the transnational networks and circulations of fascist cultures and practices.[30]

Learning from the Enemy

From 1929 to 1940, the GL group, devoting its energies to clandestine political struggle and intellectual reflection and discussion, branched out into transnational networks of emigration and conspiracy in various Italian cities. It became a point of reference for at least three generations, whose different experiences brought them together in the group and inspired their plans and discussions.

According to the sociologist Karl Mannheim, an approach focusing on 'generation-units' makes it possible to analyse 'an identity of responses, a certain affinity in the way in which all move with and are formed by their common experiences'. The idea of generation is rooted in the social, cultural, and demographic changes witnessed from the late eighteenth century onwards, which were clearly evident at the point of transition from the nineteenth to the twentieth century. Successive generations gradually acquired social and cultural consciousness, enabling them to embrace their own role in accordance with the rhythm of historical change. The increasingly close link between generation and youth acted as the driver of revolution. As a privileged form of self-representation, the concept of generation became a productive means by which to interpret history. The duration of generations depends on the variable intensity of social and

---

30 For a path-breaking take on studying communist antifascism and fascism together see Kasper Braskén, 'Communist Antifascism and Transnational Fascism: Comparisons, Transfers, Entanglements', in Arnd Bauerkämper and Grzegorz Rossoliński-Liebe (eds), *Fascisms without Borders: Transnational Connections and Cooperation between Movements and Regimes in Europe from 1918 to 1945*, New York: Berghahn Books, 2017, 288–311.

cultural change, or the unpredictable frequency of political turns. The boundaries separating different generations, however, are invisible and unstable, indeed, sometimes ambiguous, so that they often tend to inter-penetrate one another in their outermost reaches.[31]

GL was anything but a homogeneous, compact generational group. Three different generations contributed to its foundation and development. It was, in the words of Marc Bloch, a 'short generation' sandwiched between two 'long generations', which defined themselves in relation to the Great War. The short generation was the one that matured *during* the Great War; prior to that came the generation formed *before* the Great War, between the 1890s and the first fifteen years of the twentieth century, particularly in Giolitti's Italy; then came the generation who grew up *after* the Great War, between the crisis of the immediate postwar period and the establishment of Mussolini's dictatorship.

The 'short generation' of 1914–1915 comprised those born in the 1890s, including both Carlo Rosselli (1899) and Emilio Lussu (1890). In 1918 they were aged nineteen and twenty-eight respectively, and their genera-tion had directly experienced the war as a traumatic watershed moment, although only some of them had experienced it on the battlefield. This was the generation of the founders of *Ordine Nuovo*, including Antonio Gramsci (1891), who constituted one of the earliest Italian communist groups; but it was also the generation of the first Fascists. The political trajectories of the GL members belonging to this generation were compa-rable, in some ways and for a while, to those of certain early Fascists. They were characterized by their distant Risorgimento ascendancy, or at any rate their loyalty to Mazzinian tradition; by their belief in the myth of a new national revolution; by their combative interventionist passion; and by their aversion to socialist maximalism. Even those most intransigent in

---

31   See Karl Mannheim, 'The Problem of Generations', in Paul Kecskemeti (ed.), *Sociology of Knowledge*, New York: Oxford University Press, 1928, 276–322 (in particular, 306); Alan B. Spitzer, 'The Historical Problem of Generations', *American Historical Review* 73, 1978, 1353–85; Annie Kriegel, 'Le concept politique de généra-tion: apogée et déclin', *Commentaire* 7, 1979, 390–9; Jean-François Sirinelli (ed.), 'Générations intellectuelles', *Cahiers de l'IHTP*, November 1987; Pierre Nora, 'La génération', in *Les lieux de la mémoire*, tome 3, *Les France*, vol. 1, *Conflits et partages*, Paris: Gallimard, 1992, 931–71. Robert Wohl, *The Generation of 1914*, Cambridge, MA: Harvard University Press, 1979, still makes a valuable contribution.

their opposition to Fascism were, nonetheless, exposed to the appeal of Fascism as a 'generational revolt'.[32]

This inner circle around Rosselli attracted figures from an earlier generation, a 'long generation' which, for various reasons, was in harmony with the younger generation. It included eminences of anti-Giolittian culture such as Giuseppe Prezzolini (1882), as well as certain guiding lights of GL such as Benedetto Croce (1866), Gaetano Salvemini (1873), and Luigi Einaudi (1874). The founder of Fascism, Benito Mussolini (1883), like older representatives of early Fascism such as Giovanni Gentile (1875), belonged to the same generation. They had all lived through the war as fully aware adults, although the second part of their lives, so brutally interrupted by that war, was different from the first. Some of the future members of GL had been socialist militants or advocates of anti-Giolittian culture. The Great War and Fascism (and also, in Caffi's view, the Russian Revolutions and Bolshevism) provided an extraordinary, albeit not immediate, stimulus to rethink their previous trajectories and take very different directions in the 1920s or early 1930s. This generation was, in many ways, an anomaly when compared to Rosselli's Parisian leadership group: it helped trigger some of the liveliest and most controversial debates within GL.

A thin, yet significant line separated GL militants who had known, even if only briefly, pre-Fascist (and Giolittian) Italy from those who had grown up in postwar Italy and then under the Fascist regime. The slightest difference in age implied a perceptible divergence of experience. Carlo Levi (born in 1902), Nicola Chiaromonte and Mario Levi (1905), Aldo Garosci (1907), Vittorio Foa and Leone Ginzburg (1909), Massimo Mila (1910), Franco Venturi and Renzo Giua (1914), all belonged to a generation that had grown up (albeit in different circumstances in some cases) between the postwar meltdown and the early years of the Fascist regime. The precursor of this category was Piero Gobetti (born in 1901), against whose legacy many GL members (especially but not only from Turin) would continue to measure themselves: in this sense it was a post-Gobettian

---

32   See Juan Linz, 'Some Notes toward a Comparative Study of Fascism in Sociological Historical Perspective', in Walter Laqueur (ed.), *Fascism: A Reader's Guide*, Berkeley: University of California Press, 1976, 3–121; Bruno Wanrooij, 'The Rise and Fall of Italian Fascism as a Generational Revolt', *Journal of Contemporary History* 22, no. 3, 1987, 401–18.

generation. This generation, far more than others, saw the GL experience as a fundamental moment in their political formation and, more importantly, in their intellectual growth.

As regards the notion of generation, Marc Bloch argued in his *Historian's Craft*:

> Men who are born into the same social environment about the same time necessarily come under analogous influences, particularly in their formative years. Experience proves that, by comparison with either considerably older or considerably younger groups, their behaviour reveals certain distinctive characteristics which are ordinarily very clear. This is true even of their bitterest disagreements. To be excited by the same dispute, even on opposing sides, is still to be alike. This common stamp, deriving from common age, is what makes a generation.[33]

With regard to the 'stamp' that united certain early Fascists and antifascists, account should be taken of early twentieth-century Italian culture, its ambivalence and its significant persistence through later decades, and thus of the key relationship between Fascism and culture.

A critical attitude towards the Giolittian political system and style constituted one (negative) common denominator in early twentieth-century Italian culture. Under the pressure created by Giolitti's experiment in nation-building and democracy-building, a deep rift opened up between the liberal ruling class and the intellectual class, a rift that wartime interventionism first, and then Fascism and antifascism, attempted in various ways to bridge. This cultural context was the breeding ground of both Fascism and antifascism, where much of the most innovative, and explosive, material of the new century was deposited. The dynamics of this cultural context, as heterogeneous as they were ambiguous, can only be fully understood, however, if one avoids resorting to retrospective viewpoints on Fascism and antifascism. More broadly, this context was strongly marked by an ambivalent attitude to politics which passed down to later experiences like GL. On the one hand, early twentieth-century culture as it attempted to select and educate a new ruling class rejected the political parties as such, claiming to go beyond the traditional Left/Right divide. It

---

33   Marc Bloch, *The Historian's Craft*, New York: A. Knopf, 1953, 153.

was thus inspired by an idea of social and cultural change that dismissed or even denied the legitimacy, or necessity, of political means. On the other hand, it was animated by the passionate search for a 'new' style of politics, questioning the 'old' politics, seen as spoiled and corrupted, in a situation of feverish transition to mass participation in social and political life that characterized, at different levels and degrees, all of Europe at the time. In the wake of the French example, Italian culture consecrated the advent of the modern intellectual and his path-breaking interventions in the public sphere: a figure who offered to mediate between the state and civil society, who was relatively independent from the traditional centres of power and knowledge, but was also aware of the need for a nexus between theory and practice, or at least for a form of public participation and communication within the context of a nascent mass society. In sum, early twentieth-century culture featured simultaneously non-political and political, sometimes anti-political and hyper-political, motivations. Accordingly, a periodically re-emerging divide separating culture from politics persisted over time and followed a shifting rhythm of tensions, convulsions, and transformations.

Early twentieth-century intellectuals aspired to reorganizing the state. Faced with a 'long Great War', which from 1911 onwards (that is, from the Italian attack on the Ottoman Empire and its backlash in the Balkans) pushed towards mobilization, they strengthened their hold on public opinion and indulged in their pursuit of power. On the one hand, their support for intervention in the ongoing war shaped the public mood much more than their various justifications of war (democratic, nationalist, revolutionary-syndicalist, or futurist). In the feverish debates witnessed during the period of 1914–15, positions in favour of democratic neo-Risorgimento patriotism and revolutionary-libertarian syndicalist interventionism often overlapped with, and were conflated with, imperialist and nationalist orientations. On the other hand, the Great War marked a caesura that triggered sweeping political and social change and offered an opportunity for realization of the nationalizing projects long cherished by various cultural currents in the early part of the twentieth century. Fierce anti-Giolittian criticism and passionate interventionism affected public opinion to a significant extent, and resurfaced in the postwar propaganda for political renewal, reigniting divisions and conflicts within the country. Fascism transformed the anti-political slogans and energies generated by

anti-Giolittians into a hyper-political project aimed at – and successful in
– overthrowing the 'old' Italy in the name of a new, 'young' Italy. Thus, a
political regime of a different kind was to emerge – one that put an end to
intellectuals' mediation between the state and civil society, and increasingly drove their integration into the totalitarian regime.[34] In the late 1920s
and early 1930s, GL entered the by now definitive fissures of anti-
Giolittian culture between Fascism and antifascism. Faced with Mussolini's
dictatorship, Rosselli's group chose the line of radical opposition to the
regime and sought the formation of a new ruling class among émigrés and
conspirators, by challenging the Fascist relationship between politics and
culture.[35]

Paradoxically, then, the paths taken by GL and its adversary are inextricably entwined, yet with no confusion as to who the persecuted and the
persecutor were. On the contrary, it is precisely in terms of this common
ground that the reasons for their opposition can best be understood. GL
started from the complex reality of Fascism and, at the same time, set out
to find a new political, economic, social, and cultural order for Italy and
Europe that was not only radically different from Fascism, but would also
move beyond it. In a dialogue with Vittorio Foa, an ex-GL member and
friend of Leone Ginzburg, the historian Carlo Ginzburg spoke of Foa's
distinctive 'need to learn from the enemy'. Foa's fundamental 'anti-moralism' offered the opportunity to distinguish between the enemy's questions
and its answers, accepting the former and rejecting the latter.[36] This

---

34   See Luisa Mangoni, *L'interventismo della cultura. Intellettuali e riviste del
fascismo*, Rome-Bari: Laterza, 1974; Emilio Gentile, *Le origini dell'ideologia fascista
(1918–1925)*, Rome-Bari: Laterza, 1975; Emilio Gentile, *Il mito dello Stato nuovo
dall'antigiolittismo al fascismo*, Rome-Bari: Laterza, 1982; Mario Isnenghi, *Intellettuali
militanti e intellettuali funzionari. Appunti sulla cultura fascista*, Turin: Einaudi, 1979;
Gabriele Turi, *Il fascismo e il consenso degli intellettuali*, Bologna: Il Mulino, 1980.

35   See the insightful contribution by Stéfanie Prezioso, 'Fighting Fascism with
Its Own Weapons: A Common Dark Side?', in Chris Millington and Kevin Passmore
(eds), *Political Violence and Democracy in Western Europe, 1918–1940*, Basingstoke:
Palgrave Macmillan, 2015, 31–47.

36   'La fine della storia la sappiamo ... Un dialogo fra Vittorio Foa e Carlo
Ginzburg coordinato da Federico Bozzini', in Aldo Colonnello and Andrea Del Col
(eds), *Uno storico, un mugnaio, un libro. Carlo Ginzburg, Il formaggio e i vermi, 1976–
2002*, Trieste: Edizioni Università di Trieste, 2002, 96–7. The expression 'learning
from the enemy' has been traced back to Bertolt Brecht (in order to define Walter

attitude was rooted in Foa's youthful opposition to the Fascist regime, as his prison letters clearly testify. One such letter, dated 10 June 1938, offered a critique of Johan Huizinga's work, *In the Shadow of Tomorrow*, published in 1935 and translated by Einaudi as *Crisi della civiltà*.[37] Foa's judgement was decidedly negative. The Dutch historian represented a generation 'cradled and raised in the peaceful enjoyment of institutions and values that seemed untouchable, and in the confidence of their indefinite progress', that had not recovered from the 'blow dealt to that world by the Great War'. The harsh, yet astute observations of the imprisoned antifascist resulted in the formulation of a category, that of the 'whiners', to which Huizinga himself was assigned. Foa began his critique with a key question: 'How do you fight an enemy you don't know?' This was his answer:

Unlike the whiners, we (I say we because I truly hope that there are others who think as I do) do not believe in irrational actions and set ourselves the task of recognizing their rationality in order to establish the rules governing our actions. There is a huge gulf between the whiners and us, one established by our common adversaries: . . . the whiners complain about the collapse of their little world, whereas we internalize the demands that our adversaries strive to meet and enrich them with new (eternally new), higher, more complex demands. The whiners oppose their abstract model of civilization to history; we, by contrast, feel that we are an integral and active part of our own time, which we do not repudiate, indeed we feel it to be all the more our own the more it apparently seems to wrong us.[38]

Foa used the derogatory term 'whiners' to underscore the attitude of GL as distinct from that of the politicians and intellectuals stubbornly wedded to an idyllic view of the pre-1914 'world of yesterday', and as such unwilling to critically assess and understand the grim sequence of post-1914 catastrophes, collapses, defeats, shocks, and aftershocks. Like Foa, the other GL

Benjamin's intellectual strategy) by Cesare Cases, 'Imparare dal nemico', in *Il boom di Roscellino. Satire e polemiche*, Turin: Einaudi, 1990, 241–7.

37 Johann Huizinga, *Crisi della civiltà*, Turin: Einaudi, 1937 (1935).

38 Letter to his family, 10 June 1938, in Vittorio Foa, *Lettere della giovinezza. Dal carcere (1935–1943)*, Turin: Einaudi 1998, 422–6.

members acknowledged the rationale of what was usually dismissed as irrational (Fascism first and foremost), without questioning the underlying political choices based on intransigent antifascism. This attitude, at once ideological and anti-ideological, moralistic and anti-moralistic, rhetorical and anti-rhetorical, reflected the thinking of the idealist, liberal philosopher Benedetto Croce. His masterpiece, *History of Europe in the Nineteenth Century*, published in 1932, was an important source of inspiration for Foa and the other GL members. With characteristic optimism, Foa summed up the meaning of his experiences in GL using a phrase taken from Giambattista Vico's *The New Science*, which Foa read in prison, but also quoted in Croce's *History of Europe*: 'They seem to be untoward events and are opportunities.'[39] 'It was all the work of liberty,' Croce explained, 'its unique and eternal positive moment, which alone is made effective in the series of its forms and gives them their significance, and which alone explains and justifies the function fulfilled by the negative moment of subjection, with its constraints, its oppressions, its reactions, and its tyrannies, which (to quote Vico once more) seem to be "untoward events" and are really "opportunities".'[40] Although Foa and his fellow GL members questioned and dismissed Croce's consistently historicist assumptions, and interpreted this idea of liberty in their own ways as a ground for actively fighting Fascism, they undoubtedly agreed that 'having as rule of the game this very liberty . . . demands tolerance of the opinions of others, readiness to listen to and learn from opponents and in every case to know them well'.[41]

GL's willingness to learn from the enemy did not mean overcoming the friend/foe logic – far from it. The very identification of Fascism as an 'enemy' entailed the idea of irreducible opposition, which, in turn, implied the adoption of different tactics and strategies for fighting it: lengthy periods of intellectual research and editorial work alternated with shorter periods of propaganda and political action. This attitude, both ethical and cognitive, reflected a form of responsibility that linked the present with the future and therefore concerned the very relationship between politics and

---

39   Foa, *Lettere della giovinezza*, VII.

40   Benedetto Croce, *History of Europe in the Nineteenth Century*, London: Routledge, 2019 (1932), 9.

41   Ibid., 40.

culture. GL's experimental character derived from the idea of a caesura in the historical process, which Rosselli's group had been able to interpret and transform into a political and intellectual project.

So, what did GL learn from its enemy – Fascism? First, it appropriated the willingness to face the enemy by resorting to all sort of means, even those of a paramilitary nature, thanks to its links with traditions of armed volunteerism and civic patriotism. Second, it understood the importance of symbolic mobilization through the massive use of modern propaganda, designed to undermine the consensus created by the Fascist regime. Third, as opposed to the class-based culture of the Marxist Left, it internalized the need to compete for the sympathies of the middle classes at a time when they were leaning towards authoritarianism and illiberalism, or even Fascism itself. Fourth, like radical Fascist currents, it too borrowed the ideas of nationhood and Europe from the Mazzinian tradition, but applied them to various forms of revolutionary antifascism, as the grounds for the new post-Fascist (and post-imperial) political and social order. Last but not least, the GL group developed plans for a mixed economy and public policies as counter-cyclical responses to the 1930s crisis, while confronting cultural pessimism with its belief in progress, disputed as that may have been. In sum, GL's struggle to understand and combat its Fascist enemy reflected the key passions, tensions, contradictions, and dilemmas of interwar Europe.

1
Antifascism as an Experiment

Understanding Fascism Means Fighting Fascism

On 1 August 1929, Carlo Rosselli arrived in Paris on the evening train in the company of Emilio Lussu and Francesco Fausto Nitti. The three opponents of Fascism had managed to escape from their confinement on the island of Lipari – 'a big cell without walls, only sky and sea' – where they had been imprisoned since 1927.[1] Their escape on the night of 29 July was as daring as it was sensational. They swam to a boat moored off the island and then made their way to the Tunisian coast, before crossing the Mediterranean again to finally land in France. At the Gare de Lyon in Paris, three Italian exiles – Gaetano Salvemini, Alberto Cianca, and Alberto Tarchiani – were waiting for them to arrive on the train from Marseilles. For Mussolini, it was a severe setback that made headlines across half the continent, while British public opinion mobilized in favour of Rosselli's wife, Marion Cave, who had been arrested in the Aosta Valley just after her husband's flight from Lipari, and subsequently released.[2]

---

1   Carlo Rosselli, 'Fuga in quattro tempi', *Almanacco socialista*, 1931, in *Opere scelte*, vol. 1, *Socialismo liberale e altri scritti*, ed. John Rosselli, Turin: Einaudi, 1973, 515.

2   Isabelle Richet, 'Marion Cave Rosselli and the Transnational Women's Antifascist Networks', *Journal of Women's History* 24, no. 3, 2012, 117–39.

When Rosselli arrived in the French capital, the small group of exiles immediately began discussing the idea of creating a new political movement to fight Fascism and renew Italy. In October, GL was officially established.[3] Rosselli, who had long rejected the idea of going into exile, was convinced that 'captivity in the homeland could be exchanged for freedom in exile', but only on the condition that 'this hard-won personal freedom be made a means for regaining the freedom of an entire people'.[4] In Rosselli's eyes, fleeing the country was the result of chance rather than choice; its link with conspiracy was to be a close and indissoluble one.

When Rosselli went into exile in 1929, all opposition to Mussolini and his increasingly totalitarian regime had been crushed. The surviving political parties, whose members either emigrated or were conspiring against the regime from within Italy, were as fragmented as ever. The Fascist dictatorship had succeeded in bringing Italian society under its control, building up a powerful police apparatus and making deals with traditional institutions such as the monarchy, the army, and the Church, as well as with the country's main economic forces. The opposition, by contrast, which had been defeated and suppressed several times, appeared inert and hopeless, lacking in strength and perspective. Having failed to prevent the establishment of the Fascist regime, the leadership and many members of the old political parties started to move abroad in 1926. While the communists formed an active, albeit small organization that closely followed the policies of the Third International and the Soviet Union, the socialists and republicans formed the organization Concentrazione d'azione antifascista in 1927. However, these parties' activities tended to end up in sterile, dogmatic disputes within the émigré community. Convinced that the regime was about to fall, the leaders of Concentrazione antifascista limited themselves to propaganda activities that would ensure a possibly peaceful, if not legal, succession to Fascism without any dramatic rupture.

At the time, Carlo Rosselli was a man in his early thirties who wanted to be active again after a long period of confinement. Endowed with substantial family wealth, he aspired to an academic career, while he was

---

3   Its name derived from the reversal of Libertà e Giustizia, name of an anarchist group founded by Mikhail A. Bakunin in Naples in 1865: see ' "Libertà e Giustizia" e "Giustizia e Libertà" ', *Quaderni di GL* 3, June 1932, 53–4.

4   Carlo Rosselli, 'Fuga in quattro tempi', 525.

already involved in politics as a convinced socialist. In short, he found himself ideally placed to establish a group of political activists capable of breaking away from existing political organizations and traditions and of lending a new impetus to the struggle against Fascism. His willingness to sacrifice the present for the future, his desire to project the meaning of his existence into the collective dimension, and his ethical and aesthetic glorification of the political struggle – that of a small group – made Rosselli a romantic revolutionary. In his mind, action was necessary, but not sufficient. So where and how could the political struggle recommence?

Between 1927 and 1928, during his confinement on the island of Lipari, the young economist wrote his first and only book, *Liberal Socialism*, about the political battle and political theory, which was printed, with the French title *Socialisme libéral*, in Paris in December 1930. This work is divided into two closely related sections: the first offers a critical evaluation of socialism aimed at developing a new theoretical and political perspective, while the second presents Rosselli's reflections on the victory of Fascism after the Great War. The emergence and rise of Mussolini's movement and regime called for a rethinking of both the past and the future. He wrote of Fascism:

> Combating it does not mean eliminating it. Indeed, the better one understands it, the more effectively it can be fought and overcome. To understand is to overcome. Fascism is almost completely devoid of constructive values, but it has value that cannot be overlooked as experience, as a revelation of the Italians to themselves.[5]

The novel, experimental character of Rosselli's political project derived from these lines from *Liberal Socialism*. An understanding of Fascism in Italian history was the essential prerequisite for defeating it. More than 'liberal socialism', however, it was revolutionary, republican, and democratic antifascism that determined the perspective of GL, which aimed to reorganize and remobilize the forces opposed to the regime. In November

---

5   Carlo Rosselli, *Liberal Socialism*, ed. Nadia Urbinati, Princeton, NJ: Princeton University Press, 2017, 115. The original manuscript was translated into French (*Socialisme libéral*, Paris: Librairie Valois, 1930) then back into Italian (*Socialismo liberale*, Rome-Florence-Milan: Edizioni U, 1945).

1929, the first issue appeared of a bulletin entitled *Giustizia e Libertà*. *Movimento rivoluzionario antifascista*. Using a 'new language' to call for 'war' against Mussolini's regime, GL aimed to gather republicans, socialists, and democrats to fight 'for freedom, the republic and social justice', having 'put aside the party books'. It presented itself as a 'secret organization' that would 'become popular', a 'bold minority' that would 'sweep the masses along'.[6]

Despite his deep ties to England, Rosselli decided to settle in France with his wife, Marion Cave: they soon had three children. Carlo Rosselli's family fortune, which included a considerable share in a mercury mine in Tuscany, enabled him to finance not only his exile in Paris, but also many of GL's projects. However, his daily life in the French capital was full of risk. A multitude of Fascist spies, informers, and double agents, aided and abetted by the uncertain conspiracy rules of GL, threatened Carlo's work and life. The French engineer René Odin (alias 'Togo') and the Venetian count and literary critic Giacomo Antonini (alias 'Raffaello') were among the most dangerous confidants of Mussolini's political police, and these two men managed to approach Rosselli and gain his trust.

Rosselli, however, was convinced that Italy was the real political battleground: it was necessary to avoid delegating the fight against Fascism to others. Conspiracy was the result of his experience between 1925 and 1926, when the Fascist regime made its first totalitarian breakthrough, and also a response to the need for organized (possibly armed) struggle. At its core, the GL project drew on a nineteenth-century political tradition that established an organic link between revolution and conspiracy, codified by the Pisan revolutionary Filippo Buonarroti. However, above all, it looked to Georges Sorel, the main French thinker of revolutionary syndicalism, who was widely popular in Italy and appealed to figures as diverse as Benedetto Croce, Antonio Gramsci, Giuseppe Prezzolini, and Piero Gobetti. Indeed, the 'active minorities' (*minorités agissantes*) played a crucial role in his conception of the historical process.

GL's activists, driven by their desire for action, established a close-knit network of clandestine contacts, disseminated political propaganda,

---

6 [Carlo Rosselli,] 'Non vinceremo in un giorno, ma vinceremo', *GL*, November 1929, in Carlo Rosselli, *Scritti dell'esilio*, vol. 1, *Giustizia e Libertà e la Concentrazione antifascista 1929–1934*, ed. Carlo Casucci, Turin: Einaudi, 1988, 12.

secretly circulated banned books and leaflets, and carried out symbolic protests and gestures. The most sensational event involved Giovanni Bassanesi and Gioacchino Dolci, who took off in a plane from Canton Ticino on 11 July 1930, dropping propaganda leaflets over Milan as they flew over the city. These combat tactics brought together a number of different elements, including the revolutionary syndicalist heritage, interventionist and futurist culture, the actions of the Arditi (the Italian army's elite corps), and D'Annunzio's Fiume expedition. The common denominator was the heroic momentum that echoed wartime experience well beyond 1918. The young Turinese revolutionary Fernando De Rosa, for example, used Fascist-like language to express his deep sense of 'the comradeship of the trenches'.[7] However, despite the great psychological and physical courage that the conspiracy required, it soon became apparent that these demonstrative actions were essentially futile. During a period of dictatorial stabilization, the actions of GL – which were technically ineffective in the short or very short term – were guided by a predominantly pedagogical goal that would supposedly unfold over time. They helped embody and nurture an example of non-conformism based on heroic self-sacrifice.

However, a group like GL, hankering to fight the Fascist dictatorship, could not rule out the possibility of armed struggle a priori. What forms political violence should take was the subject of intense debate. Was it legitimate to resort to terrorism? And, if so, with what means and goals? Discussion of the strategies and tactics to be adopted in the struggle was accompanied by thoughts on the organizational structure of GL.[8] In 1931, Rosselli overcame his distrust of political parties and signed agreements first with the Socialist Party, and then with the entire Concentrazione antifascista. Revolutionary action in Italy was thus delegated to GL: it was a matter of maintaining contact with clandestine (socialist, democratic, or republican) groups, devising and carrying out new forms of active

---

7   Letter from Fernando De Rosa to Alberto Tarchiani, 19 September 1932. Fondo Aldo Garosci, Corrispondenza, Dossier Fernando De Rosa, Istituto per la Storia della Resistenza e della Società contemporanea Giorgio Agosti (Turin).

8   See Sergio Luzzatto, *Il corpo del Duce. Un cadavere tra immaginazione, storia e memoria*, Turin: Einaudi, 1998, 23–31, and Mario Giovana, *Giustizia e Libertà in Italia: storia di una cospirazione antifascista, 1929–1937*, Turin: Bollati Boringhieri, 2005, 97–112.

propaganda, and mobilizing forces outside the existing political parties. *La Libertà* became the newspaper of the Concentrazione antifascista, with contributions from leading members of GL. This cooperation with the aforesaid political parties, however, was looked on unfavourably by Salvemini, who had emigrated to Boston where he had begun teaching at Harvard University. In a letter sent in 1931, he advised Rosselli to continue working among the 'young people' living under the regime.[9]

In sharp contrast with the position of other antifascist émigré groups, GL's original project was based on its refusal to adopt a party structure. 'Shelving the party card' was its great motto. This idea harked back to the twentieth-century elitist theories of Gaetano Mosca, Vilfredo Pareto, and Roberto Michels, and fuelled the postwar anti-party polemics of Salvemini and Gobetti. Not surprisingly, the main proponents of the transformation of GL into a political party (especially a socialist party), such as Lussu, were far away from this culture.[10] Rosselli adopted an ambivalent position here. He was emotionally and culturally wedded to socialism's reformist tradition, and officially joined the party of Filippo Turati and Giacomo Matteotti between 1924 and 1926; nevertheless, he was aware of socialist maximalism's responsibility for the rise of Fascism in Italy. This notwithstanding, while refusing to transform GL into a political party, he acknowledged the existence of new political parties in the post-Fascist democratic republic. Therefore, he intended to test 'the microscale anticipation of the new integral liberal order of tomorrow', 'the free federation of groups that will be the parties of tomorrow'.[11] The debate over the legitimacy and adequacy of a party structure continued, with the tone changing according to the requirements of what was an increasingly bitter political struggle.

Opposition to the Italian Communist Party (PCd'I) was initially total. When Communist leader Palmiro Togliatti levelled the charge of 'social fascism' against GL, he used the sharpest, most sectarian language of the

---

9   Letter from Gaetano Salvemini to Carlo Rosselli, 8 July 1931, in Carlo Rosselli and Gaetano Salvemini, *Fra le righe: carteggio fra Carlo Rosselli e Gaetano Salvemini*, ed. Elisa Signori, Milan: Franco Angeli, 2009, 118.

10   Tirreno [Emilio Lussu], 'Orientamenti', *Quaderni di GL* 3, June 1932, 43–50.

11   Carlo Rosselli, 'Pro o contro il partito', *Quaderni di GL* 8, August 1933, 9. See also Maria Salvati, 'From the Republic of Antifascists to the Republic of Parties', in 'The Transformation of Republicanism in Modern and Contemporary Italy', special issue, *Journal of Modern Italian Studies* 17, no. 2, 2012, 220–37.

Third International, which had been adopted at the Sixth Congress of the Comintern in July–September 1928. In a period of purported radicalization of the class struggle, socialism was accused of 'fascistization'. By preventing workers from converting to communism, it was seen as allying itself with the crisis-ridden capitalist system: in a sense, it was supposed to provide that system with its most insidious (because covert) support. GL's pact with Concentrazione antifascista was equated with the 'activation of social fascism': as such, the PCd'I had to expose and denounce this move. GL's hostility to Italy's Communists was equally as strong: it accused them of treating the proletariat as a 'herd', of imposing its 'Jesuitical discipline' on workers, and of lulling them 'with the constant glorification of [their] virtues in order to make it easier for them to become the object of dictatorship by the party bureaucracy tomorrow'.[12]

By tightening its relations with other parties active among the Italian émigrés, GL feared it could lose its specific identity. Max Ascoli was especially aware of this risk. Ascoli was a law professor who had lately emigrated to New York on a Rockefeller Foundation grant and was teaching at the New School for Social Research. While acknowledging that action in Italy was not 'futile', he backed the need for a profound economic, philosophical, legal, and literary rethinking, inspired by GL: 'Once again, politics that expresses itself only in terms of politics is already doomed.'[13] Following this letter sent in December 1931, relations between Rosselli and Ascoli were interrupted, and they only resumed in 1934. In the meantime, however, the positions between the two had converged towards the attempt to 'de-provincialize antifascism', as Ascoli aptly called this endeavour.[14]

In January 1932, Rosselli began publishing the *Quaderni di GL*, in which members of the group discussed and argued about the current political, social, and cultural prospects for Italy and Europe. GL set out its own 'Schema di programma rivoluzionario', which brought together varying political cultures and experiences. This programme was aimed to

---

12 Curzio [Carlo Rosselli], 'Risposta a Giorgio Amendola', *Quaderni di GL* 1, January 1932, 40.

13 Letter from Max Ascoli to Carlo Rosselli, 30 December 1931, in Davide Grippa, *Un antifascista tra Italia e Stati Uniti. Democrazia e identità nazionale nel pensiero di Max Ascoli (1898–1947)*, Milan: Franco Angeli, 2009, 97.

14 Letter from Ascoli to Rosselli, 1 February 1934, in Grippa, *Un antifascista tra Italia e Stati Uniti*, 101.

establish 'a constructive antifascist position' building on 'the great experiences of postwar Europe' and implying 'a radical renewal of Italian life'.[15] Instead of presenting a detailed reform programme to be proposed to, and debated and approved by, the Constituent Assembly following the eventual fall of the Fascist dictatorship, it set out the 'immediate goals to be pursued during the revolutionary crisis'. The Italian crisis, in fact, consisted not of a 'simple crisis of political forms (democracy–dictatorship)', but of a 'crisis of institutions and social orders', of which Fascism was 'the most obvious manifestation'. Therefore, 'a great and modern democracy of labour' was to emerge, 'capable of establishing a new political class in a climate of true freedom'.[16]

The political culture of GL aimed to supersede the purely negative aspects of antifascism. The Fascist experience was now seen as a stimulus to the rethinking of the whole social, political, and intellectual order of Italy and Europe. Far from limiting itself to the strict rules of opposition to Fascism, GL immediately projected itself into the future of post-Fascism. In his article, published in December 1932, Nicola Chiaromonte, then an active GL conspirator in Rome, formulated his own concept of revolution and his specific contribution to the debate within the Paris group: 'Any political struggle – and even more so ours, which clearly wants to be revolutionary – deserves to succeed only if, before being waged in the name of what one *does not want*, is started and is conducted in the name of what one *does want*, in the name of (in all honesty) an ideal.' With unusual foresight, he warned that 'contempt for the adversary' could obscure 'one's sense of the real difficulties and of one's own faults'. It was therefore necessary to avoid the temptation to 'oppose a negation with the simple negation of negation', by placing at the centre of GL's thinking 'not the "restoration" of the destroyed forms, but their regeneration in new forms'.[17] A unique religious sensibility emerged in Chiaromonte's tendentially non-political message, in which the troubled Catholicism of his family and the neo-Protestant culture of the 1920s converged along with literature on the crisis of European civilization.

---

15   'Il programma rivoluzionario di "Giustizia e Libertà" ', *Quaderni di GL* 1, January 1932, 3.

16   'Chiarimenti al programma', *Quaderni di GL* 1, January 1932, 9.

17   Gualtiero [Nicola Chiaromonte], 'Lettera di un giovane dall'Italia', *Quaderni di GL* 5, December 1932, 32, 34.

In another article, published in October 1934, Chiaromonte affirmed the primacy of a revolutionary perspective that should not take the form of 'genuine antifascism, that is, an inverted Fascism', but should promote genuine social and cultural renewal.[18]

Nevertheless, it was the means of triggering this renewal that lay at the centre of the debate, and an article by Lussu in February 1934 created deep rifts within GL. Following the defeat of Social Democracy in the Weimar Republic, Lussu felt that the 'old socialism' was declining. It was necessary to 'decide to lay the foundations of a new Italian socialism: democratic and republican, class-oriented and liberal', and to found a new party that would include both the working class and the middle classes.'[19] In May 1934, growing dissent led to the dissolution of Concentrazione Antifascista, thus rendering Rosselli's group autonomous once again. At the same time, the new weekly publication *Giustizia e Libertà (GL)* saw the light of day, with the sub-heading *Movimento unitario di azione per l'autonomia operaia, la repubblica socialista, un nuovo umanesimo.* Rosselli demonstrated an extraordinary ability to capture diverse moods within his group, coalescing them into a radical political project. As 'an expression of the new generation's ideals and will to fight', GL intended to represent a special laboratory of antifascist ideology and practices, which combined a lucid analysis of Fascism with a utopian view of human and social emancipation. In May 1934, Rosselli's first editorial of the weekly *GL* read as follows:

> We are antifascists not so much and not only because we are against that complex of phenomena we call Fascism, but because we are for something that Fascism denies and offends, and violently prevents from being achieved. We are antifascists because in this age of fierce class oppression and the obscuration of human values, we insist on demanding a free and just society . . . We are antifascists because we recognize the supreme value, the reason and measure of all things in Man . . . Our antifascism therefore implies a positive faith, that is, the replacement of a world that generated Fascism with a new world.[20]

---

18   Luciano [Nicola Chiaromonte], 'Fronte unico', *GL*, 12 October 1934.
19   Tirreno [Emilio Lussu], 'Discussioni sul nostro movimento: orientamenti', *Quaderni di GL* 10, February 1934, 67.
20   [Carlo Rosselli,] 'Fronte verso l'Italia', *GL*, 18 May 1934.

Inseparable from Fascism, GL eschewed an antifascism that was the pure negation of its matrix. Rosselli was aware of the risk of indulging an exclusively negative dimension inversely mirroring the fundamental characteristics of Fascism itself. Umberto Calosso, however, placed a positive emphasis on the synchronous relationship of opposition and imitation between GL and Italian Fascism. In Calosso's opinion, in order to educate the young people who had grown up under Mussolini's regime, a 'very elementary propaganda' was needed, even 'following Hitler's example'.[21] Calosso explained that the dynamics of war taught that 'you must fight the enemy on its own ground and using its own weapons'.[22] 'Looking the enemy in the face, thoroughly examining its movements with the force of hatred': that was Calosso's chosen method.[23] Without abandoning the friend/foe logic that was GL's basic premise, and on which it continued to depend for reasons of political (if not physical) survival and moral intransigence, Rosselli's group had to learn from the enemy.

Antifascism was an essential precondition, albeit nothing more than a precondition, for the pursuit of a new post-Fascist order. However one wanted to perceive it, GL's idea of antifascism was intimately linked to the condition of living in exile. Political exile, which had initially been experienced as a contingent, provisional necessity, was gradually, reluctantly transformed into a conscious, permanent condition. However, the often sectarian and claustrophobic climate created by political emigration, a result of alienation from one's usual national surroundings, led to the radicalization of the exiles' political projects. Salvemini accused Rosselli of having become an 'outcast' like Mazzini, 'living on dreams and abstract words'.[24] In response to these harsh criticisms and others, the November 1934 edition of *GL* published a genuine 'vademecum' of antifascism, based on the clear rejection of certain attitudes prevailing among the émigré political parties:

---

21 Letter from Umberto Calosso to Carlo Rosselli, undated, Archivio Giustizia e Libertà, Sezione I, Scatola I, Fascicolo I, Sottofascicolo 23, Istituto Storico Toscano della Resistenza e dell'Età Contemporanea (Florence).

22 Umberto Calosso, 'Ballata delle donne giovani', *GL*, 15 June 1934.

23 Umberto Calosso, 'La statua di Beccaria', *GL*, 29 June 1934.

24 Letter from Gaetano Salvemini to Carlo Rosselli, 23 April 1934, in Carlo Rosselli and Salvemini, *Fra le righe*, 214.

To portray Fascism as on the verge of extinction from one moment to the next; to emphasize the importance of existing movements; to strike a bombastic, threatening tone; to exaggerate criticism and scandals, instead of attacking the fundamentals and looking at things in an organic manner; to make accusations for mainly sentimental reasons or because of the violence committed in the past; to adopt the tone of an antifascist aristocracy towards the people of the country; to appear to defend so-called pre-Fascist democracy or existing pseudo-democracies; to deny that anything useful was achieved under the Fascist regime; to question every feature of Mussolini, or with opposing exaggeration, to reduce Fascism to the figure of Mussolini; not to give sufficient emphasis to the positive aspects of antifascism.[25]

This series of positive and negative prescriptions helped define a specific psychological, political, and epistemological statute of exile among the members of GL. As we will see in the next chapter, this 'vademecum' was the result of a difficult process of development of ideas through participation in the transnational circulation of cultures, while, at the same time, it was also the product of a constant exchange of ideas with those conspiring against Fascism from within Italy. In other words, this vademecum represented a code of conduct for a 'new' antifascism that was based on criticism of the 'old' form of antifascism. But where did this 'new language' of GL come from? What were its roots and expressions? Who saw themselves as part of this new political project? To answer these and other questions, it is necessary to retrace the trajectory of GL's founders, together with some of the key points in Italian and European history during the early twentieth century.

Group Picture: Between Giolitti and Mussolini

The political and intellectual roots of GL, together with its ambivalences, contradictions, and the tortuous paths taken by its key players, need to be analysed against the background of early twentieth-century culture. All of its key figures came from Italy's social or intellectual elites. Rosselli himself was

---

25   [Carlo Rosselli,] 'I rischi dell'emigrazione', *GL*, 16 November 1934.

from an upper-class family highly critical of Giovanni Giolitti's governments, which were considered to be symbols of a corrupt and inglorious Italy.

Florence was the epicentre of an early twentieth-century cultural earthquake, driven by anti-positivist, irrational, pragmatic, and spiritual forces. The difficult relationship between culture and politics, which took various forms and involved diverse perspectives, was one of the focal points of various reviews published at the time (*Leonardo* edited by Giovanni Papini and Giuseppe Prezzolini, *Il Regno* by Enrico Corradini, *Hermes* by Giuseppe Antonio Borgese). As early as 1903, Prezzolini argued that this new cultural constellation was 'united more by hatred than by common goals'. In 1908, Prezzolini launched *La Voce*, whose contributors were individuals on the fringes of the academic system and traditional cultural networks. Expressing vehement criticism of 'the democracy of Giolitti', his Florentine journal sought to establish and educate a new ruling class, a sort of 'party' of intellectuals. *La Voce* tended to conflate politics and culture, nurturing the dubious temptation to substitute one for the other. Its contributors vacillated between a concern for the radical reform of representative democracy and a desire for its palingenetic destruction. Their often non-political, or even anti-political, mood was encapsulated in a memorable phrase penned by *La Voce* contributor Giovanni Amendola: 'We do not like Italy as it is.'[26]

Salvemini was one of the most influential figures in the group headed by Prezzolini. A historian and former Socialist Party activist, Salvemini subsequently became critical of Marxism and tended more towards the reformist line. He was among Giolitti's greatest critics, dubbing him the 'underworld minister'. Following disagreements with Prezzolini, Salvemini founded his own journal, *L'Unità*, in which he revived the debate on the reform of the educational system and of Italy's public administration, on the need for a federal system and for universal suffrage, and on the question of the development of Southern Italy. Salvemini's journal was highly critical of economic oligarchies and political parties, which were accused of distorting 'true' democracy.

Much of this cultural material had settled and become ingrained in post-unification, liberal Italy. A common substrate, perhaps the deepest, was Mazzini's mythical idea of the 'unfinished Risorgimento', which urgently called for an 'Italian revolution'. The unexpectedly rapid

---

26   Giovanni Amendola, 'Il Convegno nazionalista', *La Voce*, 1 December 1910.

construction of the new Italian state in the 1860s had provoked mixed reactions, although writers and intellectuals mostly perceived it as the realization of a centuries-old dream of independence and national unity. Fleeting initial enthusiasm was followed by growing disillusion and resentment, increasingly marked by frustration with, and recrimination against, the divide separating the 'legal nation' and the 'real nation'. Intellectuals became the principal triggers of an increasingly bitter conflict between the state and civil society during the early years of the twentieth century.

This non-political, often anti-political, culture represented the Italian dimension of a European debate largely rooted in the ideas of Maurice Barrès, Henri Bergson, Maurice Blondel, Charles Péguy, and Georges Sorel. This *ni droite ni gauche* culture was characterized by an elitism tasked with transforming primordial mass society. Notably, a virtuous aristocracy or an audacious avant-garde were called upon to infuse society with renewed moral vitality and to create an organic cultural or religious basis for that society (with emphatically nationalist connotations). The young Florentine intellectuals, who were both amateurs and iconoclasts, were in close contact with cultural figures from the Habsburg towns of Trieste and Gorizia, such as Scipio Slataper and Carlo Michelstaedter. Thanks to the latter, Central and Northern European philosophy and literature pertinent to the crisis reached Italy, introducing the works of Søren Kierkegaard, Friedrich Nietzsche, Henrik Ibsen, Karl Kraus, Sigmund Freud, and Ernst Mach.

That this early twentieth-century Italian culture was anything but provincial is shown by its appeal to a revolutionary intellectual like Andrea Caffi, who had been educated in imperial, cosmopolitan St Petersburg. Caffi was the son of a costume designer working for the Russian capital's theatres, who had joined the revolutionary student circles and semi-clandestine ranks of Russian Social-Democratic Workers' Party at an early age, had participated in the 1905 revolution, and had been imprisoned several times. He subsequently went into exile, shuttling backwards and forwards between Berlin, Florence, Zurich, and Paris. A disciple of the German philosopher and sociologist Georg Simmel, Caffi associated with Prezzolini and contributed to the pursuit of a new moral and intellectual order.

Between 1908 and 1911, *La Voce* was a meeting point for different political cultural currents: nationalism and futurism, revolutionary syndicalism and democratic reformism, intertwined in the search for a new elite.

However, between the summer of 1914 and the spring of 1915, this colourful intellectual world enthusiastically embraced Italy's entry into the war as an opportunity to carry out that 'revolution against Giolitti' that Prezzolini identified with the myth of the 'Italian revolution'. As early as 1914, Salvemini publicly advocated war against 'Prussian militarism' (meaning the Austro-Hungarian and German Empires) in the name of 'democracy'. The usual tirades against Giolitti were now accompanied by an apocalyptic crusading spirit that contributed to the troubled atmosphere of the so-called 'radiant days' of May 1915. In the meantime, Caffi went to the Argonne front as a volunteer in Garibaldi's Legion, a unit of the French Foreign Legion; he was then called back to arms in Italy in May 1915. He was aware of the 'European catastrophe', but that did not diminish his belief in the 'idealistic avant-garde groups [fasci]' who would renew Italy.[27]

Rosselli was too young to be sent to the front at that time, but he was nevertheless involved in the war. A scion of two upper-middle-class Jewish families – the Rossellis of Livorno and the Pincherles of Venice – he was born in Rome but grew up in Florence, in a strongly nationalist environment. His father's family were intent on cultivating the memory and legacy of Mazzini, who died in Pisa in 1872 at the home of one of the family ancestors, Pellegrino Rosselli. Along with his brothers Aldo and Nello, Carlo shared the interventionist beliefs of his mother Amelia Pincherle, a celebrated playwright from a liberal family close to Florentine nationalist circles at the turn of the century. After the death of her husband, Amelia was entrusted with her children's education, which she imparted according to the principles of a strict sense of duty. For her, as for many of the '1915 generation', Mazzini and the poet Giosué Carducci seemed more important than D'Annunzio and the politician Enrico Corradini, although nationalism, imperialism, and irrationalism increasingly blended together in their thinking. The Rosselli brothers enthusiastically supported the 'last war of the Risorgimento' to conquer Trento and Trieste: Carlo and Nello began publishing an interventionist student magazine, *Noi giovani*, while Aldo's death at the front in March 1916 confronted them with the tragic reality of the war in the northeastern Carnia Mountains. In the autumn of 1917, Carlo was called up, and

---

27   Marco Bresciani, *La rivoluzione perduta. Andrea Caffi nell'Europa del Novecento*, Bologna: Il Mulino, 2009, 19–57.

attended the Officers' Training School in Caserta until the spring of 1918. This made a significant mark on Rosselli's mindset, inspired by the idealism of Giovanni Gentile and based on the connection (derived from Mazzini) between will and morality.[28]

Mazzini's diverse and contradictory legacy shaped the idea of national democracy, the education of the 'people', and the political renewal of liberal Italy. While Salvemini, then a socialist, sharply criticized Mazzinian idealism, the Venetian jurist Alessandro Levi, uncle of Carlo and Nello, offered an interpretation of Mazzini's thought that emphasized the latter's openness to socialism. In the immediate postwar period, the idealist philosopher Giovanni Gentile proposed a nationalist and religious reinterpretation of Mazzini instead. Certainly, Rosselli was closer to Levi than to Gentile in terms of their respective sensibilities; but his generational affiliation meant that he succumbed to a nationalist vision of the Risorgimento. Within a few years, given the rise of Fascism – which had appropriated Mazzini's ideas – the compatibility of these interpretations became increasingly difficult (albeit not impossible).[29]

Rosselli's youthful, palingenetic language, however, echoed interventionist, nationalist conceptions. At the same time he absorbed the most innovative and creative tendencies of postwar French culture, thanks to his collaboration with Jean Luchaire, a gifted political journalist working in Florence. Due to the scarcity of sources on this period, it is difficult to know Rosselli's attitude towards the early Fascist movement. His generation's cultural education did not equip them with the means to clearly perceive the novelty and brutality of Fascism. Rosselli's affiliation with the ex-combatants' front, in which his personal experience of war and the family's traditional support for Mazzini converged, was accompanied by Salvemini and Alessandro Levi's relentless criticism of socialist maximalism. The idea that Fascism was the expression of a 'struggle of generations' was widespread in Gobetti's circle, which saw the Italy of the 'young' pitted against the Italy of the 'old'. After Mussolini's coming to power, the division between Fascism and antifascism became ever sharper; however, Rosselli's

---

28 Caroline Moorehead, *A Bold and Dangerous Family: The Rossellis and the Fight Against Mussolini*, London: Chatto & Windus, 2017.

29 Simon Levis Sullam, *Giuseppe Mazzini and the Origins of Fascism*, Basingstoke: Palgrave Macmillan 2015, 69–86.

antifascist stance (like that of Salvemini) was far from obvious or, indeed, necessary.[30] During the fierce political disputes of the postwar period, Salvemini tried to disentangle the democratic perspective from the nationalist one, but he did so in language that discredited organized parties and deepened the rift between society and politics. In his opinion, the young generation affected by the war needed to create a new political culture and establish a new ruling class. When he heard the news of the March on Rome, he did not hesitate to back Mussolini as prime minister in preference to any member of the old liberal ruling class, whom he accused of being the real culprits of Fascism. Between 1921 and 1923, previous cultural and political experiences thus prevented him from grasping the profound differences between Giolitti and Mussolini. Salvemini only began to reassess the question of formal democracy, and implicitly criticize his own hostile attitude towards Italy's prewar liberal system, after Mussolini had seized power.

Despite their friendship and agreement on 'democracy', Rosselli and Salvemini failed to agree on their opposition to Mussolini's government, their rethinking of socialism and liberalism, and their reassessment of Mazzini's legacy. While Salvemini increasingly distanced himself from politics, Rosselli drew closer to it. After Matteotti's kidnap and killing in June 1924, Carlo officially joined the United Socialist Party, although his desire for a profound revision of Marxist culture remained. Small groups began to flourish in Florence under Salvemini's leadership, but it was only after the rise of Fascism that they assumed an overtly political (antifascist) character. The most important such group was the Circolo di Cultura, founded in 1921. One of its founders was Ernesto Rossi, who had volunteered in 1916 as soon as he turned eighteen. During the wartime period, Rossi combined patriotic devotion, strong criticism of military orders, a futuristic enthusiasm for aviation, and Mazzini's sense of duty. In the postwar period he joined veterans' associations, turning his back on socialist-communist anti-patriotism and cherishing the hope of a radical renewal of the national ruling elite. This was what underlay his sympathy for early Fascism, the result of an impetuous critique of the parliamentary system

---

30 Nicola Tranfaglia, *Carlo Rosselli dall'interventismo a 'Giustizia e Libertà'*, Bari: Laterza, 1968.

and a vigorous defence of wartime sacrifice, reflected in his collaboration with the newspaper *Il Popolo d'Italia* from 1919 to 1922. The belief that a youthful, palingenetic momentum would sweep over and purify Italy continued to motivate disoriented postwar veterans for a long time thereafter. In the meantime, after completing a doctorate on Pareto's sociological thought, he taught at the Vittorio Emanuele Technical Institute in Bergamo, conducted economic research at the Bocconi University Library, and worked on Luigi Einaudi's magazine *Riforma sociale*.

The combatants' world comprised myriad figures holding different views on liberal institutions, but united in the conviction that the construction of a new nation had commenced in the wartime trenches of the Carso and Trentino mountains. At the same time, this outlook created a magnetic field that replicated the tensions, contradictions, and ambivalences of prewar anti-Giolittian culture in the far more unstable postwar context. The veterans' associations appeared uncertain and confused vis-à-vis the Fascist movement, which endeavoured to monopolize recognition of the sacrifices made by Italy's peasant infantrymen during the war. A decisive step towards antifascism was taken by the Italia Libera movement, founded in 1923 in opposition to the pro-Fascist Veterans' National Association. It brought together those prepared to organize the illegal antifascist struggle with those seeking to restore pre-Fascist liberal institutions. Carlo Rosselli was a member of Italia Libera's Florentine circle at the time.

In the autumn of 1924, in the wake of Matteotti's assassination, Giovanni Amendola founded the political group Unione Nazionale delle forze liberali e democratiche. With the aim of reforming and modernizing the nation, his 'new democracy' sought to turn the legacies of *La Voce* away from interventionist, nationalist, and authoritarian positions. Silvio Trentin, a jurist lecturing at Pisa University, participated in Amendola's project together with Rossi and Nello Rosselli. Trentin, who was from a family of landowners, members of the ruling class of San Donà del Piave, had backed, albeit reluctantly, Giolitti's governments in the name of gradual reformism. He subsequently supported intervention in the war against Austria–Hungary, in the name of the Italian nation and democracy. In his early thirties he volunteered with the Red Cross as a first lieutenant and administrator, and was subsequently assigned the position of air reconnaissance officer, in which capacity he earned numerous medals for bravery. Surprised by the crisis of liberal institutions during the postwar period, he was initially seduced by Fascism and its promises of renewal. Elected as a deputy for the Venetian Social Democrats in November 1919, his brief parliamentary experience proved disappointing; in the face of rampant *squadrismo*, his party continued to call for social peace in 1921. However, by the end of 1923, realizing that it was impossible to reach an agreement with the Fascists, Trentin had recognized the need to support the country's liberal institutions; a year later, he joined Giovanni Amendola's Unione Nazionale, and subsequently the Republican Party.[31]

The struggle against Mussolini's government during the Matteotti crisis was the backdrop to the founding of the newspaper *Il Caffè* in Milan in July 1924, which, despite various seizures, managed to publish until May 1925. Unlike Italia Libera, which sought a balance between readiness to compromise on the monarchy and opting for an intransigent anti-fascist stance, this new project, with its clear neo-Enlightenment orientation, promoted by Ferruccio Parri and Riccardo Bauer, espoused an anti-rhetorical style accompanied by polemical rigour. Parri was from a Piedmontese family that cherished the myth of Mazzini and sympathized with the democratic elitism of the early twentieth century. During the war, his desire for the radical regeneration of the nation had turned into harsh criticism of representative democracy. He had shared the interventionist and anti-socialist sentiments of early Fascism, close to the war veterans' milieu and hostile to the 'dictatorship of Giolitti'. It is difficult to say exactly when he consciously became an antifascist; what is certain is that the Fascists' March on Rome quickly removed any doubts he may still have had.[32] The other founder of *Il Caffè*, Bauer, from a wealthy Bohemian merchant family, had renounced his Habsburg citizenship so as to volunteer for the Italian army during the Great War. After attending the officers' course at the Turin Academy, he was called up in 1916, wounded several times, and awarded a bronze medal after the war. Bauer was later appointed secretary of the Humanitarian Society (a prestigious philanthropic and cultural institution based in Milan) and eventually

31   Frank Rosengarten, *Silvio Trentin dall'interventismo alla Resistenza*, Milan: Feltrinelli, 1980.

32   Luca Polese Remaggi, *La nazione perduta: Ferruccio Parri nel Novecento italiano*, Bologna: Il Mulino, 2004, 19–116 (with insightful analyses on the anti-Giolittian revolution).

adopted liberal-democratic views, contributing to the political journal *Rivoluzione Liberale*. However, he argued fiercely with Gobetti, the founder of the journal, calling for an antifascist undertaking that focused more on the political than the cultural level.

As one of the strongholds of Fascist *squadrismo*, Florence also became one of the most active centres of resistance to Mussolini's rule, which had accelerated the disintegration of Italy's liberal institutions. The Circolo di Cultura was targeted and destroyed by Fascist squads on the night of 30 December 1924, a few days before Mussolini proclaimed full-fledged dictatorship. In an oppressive situation where only clandestine action was now possible, the underground publication *Non mollare* emerged, inspiring both the representatives of Italia Libera and the members of Circolo di Cultura. This was little more than a call to rebel that circulated between January and October 1925. The struggle 'on lawful grounds, using lawful weapons, in a civilized atmosphere' was now over: a 'definitive incompatibility' had been established between Fascists and antifascists, so that it was now necessary to form 'a revolutionary elite'.[33]

Increased police surveillance of *Non mollare*'s clandestine publication resulted in Rossi fleeing and Salvemini being arrested in July 1925. The latter's trial, staged by the Fascists as an opportunity to teach their opponents a hard lesson, ended with the provisional release of the professor, who subsequently managed to flee, first to Paris and then to London, his flight marking the start of a twenty-year period of exile. Two more issues of *Non mollare* appeared before the Fascist squads in Florence launched an all-out 'manhunt' that destroyed the magazine's network, now very thin, in early October. Carlo Rosselli's involvement in this antifascist publication, however, proved decisive for his political development. Faced with the failure of the legal opposition, action became a genuine obsession for him.

On 1 May 1925, Croce broke with his previous ambiguity towards Mussolini's government to write a *Manifesto degli intellettuali antifascisti* that was designed to be a direct response to Gentile's opposing *Manifesto degli intellettuali fascisti*. This was a clear sign that Croce was reconsidering his views on Fascism and his attitude towards liberalism. Meanwhile,

---

33 'Ancora l'Aventino', *Non Mollare*, 27 July 1925, in Mimmo Franzinelli (ed.), *'Non Mollare' (1925). Con saggi di Gaetano Salvemini, Ernesto Rossi e Piero Calamandrei*, Turin: Bollati Boringhieri, 2005, 145.

Trentin was one of three university professors, following Salvemini and Francesco Saverio Nitti, who renounced their academic titles and positions: he resigned from Ca' Foscari University in Venice in December 1925. In February 1926, Trentin left Italy and moved to Auch in the south of France, where he devoted himself to rural work. For politicians and intellectuals like Salvemini and Trentin, who belonged to an older generation than that of Rosselli, the choice between surrender and exile was now clear, and they opted for the latter. The young Florentine antifascist, in contrast, considered exile the equivalent of surrender to the very end. In his view, 'an elite has to be organized in Italy that is capable of managing the opposition movement and forming the future ruling class.'[34]

Despite the climate of increasing intimidation and repression, Rosselli still believed that the most effective way of shaping a post-Fascist ruling class was to foster political research, reflection, and conversation through the publication of journals in Italy. With this purpose in mind, from March to October 1926, he edited the journal *Il Quarto Stato* in Milan together with Pietro Nenni. Nenni had shared the insurrectionary radicalism of the Romagna region's republican tradition as a young man, before joining the campaign in favour of intervention in the 1914–15 war, and he supported early Fascism in the period 1919–20. He then moved closer to the positions of the Socialist Party, and eventually became the leader of its revolutionary wing, becoming editor of *Avanti!* as of 1923. While Rosselli's earlier initiatives had depended on the contingencies of the political struggle against Mussolini's regime, this journal, which still circulated freely, represented a first thoughtful attempt to create a 'new socialist generation'. 'Why were we beaten?' This was the key question, one that called for the 'strongest self-criticism' in order to fathom the 'reasons for defeat' during the postwar period. In confronting 'pure Marxist ideology', Rosselli did not hesitate to distance himself from Turati's older generation, thus triggering a lively debate on the matter.[35]

Il Quarto Stato claimed to thoroughly review the question of the relationship between socialism and democracy within the context of its stated

---

34   Letter from Carlo Rosselli to Gaetano Salvemini, 29 September 1925, in Carlo Rosselli and Salvemini, *Fra le righe*, 97.

35   [Carlo Rosselli,] 'Autocritica', *Il Quarto Stato*, 3 April 1926, in Carlo Rosselli, *Opere scelte*, vol. 1, 129–32.

opposition to the Soviet model. Among the journal's contributors was Caffi, who provided first-hand knowledge of the various revolutionary cultures of Europe. The allure of the Russian Revolutions had briefly propelled him into the maelstrom of Russia's civil wars and into the ranks of the Bolsheviks. Arriving in Rome from Moscow in 1923, he was attracted to Salvemini's democratic milieu, and he established contact with Russian émigrés (both social revolutionary and counterrevolutionary) in Italy. He also wrote essays of unusual clarity on the Russian revolutionary process and the new Bolshevik regime for the democratic journals *Il Popolo, Volontà*, and *La Vita delle Nazioni*, as well as in Curzio Malaparte's Fascist-revolutionary weekly, *La Conquista dello Stato*. In the uncertain months between Matteotti's assassination and Mussolini's proclamation of dictatorship, he oscillated between various radical positions based on intellectual elitism, a distrust of the masses, and the prospect of revolutionary change. It was only between 1925 and 1926 that Caffi joined the opposition to the Fascist regime before fleeing to Paris, out of fear of imminent arrest.

In November 1926, the regime passed the Special Law for State Security. With the dissolution of political parties, the suppression of freedom of expression and assembly, and the establishment of the Special Court, the dictatorship was placed on a legal footing. Rosselli and Parri helped set up a clandestine network for rescuing key figures opposed to the regime. The most sensational operation involved the expatriation of Turati, the old Socialist leader then living in Milan in a climate of increasing intimidation. His escape was organized by Rosselli, Parri, and Sandro Pertini, a young lawyer from Savona who had fought in the Great War and joined the Socialist Party after Matteotti's murder. Although the operation was successful, Rosselli and Parri were arrested, and imprisoned in Como from December 1926 to September 1927. During their trial in Savona, their defence was based on the systematic denial of Fascism's purported role as the sole heir to the tradition of the Risorgimento, and to victory in the Great War. They rejected the Fascists' accusations of anti-patriotic defeatism. Rosselli explained that he wanted Turati's flight from Fascist Italy to provide 'living proof of the definitive rift between two Italys, between two moral races, between two opposing views of life'.[36]

---

36 Carlo Rosselli, *Lettera al giudice istruttore* (no date, but August 1927), in *Opere scelte*, vol. 1, 492.

In June 1927, his brother Nello was arrested in Florence and sentenced to five years' confinement on the island of Ustica; he was released in early 1928. Compared to Carlo, Nello was much less willing to engage in political activism, although he did participate in the work of the Circolo di Cultura, the Unione Nazionale, and the clandestine journal *Non mollare*. Under the intellectual guidance of Salvemini he had begun studying the history of the Risorgimento, and this led him to publish his first book, *Mazzini e Bakunin* (1927). Nello analysed the early history of the Italian workers' movement and at the same time examined the limits and contradictions of the republican project for emancipation in terms of the social question.[37]

Carlo Rosselli was held for two more months in Savona prison; he was then confined on the island of Lipari, where he met and got to know Emilio Lussu. The life of Lussu, the son of small landowners in Armungia in Sardinia, had been deeply marked by the Great War. Called to arms while studying in Rome, he had been deployed in the ranks of the Sassari Brigade in the Carso region (close to Trieste). His love of hunting and adventure were fully expressed in the courage he displayed at the front. Lussu was promoted to the rank of captain in 1916 and was decorated on four separate occasions. He became a wartime legend in Sardinia and was elected to Parliament, where he maintained his fighting spirit. He founded the Sardinian Action Party, a combination of peasant classism, regional autonomism, and federal reformism, and sought to establish a dialogue with the Socialist Party during a period of intense social unrest in Italy. However, his rather insular political outlook and militant attitude meant that he only later became aware of the Fascist movement's threat as a novel political force. Between the end of 1922 and mid-1923, Lussu saw the opportunity for the renewal of regional public life through a merger of the Sardinian Action Party with the National Fascist Party. He was thus on very close terms with early Fascism, from which he later distanced himself due to the authoritarian policies and continued violence of Mussolini's new government. His decision to take up the antifascist cause was sealed by a tragic personal event: the killing of a Fascist during a raid on his home in Cagliari in October 1926. Although he was judged to have acted in self-defence and

---

37 Nello Rosselli, *Mazzini e Bakunin. 12 anni di movimento operaio in Italia (1860–1872)*, Turin: Einaudi, 1927.

was subsequently acquitted by the Special Court after almost a year of preventive detention, Lussu was sentenced to confinement for reasons of public security.[38] In November 1927 he was deported to Lipari, where Carlo Rosselli arrived the following January. The two finally managed to escape on 27 July 1929. By this time, Rosselli had set out his political vision in an unpublished manuscript entitled *Socialismo liberale*.

Blending Liberalism, Democracy, and Socialism

In an interview given in September 1929, a few weeks after his arrival in Paris, Rosselli laid out the premises of his political action. He opposed 'the aspiration to be part of History with a capital H, to establish the civil status of one's time with perfect precision, and to follow the path laid down by Marxism'. His voluntarism, however, was tempered by a rejection of 'blind' action 'unsupported by reason and unilluminated by morality'. This close connection between thought and action, which harked back to Mazzini, awakened the need for a 'courageous examination of one's conscience' that reconciled socialism with freedom, understood as 'a means and an end', in all areas of individual and collective life. On this occasion, Rosselli publicly announced that while confined he had written a book on political theory and struggle that he would soon have printed in France. The book in question was entitled, in French, *Socialisme libéral*.[39]

This volume, which was only published in Italian (under the title *Socialismo liberale*) much later in 1945, was the result of almost ten years of research and reflection. While trying to get his bearings among the conflicts and dilemmas of the postwar period, Carlo Rosselli had begun to examine the economic role played by trade unions. First he studied economics at the Cesare Alfieri Institute in Florence (1921), and then law at the University of Siena (1923). Early on in these studies, Rosselli took a keen interest in theoretical problems, outlining possible responses to the

---

38   Giuseppe Fiori, *Il cavaliere dei Rossomori: vita di Emilio Lussu*, Turin: Einaudi, 2000.

39   Carlo Rosselli, 'Pensiero e azione per la conquista della libertà', interview with *L'Italia del Popolo. Bollettino quindicinale della Federazione repubblicani italiani residenti in Europa*, 30 September 1929, in *Scritti dell'esilio*, vol. 1, 3–9.

ideological and political crisis that had begun with the defeat of Italian socialism in the postwar period. He conceptualized socialism as a faith drawing on the moral character of politics; he opted for a universalist rather than a class approach; and he recognized the superiority of democracy as the means and end of action. Rosselli thus envisaged a variety of paths to socialism, ruling out the necessity of violent means in Italy to transform the nation's political and social order. However, he did not deny that elsewhere, as in Russia, violent revolution had been (or might be) necessary.

Over two periods spent in London during the summer of 1923 and the autumn of 1924, Rosselli made contact with members of the British Labour Party, and attended the London School of Economics. Thanks to Richard Tawney, a scholar of the English labour movement, Rosselli made the acquaintance of the most important figures in the Fabian Society and the 'guild' movement (notably G. D. H. Cole). He not only adopted a clearly-defined political position, he also engaged in a series of theoretical and practical experiments inspired by 'healthy English empiricism', alien to the 'blind and tortuous dogmatism' of Italian socialism.[40] The articles published between 1923 and 1924 in *Critica sociale*, *Rivoluzione liberale* and *Giustizia* conveyed the political views and vocabulary of British Labourism and guild socialism. Rosselli advocated the need for a socialist party and socialist practice characterized by a 'liberal method'. The socialist movement, he argued, must be rooted in federative associations (leagues, cooperatives, grassroots cultural institutions) and proceed 'not from the top down, not from the centre to the periphery, but the other way around'. In his eyes, the socialist movement's demand for workers' control corresponded to the need not only for economic autonomy, but also for ideal autonomy, since each worker wanted to affirm 'his dignity as a human being both inside and outside the factory'.[41] Although interested in the gradualist, democratic collectivism of Sidney and Beatrice Webb as theorized in their *Industrial Democracy* (1897), Rosselli primarily internalized the libertarian, anti-statist, cooperative socialism of Cole as set out in his

---

40   Carlo Rosselli, 'La crisi intellettuale del partito socialista', *Critica sociale*, 1–15 November 1923, 325–8.

41   Carlo Rosselli, 'Liberalismo socialista', *Rivoluzione liberale*, 15 July 1924, 114–16.

Guild Socialism Re-Stated and Social Theory (1920). The end of the Great War ushered in a short-lived period of experimentation with industrial democracy in England; projects such as the Whitley Councils breathed new life into theories of pluralism. Cole, notably, developed a pluralist conception of society rooted in the trade unions and closely linked to the working class, but he did so without developing a class perspective. The democratic polity – a departure from the rigid framework of centralized state institutions – derived its legitimacy and unity from its ability to create local and regional forms of self-government, to represent people's economic interests, and to protect individual ethical autonomy.[42]

The British experience led Rosselli to tone down his negativity towards political parties, which was rooted in the elitist culture of Mosca and Pareto. British thinking on pluralism saw the Labour Party as playing an essential role in promoting a reformist, evolutionary approach to liberal socialism. Drawn to the gradualist socialism of the Labour Party and the trade unions, Rosselli was particularly interested in a current of liberal renewal that had emerged in early twentieth-century Britain in the face of the new challenges epitomized by mass politics. In contrast to Old Liberalism, New Liberalism was concerned with responding to the demands of the world of labour, by ensuring effective improvement in the social conditions of the working classes originating from the Industrial Revolution so as to prevent their greater radicalization. The benchmark works of this school of thought were *The Crisis of Liberalism: New Issues of Democracy* (1909), by the economist John A. Hobson, and *Liberalism* (1911) by the sociologist Leonard T. Hobhouse. In the early 1920s, Rosselli probably read both of these works, which developed a pluralist view of liberalism with certain points of contact with socialism. According to the Italian philosopher Guido De Ruggiero, Hobhouse's work offered 'the best formulation of the new English liberalism of the twentieth century', in which property rights, the right to work, individual liberty and social justice were all acknowledged together. When Rosselli read De Ruggiero's 1925 *Storia del liberalismo europeo* during his confinement, he found the most authoritative confirmation of his own working hypothesis, namely:

---

42 See Marc Stears, *Progressives, Pluralists, and the Problems of the State: Ideologies of Reform in the United States and in Great Britain, 1909–1926*, New York: Oxford University Press, 2002.

'Socialism means several things, and it is possible that there is a liberal socialism, just as there is an illiberal one.'[43]

Rosselli pursued business studies and an academic career, arriving in Milan in the autumn of 1923 as Einaudi's assistant at the Institute of Political Economy at Bocconi University. In November 1924, he began lecturing in political economics and political economic institutions at the Business School. As a political activist he shuttled between Genoa and Milan to help organize the ranks of the antifascist plotters, while as a scholar he lectured on Alfred Marshall's *Principles of Economics* and John M. Keynes's *Monetary Reform*. Carlo's closeness to the English world was undoubtedly encouraged by his marriage to Marion Cave in Milan in June 1926. Born in 1896 to a Quaker family from Uxbridge and educated at St Paul's Girls' School in Hammersmith, she got a degree in French and Italian at Bedford College. Fascinated with the socialist struggles taking place in postwar Italy, in September 1919 she moved to Florence on a scholarship from the Italian-British League, and fell in with Salvemini's network in early 1921. She helped him learn English, and he got her a job teaching English at the British Institute in Florence, and then at the University of Florence. She became increasingly involved in the Circolo di cultura, where she met Carlo Rosselli. Despite Marion's clear antifascist stance, she was kept apart from Carlo's main political activity.[44]

After being arrested and convicted for his political opposition to Fascism, Rosselli continued his scholarly activities from his reclusion on the island of Lipari. At first glance, it may be a surprise to discover that Carlo Rosselli's only complete work was written in one of the situations typical of Fascist repression, that is, confinement on an island. In fact, confinement and imprisonment under the Fascist regime certainly circumscribed and conditioned, but did not prevent, intellectual activity. Arbitrary, albeit rather loose, forms of censorship allowed many books to slip through the net and circulate, while conversations between prisoners, albeit under surveillance, were permitted, and writing notes on readings

43   Guido De Ruggiero, *Storia del liberalismo europeo*, Milan: Feltrinelli, 1962 (1925), 152.

44   Isabelle Richet, *Women, Antifascism, and Mussolini's Italy: The Life of Marion Cave*, London: I.B. Tauris, 2018.

was tolerated.[45] During his confinement on Lipari between 1927 and 1929, Rosselli, although deprived of his library, had the opportunity to read extensively, and this resulted in the clandestine drafting of the manuscript for *Liberal Socialism*. Hidden between the strings of an old piano, the manuscript was secretly taken off the island by Rosselli's wife, and then carried from Italy to France. Mussolini's regime thus not only failed to keep the lid on a clever and driven enemy determined to fight it to the bitter end, but could not prevent the circulation of an important book, as yet unpublished but destined to arouse considerable interest abroad.

Like Gobetti, Rosselli was convinced that the Italian problem was first and foremost 'the problem of liberty'. In *Liberal Socialism*, he depicted Fascism as inscribed within a pattern of Italian history dominated by authority and discipline, and marked by the absence of autonomy and responsibility. At the heart of his vision lay the contrast between Italy and 'modern' Europe, for Italy had not known the wars of religion, 'the principal leaven of liberalism, the birth pangs of modern man'. According to Rosselli, despite Fascism's revolutionary proclamations, it was instead 'the most passive development in Italian history'.[46] Nonetheless, he believed that the Great War had crystallized certain characteristics of Italians in the new political movement:

> Fascism is not explicable purely in terms of class interests. Its goon squads did not come into being solely because they were subsidized by angry, reactionary social elites. Factiousness, the spirit of adventure, romantic inclinations, petit bourgeois idealism, nationalistic rhetoric, feelings aroused by the war, the restless desire for something, anything at all, as long as it was new – without motives like these there would have been no fascism.[47]

Rosselli thus appropriated Gobetti's successful formula of the 'autobiography of the nation' with which to portray a vision of Fascism as a moment

---

45   See Marco Bresciani, 'La repressione degli intellettuali', in Sergio Luzzatto, Gabriele Pedullà, and Domenico Scarpa (eds), *Atlante storico della letteratura italiana*, vol. 3, *Dal Romanticismo a oggi*, Turin: Einaudi, 2012, 623–44.

46   Carlo Rosselli, *Liberal Socialism*, 103–4.

47   Ibid., 107–8.

of revelation in Italian history. Paradoxically, this deterministic and teleological outlook, based on the characteristics of the Italian people, coexisted with an energetic affirmation of the desire for revolution. Rosselli belonged to a new generation that was 'idealistic, voluntaristic, and pragmatic' and that did not understand 'the materialistic, positivistic, and pseudo-scientific language of the elders'. However, in the first section of *Liberal Socialism* it was above all his critique of Marxism that enabled Rosselli to break with the sense of the continuity of national history, and to correlate Gobetti's problem of freedom with a new socialist perspective. While hitherto he had favoured Mazzinianism and Labourism, radical liberalism and guild socialism, he now developed a systematic theoretical evaluation of revisionism (from Eduard Bernstein to Georges Sorel, Antonio Labriola and Rodolfo Mondolfo). With regard to Marxian thought, Rosselli adopted in particular Croce's approach aimed at 'accepting what is vital and rejecting *openly and definitely* everything erroneous, utopian, and contingent in Marxism'. Marx's thought was thus seen as belonging to 'a phase that was certainly essential but that is now outmoded in the history of the socialist movement'.[48]

Rosselli was neither Marxist nor anti-Marxist; he was consciously post-Marxist. Central to his critique of Marxism was his rejection of the determinism that had characterized the Second International. Rosselli's reading of *The Psychology of Socialism*, published in 1926 and translated into French in 1927 as *Au-delà du marxisme*, proved crucial in this regard. Its author, the Flemish socialist Hendrik de Man, who had developed his ideas mainly during his prewar experience in Leipzig, a cradle of radical Marxism, belonged to the 'frontline generation'. Postwar developments involving Europe and America taught de Man the inherent strength of capitalism (organized along Taylorist lines), while he believed that the Bolshevik Revolution highlighted the need to reconcile socialism with nationhood and democracy. De Man thus began to review the psychological foundations of dialectical materialism, which led him to strongly criticize philosophical determinism. He stressed the key role of the will in the historical process, recognized the value of education, and developed the thesis of the separation of means and ends, previously advocated by the

---

48   Ibid., 50, 72–3.

German Social Democrat Eduard Bernstein.[49] Following de Man, Rosselli argued for 'an injection of ethics and a voluntaristic orientation' to socialism that would allow it to achieve 'the progressive actualization of the idea of liberty and justice among men.'[50]

However, unlike de Man, whose thinking was shaped by his Marxist education and his experience in the German social-democratic ranks, Rosselli focused primarily on the relationship between socialism and liberalism. He owed this focus to the French scholar Élie Halévy, a friend of Croce and Salvemini, whom Rosselli had met in Florence in 1925. They shared an interest in postwar Britain, on which Halévy had published a series of articles between 1919 and 1922: these articles dealt with the needs of economic recovery, the possibilities of trade-union control through the Whitley Councils, and the novelty of the libertarian, anti-state politics of guild socialism. Both Rosselli and Halévy were searching for a socialism that could reconcile individual rights and social cohesion.[51] The cycle of war and revolution that had devastated Italy and Europe between 1914 and 1922 led to the maximum expansion of state institutions and curbed individual freedoms and social autonomy. Rosselli therefore rejected any political project designed to make the state 'the administrator and universal controller of the rights and liberties of all'.[52] A reading of Halévy's major works (*The Growth of Philosophic Radicalism* and the first volume of

49   Peter Dodge, *Beyond Marxism: The Faith and the Works of Henri de Man*, The Hague: Nijhoff, 1966; 'Sur l'œuvre de Henri de Man', Colloque international organisé par l'Université de Genève, 18–20 juin 1973, sous la présidence de Ivo Rens et Michel Brélaz, *Revue européenne de sciences sociales* 31, 1974; Michel Brélaz, *Henri de Man: une autre idée de socialisme*, Genève: Éditions des Antipodes, 1985; Tommaso Milani, *Hendrik de Man and Social Democracy: The Idea of Planning in Western Europe, 1914–1940*, Basingstoke: Palgrave Macmillan, 2020 (especially 85–90, as for his relationship with Rosselli).

50   Carlo Rosselli, *Liberal Socialism*, 77–8.

51   See Michele Battini, 'Carlo Rosselli, "Giustizia e Libertà", and the Enigma of Justice', in 'The Transformation of Republicanism in Modern and Contemporary Italy', special issue, *Journal of Modern Italian Studies* 17, no. 2, 2012, 205–19; Ludovic Frobert, *République et économie (1896–1914)*, Lille: Presses Universitaires du Septentrion, 2003; Ludovic Frobert, 'Élie Halévy's First Lectures on the History of European Socialism', *Journal of the History of Ideas* 68, no. 2, 2007, 329–53; and, most recently, K. Steven Vincent, *Élie Halévy: Republican Liberalism Confronts the Era of Tyrannies*, Philadelphia: University of Pennsylvania Press, 2020.

52   Carlo Rosselli, *Liberal Socialism*, 92.

History of the English People in the Nineteenth Century), on the other hand, comforted Rosselli with regard to his harsh judgement of individualism, and revealed the prospect of compatibility between liberalism and a 'new' form of socialism. As early as the very first lines of *Liberal Socialism*, the young Italian economist rejected any teleologically predetermined view of socialism and argued for a possible convergence between socialism and liberalism:

> Liberalism has gradually become cognizant of the social problem and no longer appears automatically bound to the principles of classical, Manchesterian economics. Socialism is stripping itself, though not easily, of its utopianism and acquiring a new awareness of the problems of liberty and autonomy.
> Is liberalism becoming socialist, or is socialism becoming liberal?
> The answer is, both at the same time.[53]

Rosselli thus interpreted the socialist movement as the heir to liberalism, the bearer of a dynamic idea of freedom embodied in history as an open-ended process. Understood as one of the possible outcomes of social and political developments and conflicts, socialism became a 'philosophy of liberty'. Liberalism and socialism were by no means opposed to each other, but were linked through an organic, mutually beneficial relationship: 'Liberalism is the ideal force of inspiration, and socialism is the practical force of realization.'[54] In its original theoretical formulation, stemming from Bentham's utilitarianism, this philosophy harked back to the democratic radicalism of John Stuart Mill, and his opposition to the Manchester liberalism of Richard Cobden. Rosselli, in turn, held that 'for liberalism, and hence for socialism, observance of the *liberal method*, that is, the democratic method, of entering the political contest is fundamental'. He identified this method, 'utterly permeated with the principle of liberty', with the practice of 'self-government'. The principle of popular sovereignty, the representative system, the respect for the rights of minorities, and the rejection of the use of force, together constituted not only 'a complex of rules of the game ... intended to ensure the peaceful

---

53   Ibid., 6.
54   Ibid., 84, 87.

coexistence of citizens, social classes, and states' but, above all, 'a sort of *pact of civility*'.[55]

In 1926–28 Rosselli's political thought took the form of republicanism characterized by constitutional government, individual liberties and increasing political and social rights. Different from Marxism, grounded in the industrial and urban society, his idea of liberal socialism was much more appropriate for a still mostly peasant society, like the Italian one of the time.[56] In the young Florentine economist's mind, however, the relationships between liberalism, democracy, and socialism were continuously mutating, and represented a constant blending of these different (albeit not incompatible) traditions. This was the characteristic trait of an experimental approach that emerged from the 'non-conformist' cultures of the 1910s and that engaged with the French intellectual climate of the 1920s and 1930s. For example, *Socialisme libéral* was published in December 1930 by the publishing house founded by Georges Valois, an infantry officer wounded and decorated during the Great War and a member of Action française until 1925. That year he founded the Faisceau movement, reflecting his professed (but short-lived) admiration for Mussolini. Then, in 1928, he founded the Republican Syndicalist Party and launched the journal *Cahiers bleus*, whose contributors included Pierre Mendès France, Édouard Berth, Bertrand de Jouvenel and Marcel Déat. Aside from any contingent political choices, Valois advocated a modern, technocratic, corporatist outlook that recognized the role of producers and entrepreneurs, and that was based on the lessons of the war economy: he thus proposed the creation of a 'syndicalist republic' instead of a parliamentary republic.[57] In the early 1930s, Rosselli and Valois shared an unprejudiced desire for a radical renewal of politics.

While the French socialist or 'non-conformist' press showed some interest, at the time of publication of *Socialisme libéral* in December 1930 the work was received coldly, even critically, by the socialist and communist

---

55   Ibid., 94.

56   My thanks to Giovanni Levi for suggesting this social root of Rosselli's liberal socialism.

57   See Allen Douglas, *From Fascism to Libertarian Communism: Georges Valois Against the Third Republic*, Berkeley: University of California Press, 1992, and Olivier Dard, *Le rendez-vous manqué des relèves des années 30*, Paris: Presses Universitaires de France, 2002, 29–34.

émigré press. However, it did not constitute the original benchmark text for GL's members. Rather than a chosen doctrine or a party affiliation, the reality GL was faced with was one that demanded urgent answers. While Rosselli's theoretical research began with the reasons for the defeat of socialism, his political reflections and actions centred on the reasons for Fascism's victory. It was only by observing, and learning from, the enemy that Rosselli managed to come up with a new antifascist perspective.

The Turtle Conspiracy

Far from constituting a compact, disciplined movement, GL was an open, heterogeneous universe of informal, fluid, indeterminate connections, only some of which were subject to the rules of clandestine operation. Personal friendships, intellectual coteries, and shared experiences in the sphere of political activism, came together to form GL. The impetus from the Parisian émigré community was decisive; however, GL's groups in Italy drew on pre-existing conspiratorial networks that were reactivated and readapted despite the repression prevalent at the time. Indeed, on the liberal-democratic, socialist, and republican sides, all forms of organized opposition had run out of steam or had simply disappeared by 1928. Between 1929 and 1930, numerous small groups of GL members formed in cities and provinces throughout Italy. These comprised the liberal-democratic core in Milan, the variegated post-Gobettian milieu in Turin, the surviving members of Italia Libera and *Non mollare* in Florence, the Republican network in Rome, the former members of the Sardinian Action Party and the Republican Party in Sardinia, and the Italian, Slovenian, and Croatian Republican groups in Trieste and Istria. What was unusual among the variegated antifascist forces anchored to national tradition was, above all, their efforts to unite with political exponents of the linguistic minorities present in Italy. Fascist repression was particularly fierce in the border areas that had shifted from Habsburg to Italian sovereignty: hence the formation of the armed group TIGR (Trst, Istra, Gorica, Rijeka), which established relations with GL.

However, the first real GL group operating in Italy was organized in Milan, thanks above all to Riccardo Bauer and Ernesto Rossi. Rossi helped define the general line of GL by underscoring the need to take a liberal-democratic direction through correspondence and direct contact with the Paris GL community. In the summer of 1930, Rossi, together with Salvemini, wrote the pamphlet *Consigli sulla tattica*, offering reflections on the tactics and objectives of the revolutionary struggle, which the authors foresaw as being 'long and very hard'. They combined a call for mass 'passive resistance' with the small group's attempted 'revolutionary organization', an encouragement of illegal proselytizing with the rejection of terrorism. A new Paris edition of the pamphlet was signed by Rossi and Bauer, but being written after their arrest, it was probably revised by Lussu. It contained several significant changes, including the urgent call for a paramilitary structure and for insurgency preparations through trained, disciplined groups, ready 'for the risks of action'.[58] However, GL's Milan cell did not last long. In October 1930, a police raid following a report by the spy Carlo Del Re led to the arrest of its main representatives. During the subsequent interrogations and trials, the defendants strongly emphasized the ideological link between the legacy of Italy's Risorgimento, wartime voluntarism, and liberal democratic principles, which they believed fed both aversion to Bolshevism and opposition to Fascism.[59]

Following the demise of the Milan group, Turin became GL's main organizational and intellectual centre in Italy. As the scene of factory occupations in September 1920, Turin had consolidated its place as the true capital of the Italian labour movement, and the Fascist regime had less of a foothold here than elsewhere in the country. After the suppression of the Communist Party, however, there was nothing left in Turin that resembled an organized form of political opposition. Rather, networks of isolated individuals and forms of solidarity between students and faculty emerged: this heterogeneous, open universe was different from communist cells, and as such was more vulnerable. Of course, each of these individuals held their own political convictions (be they liberal-democratic, republican, or socialist), and yet there was a willingness to find common ground for opposing the regime. GL's Turin group was formed at the end of 1929 upon the initiative of the Milan group, which was in contact with Aldo Garosci.

Garosci had attended the Istituto Sociale in Turin, an old Jesuit school that was one of Turin's elite educational institutions. He was taught by

---

58   Giovana, *Giustizia e Libertà in Italia*, 89–97.
59   Ibid., 182–95.

Francesco Ruffini, professor of the history of canon law and religious liberty. Hence the young Garosci's passion for sixteenth-century politics, religion, and literature: his first writings on the subject were published in Piero Gobetti's last journal, *Il Baretti*. At the time, Garosci shared his historical interests and political perspectives with his cousin Giorgio Agosti, who had attended lectures at the University of Cracow in 1931 given by Stanisław Kot, one of the leading experts on the Reformation. Agosti had inherited his passion for Polish culture (literary and historical) from his mother; but, like Garosci, he chose to study law under Gioele Solari, a legal philosopher and historian of modern political thought. His antifascism operated on a cultural rather than a political level. Agosti described the state of isolation experienced by those choosing conspiracy using the following, fascinating image: 'Although we all live isolated lives, enclosed in our shells like turtles, when we cautiously stick our head out from our shell, we see another head cautiously peeking out.'[60]

Most of these 'heads' – these isolated individuals – were inspired by Gobetti's legacy and memory. Against the backdrop of the dictatorship now in power, Piero's commemoration at the University of Turin in February 1927 took on an implicitly political significance. Garosci guardedly attended the commemorative service, together with his friend De Rosa with whom he had completed the first year of his studies at the Istituto Sociale. At that time, he was only aware of the idea of 'liberal revolution'. However, his friendship with Carlo Levi, with whom he served a journalistic apprenticeship with Gobetti, was particularly important for his decision to join in conspiracy against the Fascist regime. Although he had studied as a physician, it was thanks to his lessons with the painter Felice Casorati, his dialogue with the art historians and critics Lionello Venturi and Edoardo Persico, and his discovery of the Paris School (especially the lights and colours of Amedeo Modigliani and Chaïm Soutine's works) that he soon discovered his true vocation as an artist. Between 1928 and 1931, Levi joined a European-inspired group of painters as his impatience with the provincial, plebeian conformism imposed by the Fascist regime grew. Levi's periods spent in the French capital intensified

---

60   Letter from Giorgio Agosti to Emilio Castellani, January 1940, in Giovanni De Luna, 'Giustizia e Libertà, la cospirazione delle tartarughe', *La Stampa*, 21 May 2000.

during the late 1920s and early 1930s, allowing him to get closer to GL and to liaise between the regime's opponents operating clandestinely in Turin and the Italian antifascist exiles in France. He was considered the most charismatic figure of the initial GL group in Turin. This was soon joined by a number of young people growing up under the Fascist regime, who following their own inclinations were to come together in small groups of friends.

Attendance at the Liceo Classico (Grammar School) D'Azeglio in Turin was of crucial importance for the education of exceptionally gifted adolescents such as Leone Ginzburg, Giorgio Agosti, Norberto Bobbio, Massimo Mila, and Cesare Pavese. These students were taught Italian literature by Umberto Cosmo and Augusto Monti. The latter, a contributor to the journal *Rivoluzione liberale* and a close friend of Gobetti, gathered a cluster of young students around him. One of them was Ginzburg, a precocious young man by virtue of his personal circumstances; he had been born in Odesa during the late Russian Empire to an educated and affluent Jewish family. When the Great War broke out, the Ginzburg family were holidaying in the Versilia area of Tuscany. While his family hurriedly returned to Odesa, Leone was entrusted to the care of his governess Maria Segre in Viareggio, where he attended primary school and middle school from 1916 on. He then continued his studies at the Liceo Classico Gioberti in Turin, where he had moved with his entire family after their flight from the Russian civil wars in 1919. Ginzburg completed his schooling at the Liceo Classico D'Azeglio before enrolling at Turin University's Faculty of Humanities, where he subsequently graduated in French literature.

Ginzburg belonged to Croce's circle of close friends. The Neapolitan philosopher and historian often stayed in Piedmont, where he met Einaudi, Solari, Ruffini, Luigi Salvatorelli, and Lionello Venturi. In the minds of this Turin group, 'Don Benedetto' embodied that 'open conspiracy of culture' that he himself had evoked in his work *Storia d'Italia dal 1871 al 1915* with regard to the 'preparation of minds and souls' for the Risorgimento.[61] Despite his now avowed opposition to Fascism, he adopted a prudent strategy: to shield one's free thinking while not disregarding subsequent threats to one's physical existence under the dictatorship. When he

---

61   Benedetto Croce, *Storia d'Italia dal 1871 al 1915*, Bari: Laterza, 1967 (1928), 25.

reprinted Torquato Accetto's seventeenth-century treatise *Della dissimulazione onesta* in 1928, he thus noted that 'the art of faking, simulating and dissimulating, of trickery and hypocrisy' was practised 'because of the illiberal conditions of the society of the time'.[62]

In May 1929, Umberto Cosmo and others drew up a letter offering their support to Croce, whom Mussolini had called a 'shirker of history' following Croce's speech to the Senate opposing the Lateran Pacts. The letter's signatories included Massimo Mila, a student of Monti and scholar of music history who had grown up in a Piedmontese family characterized by both nationalist and royalist loyalties. Until then, he had only cultivated humanistic interests such as poetry and the piano, without expressing himself politically. A decisive factor in Mila's new-found political commitment was his meeting with Gian Carlo Pajetta, who tried in vain to convert him to communism. Ginzburg, however, notwithstanding his friendship with Croce, refused to sign the letter of support following Mussolini's attack. Indeed, Ginzburg consistently renounced all forms of political opposition until he was officially granted Italian citizenship in October 1931. Probably only full membership of the national community that had been created by the Risorgimento could justify, in the eyes of this stateless young man, his participation in the antifascist conspiracy.[63] His study of the relationship between the Russian radical intellectual Aleksandr I. Herzen and the Italian patriots Garibaldi and Mazzini in 1848 helped justify this decision.[64]

While fascists and antifascists argued over the historical significance and political value of the Risorgimento, Ginzburg thus started a process of Italianization, and his claim to Italianness represented a radical departure from a previous merely intellectual life that was forced to political commitment under dictatorial conditions. From that moment on, Ginzburg carefully prepared himself for the role of conspirator, in a manner reminiscent of the nineteenth-century Russian revolutionary intelligentsia he was familiar with. In the summer of 1932, together with Croce, he travelled to

---

62   Benedetto Croce, 'Torquato Accetto e il trattatello della "Dissimulazione onesta" ', *La Critica* 6, 1928, 221–6, in *Nuovi Saggi sulla letteratura del Seicento*, Bari: Laterza, 1931, 58.

63   Gianni Sofri, 'Ginzburg, Leone', in *Dizionario Biografico degli Italiani*, Rome: Istituto della Enciclopedia Italiana, 2000, 56.

64   Leone Ginzburg, 'Garibaldi e Herzen', *La Cultura* 4, 1932, 726–49.

Paris, where he had the opportunity to meet Rosselli and get involved in GL before returning to Turin.

Turin boasted a 'bourgeois' social and intellectual milieu, and some of the members of that milieu were prepared to form an alternative elite to that of the Fascists. In August 1931, a report from the PCd'I's clandestine leadership in Turin examined the possibility of approaching and recruiting members of GL who were already operating on the lines of a 'fairly advanced' programme and had become 'radicalized'. Although they rejected the idea of the dictatorship of the proletariat and were critical of the Soviet experiment, they admitted that 'only the working class could be expected to do anything against Fascism'.[65] In fact, in the autumn of 1931, Garosci, together with the republican activist Mario Andreis and the libertarian Luigi Scala, assistant professor of natural sciences at the university, managed to print 4,000 copies of the clandestine newspaper *Voci d'officina* and to distribute three numbers of the paper in the factories of Turin. Renzo Giua, then a young student of Romance philology and son of Michele Giua, professor of chemistry, was one of those involved in this enterprise. The main topics covered in this cyclostyled paper were an analysis of the catastrophic crisis of capitalism, a call for all antifascist forces to work together, and a denunciation of the agreements reached between the Catholic Church and the Fascist regime. *Voci d'officina*'s relationship with the Fiat factories, sporadic and precarious as ever, was nonetheless reflected in the use of revolutionary language advocating the construction of a 'workers' state'.

In the winter of 1931, Amendola's mission explored the possibility of reaching an agreement with the Turin members of GL. However, the willingness of Andreis and Vittorio Foa to engage in dialogue with the communists was thwarted by Garosci's hostility and Carlo Levi's uncertainty. Then, in December 1931, Andreis and Scala were arrested, convicted by the Special Court and held in the prisons of Piacenza and Castelfranco Emilia (until the amnesty in December 1934). Renzo Giua was arrested in January 1932, but released a few months later. Garosci took the

---

65   'Relazione comunista su "GL a Torino", agosto 1931', in Domenico Zucaro, 'Socialismo e democrazia nella lotta antifascista, 1927–1939. Dalle carte Nenni e dagli archivi di Giustizia e Libertà e del Partito comunista', *Annali della Fondazione Giangiacomo Feltrinelli* 25 (1986–87), 106–7.

opportunity to go abroad, leaving on a regular passport the night before his scheduled arrest. He settled in Paris, where he met Rosselli and continued his studies while working in the art studio of Lionello Venturi, who financed his period of exile. For his part, the great art historian had recently arrived in Paris with his son Franco. The Venturi milieu that had formed in the cities of Modena and Turin was steeped in the nationalist attitudes of early twentieth-century culture, with its interventionist yearnings and anti-socialist tendencies, all of which were exacerbated by the Great War. Venturi's distaste for the plebeian, brutal character of Fascism was accompanied during the postwar period by the hope that the regime would fulfil its national mission. Lionello's refusal in November 1931 to take an oath of allegiance to the regime and his decision to remain abroad in early 1932, combined with his early retirement from the university, abruptly ended his relations with the regime. His son Franco, who attended the Liceo Classico Alfieri, was then arrested on suspicion of antifascist activities and released shortly thereafter: Franco subsequently decided to go to Paris, where he enrolled at the Sorbonne and became close to Rosselli through Garosci.[66]

Their collaboration with the Florentine cultural magazine *Solaria* led Garosci to establish a close relationship with Chiaromonte, although differences and tensions in the understanding of politics soon arose between the two. After making contacts with Rosselli in the French capital in the spring of 1932, Chiaromonte became the leader of the GL conspiracy in Rome. Born in a village in southern Italy near the town of Potenza, he had received a strict religious education and had attended the Collegio Massimo, a Jesuit institute in Rome. In the immediate postwar period, at a young age he had been drawn to the myth of D'Annunzio and Mussolini before developing a deep distrust of the organizational tools of modern politics. Despite his having studied law, his main interests were of a philosophical, literary, and religious nature. In the latter half of the 1920s and the early 1930s, Chiaromonte contributed to the liberal newspaper *Il Mondo* and to the neo-Protestant magazine *Conscientia*. Between 1932 and 1934, he helped organize a small circle of intellectuals who spoke out against Mussolini's regime and its use of political violence. This circle comprised intellectuals and writers such as Alberto Moravia, Ugo La Malfa, Mario Soldati, and Corrado Alvaro, and also involved them in

---

66   Adriano Viarengo, *Franco Venturi tra politica e storia*, Rome: Carocci, 2014.

clandestine operations. It was especially with Moravia, a cousin of the Rosselli brothers and friend of Caffi, that Chiaromonte shared his frustration with the rhetoric of the Fascist regime and his rejection of 'bourgeois' society.[67]

In sum, in the early 1930s, GL managed to establish a subtle, fragile yet persistent series of relationships with those underground groups in Italy that shared Rosselli's political project. These groups continued to foster Gobetti's memory and legacy, and this led to a willingness to act (especially in Turin) that also circulated in the GL networks beyond Italy's borders.

In the Shadow of Piero (But Not Only)

Piero Gobetti's posthumous fortunes, the permanence of his intellectual legacy and the variety of his interpretations, belong to the twentieth-century history of Italy. The direction taken by Gobetti was to considerably influence the postwar generation, whose expectations, anxieties, and dilemmas he seemed to embody. With precocious enthusiasm, the young intellectual from Turin tried to transfer to the new context those questions that had been posed by the 'idealist' culture (from Prezzolini to Giovanni Gentile, but especially by *La Voce*) of the period prior to the Great War. His feverish endeavours of editorial organization and cultural mediation were even more important than his original desire for intellectual renewal. Gobetti absorbed the elitist culture of early twentieth-century Europe through his relationship with Salvemini and Luigi Einaudi, but its acceptance was also indebted to Mosca, Pareto, and Sorel. He honed his instinctive distrust of political parties and hoped for the formation of a new ruling class. Gobetti was attracted to both Giovanni Gentile and Benedetto Croce, to the nationalist rhetoric of the war veterans and to the heroic morality of the workers' movement; as such, he became an advocate of an anti-Giolittian ethics that tended to lump Mussolini and Giolitti together in a drastically negative vision of Italian politics, before becoming a strict antifascist between 1921 and 1922. After the March on Rome, Gobetti

---

67 See Cesare Panizza, *Nicola Chiaromonte. Una biografia*, Rome: Donzelli, 2017, 15–68.

memorably expressed his 'physiologically innate' antifascism, which represented the 'stylistic antithesis' of 'the other Italy' – that is, the Fascist one. However, rather than being a conscious, precocious point of departure, Gobetti's antifascism was a difficult, yet subsequently unquestioned, point of arrival.[68]

Rosselli visited Gobetti in Turin in late 1922 and early 1923, and contributed to the periodical *La Rivoluzione liberale*. However, no genuine friendship developed between the two. While they shared an interest in the relationship between liberalism and the workers' movement, which they both considered crucial to the future social order, they differed in their views on socialism. In Gobetti's mind, socialism was a perspective worn away by postwar conflicts that had encrusted the vital core of Marxian thought; in Rosselli's view, on the other hand, socialism could potentially revitalize liberal methods. However, Rosselli shared Gobetti's interpretation of Fascism as the 'autobiography of the nation' and the idealists' conception of liberalism. In a 1932 article reminiscent of Gobetti's thinking, he praised liberalism as a 'state of mind', 'a virile faith founded on reason', and affirmed the complete identification of liberty and modernity.[69] Overall, Caffi felt that the leader of GL was being 'too optimistic' about the fate of liberalism, which was 'to be resurrected (transfigured) after the catastrophe of 1914'. What was needed was a 'tremendous revolution' that would 'bring a certain kind of liberalism back to European societies'.[70] However, in keeping with Rosselli, Carlo Levi argued that 'the inherited inability to be free', 'the habit of liberating indulgence' and 'the fear of passion and responsibility', together constituted the essence of Fascism as the 'autobiography of the nation' that could only be eradicated by 'integral liberalism'.[71]

The question of the 'missed Reformation', which was also part of Carlo Levi's view, was intended to underline the lack of civic and

---

68   Piero Gobetti, 'Elogio della ghigliottina' and 'Questioni di tattica', *Rivoluzione Liberale*, 23 November 1922.

69   Curzio [Carlo Rosselli], 'Liberalismo rivoluzionario', *Quaderni di GL* 1, January 1932, 25.

70   Letter of Andrea Caffi to Carlo Rosselli, 30 January 1932, in Alberto Castelli, 'Il socialismo liberale di Andrea Caffi', *Storia in Lombardia* 2, 1996, 158.

71   R. S. [Carlo Levi], 'Seconda lettera dall'Italia', *Quaderni di GL* 2, March 1932, 11–12.

communitarian spirit, in the sense of a new national pedagogy. This debate stemmed from the post-Risorgimento period, when the first critical assessments were made of the construction of the Italian nation-state. These, in turn, were inspired by ideas circulating during the first half of the nineteenth century, thanks to works such as Simonde de Sismondi's *Histoire des républiques italiennes du moyen âge* and Edgar Quinet's *Les révolutions d'Italie*. The ongoing debate received an important impetus from Francesco De Sanctis and other leading exponents of Neapolitan Neo-Hegelianism. In their eyes, the sixteenth-century religious Reformation constituted a precondition for any modern revolution. Gobetti saw this reflection as reshaped by the amateur journalists Alfredo Oriani and Mario Missiroli regarding the flaws and failures of Italian nation-building. In addition to Oriani's thesis of state unification as a 'royal conquest', Missiroli reformulated the theme of the Risorgimento as a 'failed revolution' due to the 'missed Reformation'. This critical point, however, had less to do with the rivalry between Catholicism and Protestantism in the sixteenth-century Italian peninsula than with frustrations with the late nineteenth-century liberal state.[72]

The reappraisal of this complex legacy – which consisted more of dazzling insights than convincing observations – became the subject of claims made by, and competition among, liberal democrats, socialists, and communists. GL's members, invoking the heroic myth of Gobetti and the enduringly suggestive power of his ideas, then chose to adopt notions that were anything but Gobettian in the true sense of the word.[73] In the first phase of the development of GL, the reference to Gobetti's understanding of liberalism offered a broader political platform for achieving Rosselli's task. The dispute over the legacy of *Rivoluzione liberale* became increasingly bitter in 1930, when Togliatti published a draft of an essay by Gramsci (then in prison) laying the groundwork for the partial rehabilitation of Gobetti by the Italian Communists. Gramsci's essay was then

---

72 See Laura Demofonti, *La Riforma nell'Italia del primo Novecento. Gruppi e riviste di ispirazione evangelica*, Rome: Edizioni Storia e Letteratura, 2003, 149–297.

73 See Ersilia Alessandrone Perona, 'L'uomo Gobetti e la sua formazione', in Valentina Pazé (ed.), *Cent'anni. Piero Gobetti nella storia d'Italia*, Milan: Franco Angeli, 2001, 19–43, and Alessandrone Perona, 'Alle radici della fortuna di Piero Gobetti', in Alberto Cabella and Oscar Mazzoleni (eds), *Gobetti tra Riforma e rivoluzione*, Milan: Franco Angeli, 1999, 119–56.

taken up by an article written by Giorgio Amendola, entitled 'Con il proletariato o contro il proletariato? Discorrendo con gli intellettuali della mia generazione', published in 1931. In this important text, the son of Giovanni Amendola – a representative of liberal-democratic antifascism who had been assassinated by Fascist squads in 1926 – justified his recent membership of the PCd'I. Rereading Gobetti through Gramsci, he defined him as an 'elder brother and secure leader' who had broken with the past and recognized the 'great force of tomorrow: that of the proletariat'. In a following article, Togliatti invoked Gobetti's revolutionary legacy as opposed to Rosselli's 'social fascist' stance.[74] GL perceived Togliatti's attack as a clear moment of rift and a sign of irreducible divergence. In his reply to Amendola, Rosselli portrayed Gobetti as a master and leader who had recognized the 'decisive role of the proletariat in the antifascist struggle'. He argued, however, that the formula of 'liberal revolution' was very different from that of official communism. Gobetti's 'renewal program' postulated the 'moral autonomy of the individual and the free conflict of groups and classes', which entailed a 'slow and laborious process of self-improvement and self-education of the masses', for which 'the environment and method of freedom, strictly conceived' were fundamental prerequisites.[75]

While Rosselli asserted the complete dissimilarity between Gobetti and Gramsci, between the members of GL and the communists, another response to Amendola and Togliatti came from Calosso, a unique interpreter of postwar culture in Turin. Like Gobetti, he had graduated from the University of Turin, with a dissertation on the political thought of the eighteenth-century Piedmontese dramatist and poet Vittorio Alfieri. Along with Gramsci, Togliatti, and Angelo Tasca, he had frequented the Turin section of the PSI and supported the revolutionary, idealist interventionism of the minority of Turin's socialists. After fighting in the war, Calosso collaborated with *L'Ordine Nuovo* as a political editor and literary

---

74 For these references, see Antonio Gramsci, 'Alcuni temi della quistione meridionale', *Lo Stato Operaio*, January 1930, 9–26; Giorgio Amendola, 'Con il proletariato o contro il proletariato? Discorrendo con gli intellettuali della mia generazione', *Lo Stato Operaio*, June 1931, 309–18; Ercoli [Palmiro Togliatti], 'Sul movimento di "Giustizia e Libertà" ', *Lo Stato Operaio*, September 1931, 463–73.

75 Curzio [Carlo Rosselli], 'Risposta a Giorgio Amendola', *Quaderni di GL* 1, January 1932, 33–40.

critic and became a communist, before approaching GL in 1931. In an essay published in the *Quaderni di GL* of August 1933, Calosso retrospectively examined his experience with *Ordine Nuovo*, analysing 'the doctrinarism' with which Gramsci had foreseen a Soviet-style revolution in Italy in 1919–20, and had misunderstood the novelty of Fascism. He recognized that Gramsci's modern culture had attracted Gobetti and underlined that they had in common a 'demand of autonomy'. In this sense, *Rivoluzione liberale* was the heir to *Ordine Nuovo*.[76] Questioning the communist claim that the young Turin intellectual was a 'fellow traveller', Calosso thus created a new political myth based on the 'liberalism' of both Gramsci and Gobetti. For his part, Carlo Levi, who emphasized Gobetti's closeness to the 'young communists', had argued that *Ordine Nuovo* was 'the workers' equivalent' of *Rivoluzione liberale*.[77]

No one was better placed than Levi to establish a sense of continuity between GL and Gobetti's legacy by moving from private to public memory. For his generation, writing about Piero Gobetti meant 'embracing those ideas and desires that, through his work, [had] been inherited by the best of Italy's younger generation, and as such [had] transformed individual, ideal histories into a common process, a common civilization'.[78] As was often the case, this article was unsigned, although anonymity complied not only with the rules of clandestine work, but also with the idea of collective representation. Carlo Levi wanted to pass on a legacy resulting from a privileged personal and generational experience. Gobetti had provided Italians with 'a theory of politics, a morality of freedom, the instrument with which to create a political class', as well as a 'myth of action'.[79] Ginzburg was in full agreement with Levi, when claiming that GL's programme was the 'natural, spontaneous continuation' of *Rivoluzione liberale*: it was necessary to 'profoundly undermine

---

76   Fabrizio [Umberto Calosso], 'Antonio Gramsci e l'Ordine Nuovo', *Quaderni di GL* 8, August 1933, 75, 79.

77   [Carlo Levi,] 'Piero Gobetti e la Rivoluzione Liberale (dall'Italia)', *Quaderni di GL* 7, June 1933, 40.

78   Ibid., 33. See David Ward, *Carlo Levi. Gli italiani e la paura della libertà*, Florence: La Nuova Italia, 2002; for a different point of view, see Vittorio Foa, 'Carlo Levi "uomo politico" ', in *Per una storia del movimento operaio*, Turin: Einaudi, 1980, 43–52.

79   [Levi,] 'Piero Gobetti e la Rivoluzione Liberale', 41.

the basis of people's practical existence' in order to change 'their moral relations'.[80]

The Turin members of GL contributed decisively to the formulation of the 'Schema di Programma di GL' with which GL aimed to constitute 'a republican state that establishes the broadest democracy and relies essentially on the working classes and their autonomous organizations'.[81] At the same time, those same members did not hesitate to reiterate the need for a radical stance in favour of factory councils. In September 1933, Ginzburg (perhaps together with Carlo Levi) published an important article in which he attempted to bestow a dual meaning on the concept of autonomy, one moral and the other juridical – 'the latter appearing to be virtually the historical variety of the former'. In both meanings, autonomy – identified with the 'religion of liberty' (in Gobetti's rather than Croce's view) – contributed to affirming 'the moral value of politics' and making it 'the instrument of a renewal of civilization'. Ginzburg thus recognized the inherently paradoxical and ambivalent character of revolutionary politics: 'awakening the spirit of liberty, while at the same time denying it, by giving it a form' and 'creating a state by anarchical means'. This revolutionary perspective was linked to a historical perspective that denied the existence of any form of democracy in prewar Italy: 'In Italy, parliament and political parties were finished as liberal institutions, even before Fascism asserted as much through its totalitarianism.'[82] Ginzburg's benchmarks were instead the workers' assemblies, the factory committees, and the workers' and peasants' councils of 1919–20, as being 'among the few examples of early democracy that reflect the character of our people and demonstrate their political maturity, their ability to pursue their ideals'. This spontaneous link between economic autonomy and the general principle of self-government embodied in the Soviet, heightened the 'liberal value' of the Russian Revolution.[83]

The roots of this reflection were certainly not disconnected from the Russian progressive milieu to which the entire Ginzburg family belonged.

---

80   M. S. [Leone Ginzburg], 'Ipotecare il futuro (dall'Italia)', *Quaderni di GL* 10, February 1934, 75–6.

81   'Schema di programma', *Quaderni di GL* 1, January 1932, 1.

82   M. S. [Leone Ginzburg], 'Il concetto di autonomia nel programma di G.L.', *Quaderni di GL* 4, September 1932, 7, 10.

83   M. S. [Leone Ginzburg], 'Chiarimenti sul nostro federalismo. Dall'Italia', *Quaderni di GL* 7, June 1933, 48–56.

Ginzburg's father was a constitutional democratic (or 'Cadet'), his mother a 'Labourite', his brother Nicola a social democrat, and his sister Marussia a revolutionary socialist. Accordingly, Leone reproached Gobetti for his inability to 'understand the positive value of a tradition' – the populist and social-revolutionary tradition – that had appreciated the importance of the peasantry. Yet, he agreed with the Gobettian view that Lenin and Trotsky represented 'a constructive element', 'a liberal tendency', which would accelerate the Europeanization of Russia.[84] Gobetti was convinced that in the face of the crisis of the rule of law, and sometimes of the state *tout court* (as in the former Russian Empire), it was necessary to replace – or at least supplement – the legal conception of liberalism, centred on defining the limits of state power, with an ethical vision based on the desire for the radical renewal of the ruling class. The workers' movement elite was to contribute to its selection and formation. This reproposition of Gobetti's 'paradox of the Russian spirit' was now completely anachronistic for the purpose of understanding the reality of Stalin's dictatorship during the early 1930s; however, within the context of the struggle against Mussolini's dictatorship, it allowed Ginzburg to revive the need for a long-term cultural battle.[85]

Rather than the shadow of Gobetti, it was the shadow of the postwar period, replete with violent disputes and unprecedented solutions, that hung over the bitter controversy between Amendola and Rosselli, the (self-)critical reappraisal of Calosso's experiences in *Ordine Nuovo*, and the assorted historical-political notions posited by Levi and Ginzburg. Many parts of Europe had witnessed attempts at production management, workers' control, and industrial democracy, based more or less directly on the example (and myth) of workers' and peasants' councils, although not infrequently experienced as the intensification of a class struggle tending towards anarchy. The lessons drawn from these bold but often short-lived experiments were as varied as ever: in any case, it was commonly believed that social change should be preceded and accompanied by ethical and cultural change.[86]

---

84   M. S. [Leone Ginzburg], 'Gobetti e il significato della rivoluzione russa', *Quaderni di GL* 5, December 1932, 88–92.

85   Gobetti's articles on the Russian Revolution were published posthumously in *Il paradosso dello spirito russo*, Turin: Edizioni del Baretti, 1926. His vision was deeply shaped by Caffi (Piero Gobetti, 'Rassegna di questioni politiche. Esperimenti di socialismo', *Energie nove*, 25 July 1919, 132–9, in *Scritti politici*, 138–53).

86   Charles Maier, *Recasting Bourgeois Europe: Stabilization in France, Germany,*

During the 1919–20 period, Turin was the setting for a series of tense social struggles and strikes. For Gobetti, those 'Red Years' had helped enhance the conflict, seen as a moral mould for the development of the workers' movement, while, at the same time, representing a point of discontinuity with respect to Italy's history. On the other hand, the intense succession of workers' battles at the Turin car factory (FIAT) had given rise to the myth of workers' councils, the most sophisticated theorist of which was Antonio Gramsci. In the view of *Ordine Nuovo*, however, the works councils not only represented a solution to the head-on clash of capital with labour, but they also overshadowed a new overall arrangement inspired by a vision of communism native to Italy. Whereas in the view of GL's members, in particular Levi and Ginzburg, the lessons of the 'Red Years' remained controversial. Insofar as their interpretation of Gobetti's legacy linked the concept of autonomy to the 'religion of freedom' perspective (which Gobetti mentioned in defining Vittorio Alfieri's faith), their evaluation of the council experience represented an alternative to Gramsci's class-based approach. In Levi and Ginzburg's minds, the ethical and legal principles of self-government, combined with a federalist programme, became not only the decisive key to interpreting the history of Fascism as an 'autobiography of the nation', but also, and above all, a cultural instrument to be used to reverse its dramatic course. However, the continuous comparison with *Rivoluzione liberale*, and the consequent impatience with parliamentary democracy and party mediation, continued to convey a considerable degree of ambivalence towards politics within GL. The antifascist option acted like a reagent, dissolving these ambivalences, which had originally coalesced to form a non-political culture, and regenerating them in other forms.

Garosci in Paris was formulating a different stance on the Gobettian legacy he had become familiar with in Turin, and was increasingly sceptical of these very ambivalences. In a letter to Rosselli written in 1931, Garosci expressed his perplexity at GL's proposed programme, and

and Italy in the Decade After World War I, Princeton, NJ: Princeton University Press 1975; Geoff Eley, *Forging Democracy: The History of the Left in Europe 1850–2000*, New York: Oxford University Press, 2002, 220–9; Jan-Werner Müller, *Contesting Democracy: Political Ideas in Twentieth-Century Europe*, New Haven, CT: Yale University Press, 2011, 49–90.

reproached the exiles for an idea of freedom that was 'a little too closely tied to certain external forms of freedom', such as Parliament.[87] However, from his very first article in *Quaderni di GL* published in January 1932, he took as his starting point the need to rethink the political dilemmas of the early postwar period, which could no longer be seen as limited to the question of the technical capacity required for factory management. The disruptive experience of Fascism – perceived 'as a reaction against the workers' cause and against the cause of democracy' – had called for 'workers' freedom' to be coupled with the vindication of 'lost freedoms', in order to form an 'inseparable asset in the antifascist struggle'.[88]

With hindsight, Garosci formulated a clear critical interpretation of Gobetti's thought and legacy which, in his opinion, was fundamentally flawed in the following respects: its ideology of national character, which was incapable of grasping the 'European novelty of Fascism'; and its rejection of reformist policy and democratic compromise, leading to 'totalitarianism' as the distinctive feature of postwar socialism. GL had managed to overcome these flaws stemming from Gobetti's heritage because of what Garosci called its 'experimental' character, shaped by exile.[89] Nevertheless, what had the experience of exile meant for GL? Who were the group's interlocutors and points of reference in French and European cultural life? We shall explore this matter in the next chapter, investigating the trajectories and networks of GL's most representative members.

87   Letter from Magrini [Aldo Garosci] to Rosselli, undated (but end of 1931), in Aldo Agosti, *Rodolfo Morandi: il pensiero e l'azione*, Bari: Laterza, 1971, 153.

88   Mag. [Aldo Garosci], 'Il problema della libertà operaia', *Quaderni di GL* 1, January 1932, 21–4.

89   Un liberalsocialista di G.L. [Aldo Garosci], 'Il passato nel presente. Eredità gobettiana da respingere e da accettare', *Nuovi Quaderni di GL* 1, 1944, 82.

2

Exile in Paris as a Laboratory

Fascism, 'The Autobiography of a Nation', or of Europe?

Like most of their contemporaries, Rosselli, Lussu, Salvemini, Trentin, Rossi, and Ascoli struggled to decipher the novel, radical nature of early Fascism during the impending civil war of 1919–22. Their culture, steeped in anti-Giolittian sentiments, interventionist zeal, and militant intentions, had not permitted any early framing of the phenomenon. Rather, their non-political tendency had led them to identify every outcome of the postwar crisis with Giolitti's prewar period, or to underestimate the considerable discontinuity between the two. Some of them were slow to recognize the real threat posed to liberal and parliamentary institutions. Others were lured by the message of radical renewal spread by Mussolini's movement. Once they had become convinced antifascists, they were ready to take Fascism seriously and to understand it better than many socialists, communists, or liberals. Rosselli and his comrades persisted with their uncompromising opposition, but, paradoxically, their antifascism was profoundly and inseparably linked to Fascism itself. In order to understand the specificity of GL and its antifascist counterproposal, this nexus cannot be underestimated. Rosselli, in fact, considered 'Fascism and not pre-Fascism as the starting point', as '*normality*'.[1]

---

1 [Carlo Rosselli,] 'I pericoli dell'esilio', *GL*, 16 November 1934.

GL's publications did not offer any unified body of analysis, let alone a coherent theory of Fascism. On the contrary, they presented a variegated range of often dissonant perspectives that alternated between conventional views and enlightening insights. Both the lingering influence of the anti-Giolittian culture of GL, and subsequent emphasis on continuity in Italian history, resulted in dismissive definitions of Fascism: consequently, there prevailed a certain underestimation of the novelty of Mussolini's regime and its growing stability and popularity. The main interpretations advanced in this initial phase, which were to resurface from time to time, revolved around the use of two metaphors: the first was Fascism as the 'autobiography of the nation', the second was Mussolini's dictatorship as the 'prison' of the 'Italian people'. The first metaphor smoothed over the discontinuity between post-Risorgimento liberal Italy and the Fascist experience of the postwar period. The second metaphor overstressed the responsibility of traditional institutions (monarchy, army, bureaucracy, and Church), and reduced the relationship between the Fascist regime and Italian society to one of pure repression and violence. Both interpretations, however, prevented the members of GL from understanding fascism as simply a class reaction.

At first, GL's reflections were primarily focused on the national political context. A broader analytical framework soon began to emerge, however, seeking to comprehend the radical, ambiguous novelty of Fascism in postwar Europe, its chaotic and violent character, its vehement reactivity to other mass movements (such as Bolshevism), its independent, brute force arising from the experience of war, but not without coming up against substantial social, economic, and institutional interests along the way. Gobetti's image of Fascism as the 'autobiography of the nation' was interwoven with, and superimposed on, the interpretation of Fascism as the product and outcome of postwar Europe. The two exiles who worked most intensively on the study of Fascism in the late 1920s and early 1930s, Salvemini and Trentin, initially took a national approach to the postwar crisis and its developments, but went on to raise the more general problem of the relationship (and conflict) between democracy and Fascism.

During his periods of exile in Paris, London, and Boston, Salvemini worked on countering Fascist propaganda and on explaining the origins and ascent of Mussolini's dictatorship. Set against the backdrop of Giolitti's Italy, now understood as a 'democracy in the making', Fascism appeared as the expression of a serious 'deviation', which Italy – like part of Europe – had followed in the after-math of the Great War and the Russian Revolutions. Salvemini believed that the 'postwar neurosis' that led to the 'civil war' of 1920–22 was fuelled by socialist revolutionary irrationalism and the waves of collective fear that followed, as well as by the complicity of state authorities in the Fascists' illegal actions. Accordingly, Salvemini pointed out that the dismaying novelty of Mussolini's movement should be evaluated as a plausible, albeit brutal, response to the slow but inexorable decline of liberal institutions.

Trentin, for his part, shared the liberal conception of the state as a public organization designed to protect individual liberty through the rule of law and the monopoly of violence. More than anyone else, he was aware of the 'unforeseen catastrophe of the state' that resulted from the 'anarchy' and 'arbitrariness' of public life after 1918. In a context where violence tended to be shifted from the sphere of law to the sphere of action, Fascism had taken this process to the extreme. After the 'destruction of law', the subsequent 'legalization' of dictatorship marked the triumph of 'antidem-ocracy'. By using this historical-legal key to the interpretation of events, Trentin accounted for the general tendencies of the postwar European crisis of law and institutions, of which the Fascist regime had become an exceptionally brutal version.[2]

Caffi's view of Fascism was the result of his particular experience. Between 1914 and 1922, the Great War and the Russian Revolutions had disrupted his life, with the promise of change and bitter disappointment rapidly alternating and consuming one another. The Russian-born intel-lectual combined the analyses offered by Luigi Salvatorelli, Benedetto Croce and Gioacchino Volpe with the views of the British classical histo-rian, Goldsworthy Lowes Dickinson. The latter, in his 1917 work *The Choice Before Us*, had already warned of the devastating consequences of war and revolution for European societies. Caffi viewed Fascism – like Bolshevism, albeit in different ways – as one aspect of the catastrophic European crisis that had begun in the summer of 1914. Somewhat unusu-ally, he studied Fascist ideology, which most antifascists dismissed as a

---

2   Silvio Trentin, *L'aventure italienne. Légendes et réalités*, Paris: Presses Universitaires de France, 1928. Trentin developed some of these themes in *Les trans-formations récentes du droit public italien. De la Charte de Charles-Albert à la création de l'État fasciste*, Paris: Giard, 1929, and *Antidémocratie*, Paris: Librairie Valois, 1930.

predictable, irrelevant, irrational babble or simply the limp repetition of the reactionary repertoire. An unpublished manuscript of his traced the roots of Fascist ideology to late nineteenth- and early twentieth-century European culture. He explored the anti-political trends attracting 'nonconformist' intellectuals, as well as the appeal of Fascism to the 'younger generations' as a force for social change. While on the one hand Caffi linked Fascism to a lengthy, 'reactionary', 'counterrevolutionary' tradition dating from the French Revolution, on the other hand he traced the specificity of Fascism to the Great War's destructive impact on Italian and European societies.[3] A kind of 'primitivism' had led, after 1914, to the total dissolution of social relations and an abnormal development of political institutions. This socio-political regression had thus contributed to the ' "psychological" preparation of Fascism's early recruits'. It was the Great War that had produced this 'new kind of adventurer', men driven by 'fanatical enthusiasm', who formed a 'military system of government' based on 'that wretched surrogate of "consensus" obtained by force'. Mussolini's regime meant 'an extension of militarism to all branches of administrative and social organization, carried out with a ruthlessness and to extremes to which, at least among Western peoples, no "warlike" ruler had ever ventured'.[4] Caffi's use of the term 'militarism' to describe the regression to a more primitive regime of political and social relations was a direct reference to a tradition established by Saint-Simon, Auguste Comte, and Herbert Spencer. 'Militarism', understood from the perspective of Spencer's sociology and revised by Pitirim Sorokin, the Russian sociologist with revolutionary socialist positions, was a key to deciphering the illiberal, tyrannical phenomena that had been arising since 1914.

While Caffi focused on the discontinuity represented by the Great War and its lingering political, social, and cultural aftershocks, Rosselli was primarily influenced by Hitler's rise to power. Indeed, 30 January 1933 marked a turning point in his life and shaped the political and intellectual development of the entire GL group. Rosselli almost immediately perceived

---

3   Andrea Caffi, *La dottrina fascista* (1932), 65–6, Archivio Tasca, Italia fascista, Politica, F.F. 1 – 54/25, Fondazione Giangiacomo Feltrinelli (Milan). Caffi's starting point was the *Fascism* entry, elaborated by Mussolini and Gentile, in the Italian Encyclopaedia published by Treccani, 1932.

4   Caffi, *La dottrina fascista*, 66, 77, 56–7, 63, Archivio Tasca.

the hiatus that the Nazi leader's appointment as German chancellor would trigger in international affairs. He was convinced that 'fascism', including National Socialism, constituted a 'terrible digger of the graves of worlds, of myths, of people', a historical 'rupture'.[5]

Between 1933 and 1935, the magazine *Quaderni di GL* and the weekly *GL* discussed the centrality of fascism to understanding Europe at the time. According to Chiaromonte, the Fascist dictatorship was based on the 'practice of mass consensus', organized through collective ceremonies and events that aimed to involve popular masses and to abolish any form of individuality. 'Fascisms are not governments from above, but from below; dictatorships of the mob, not in the sociological sense, but more precisely in the moral sense.'[6] Chiaromonte wrote an extensive essay that was published in *Quaderni di GL* in January 1935, under the title 'La morte si chiama fascismo'. He was convinced that 'the two main fascisms, the multitude of pseudo-fascisms and the threatened fascisms' were to 'gradually express and crystallize a rather frightening phenomenon at the political level', namely 'the moral, social, political, and economic decay of Europe since 1914'. The European crisis had led to the degeneration of the modern state into a 'state outside the law', in which 'administration takes the place of politics, and command takes the place of law'. In an ironic sense, 'tyranny', understood as 'extreme disorder', thus represented the most consistent negation of the state. The revolutionary character and magnitude of the crisis triggered by the Great War and its aftershocks, had led to the 'paradox of modern reaction', which consisted of 'being forced, if not to pursue a concrete, specific objective, at least to stir the masses'. After highlighting this unique mix of reactionary and revolutionary aspects in 'Italian and German fascism' – in his view, 'the most perfect forms of modern tyranny' – Chiaromonte acknowledged that 'the combination of situations and the weakness of political methods' made Europe 'the ideal breeding ground for tyrannies'. His approach to fascism focused on the contingent situations of crisis that had triggered political and social experiences and practices across Europe in ways that were as extreme as they were spontaneous: indeed, 'fascisms are instructive because they show how a state fails, that is, how a state becomes

---

5   [Carlo Rosselli,] 'Italia e Europa', *Quaderni di GL* 7, June 1933, 3.
6   Sincero [Nicola Chiaromonte], 'Ufficio Stampa (dall'Italia)', *Quaderni di GL* 9, November 1933, 78–9.

tyrannical'. In his opinion, 'modern tyranny' could only be exercised through the 'subjugation of all in the name of all', since the masses could only be dominated by 'a certain conception of the common interest' that was identified with the 'myth of national salvation'. The 'revolutionary' character of fascisms lay in their ability to represent 'the mass, that is, that indefinable pulp, the fatal product of the decomposition of the traditional society subjected to the action of the modern state and industrialism, which takes the form of the modern masses'. In this perspective, a fundamental aporia finally surfaced: 'The profundity of the phenomenon that bears the political name of fascism is bestowed by the presence of the masses. The superficiality of the fascist order consists in offering a political-technical solution to an enormous social question.'[7]

Since the 1890s, social psychology – from Gustave Le Bon to Scipio Sighele – had analysed the rise of mass society and the emerging link between collective behaviour and the charismatic power of political leaders, and in doing so had claimed to identify constant laws of history. Chiaromonte's analytical endeavours were instead the fruit of a philosophical sensibility that, from Plato to Ortega y Gasset (via Tocqueville and Burckhardt), had reconsidered the relationship between the masses and the elite in terms of its moral implications. This gave rise to a critical view of contemporary society, imbued with a certain 'aristocratic' logic, which enabled him to understand the dynamics that led fascism to be considered as a seemingly credible (yet ultimately catastrophic) solution to the European crisis. Chiaromonte, who had studied Nietzsche in depth, ended up criticizing relativism and historicism, which he accused of legitimizing the cult of action. However, he tempered his sharp philosophical critique of activism with a firm support of antifascism. In this regard, his combination of political and non-political attitudes perfectly embodied GL's distinctive characteristic – namely, to 'understand the enemy instead of being shocked and bowing before its monstruosity'.[8]

Chiaromonte's essay left a deep impression on the GL group. In the months that followed, Rosselli drew on the basic arguments of 'La morte si chiama fascismo' to try to understand the future of a Europe under

7   Sincero [Nicola Chiaromonte], 'La morte si chiama fascismo', *Quaderni di GL* 12, January 1935, 40–2, 58–9, 60–1, 65.

8   Verus [Nicola Chiaromonte], 'La crisi morale del fascismo', *GL*, 15 June 1934.

increasing pressure from Hitler and Mussolini's regimes. In January 1935, an article appeared on the Saar referendum in favour of unification with Nazi Germany, in which Rosselli's view of the masses – as 'the brutal, ignorant, powerless, feminine prey of those who shout the loudest, of those who have the most money, of those who have the greatest power and success' – mirrored a reiteration of the collective psychology of Le Bon and Sighele more closely than Chiaromonte's view did. However, they came to similar conclusions: 'Fascisms are the most perfect mass regimes in history, in which man disappears to become a fraction of a procession, a hosanna, a plebiscite, an army.'[9] With illuminating insight (despite some blind spots), Rosselli identified the emotional mobilization of the masses as the crucial instrument of modern dictatorships. Yet he also sketched a sometimes very realistic view of the relationship between Mussolini's regime and Italian society: 'Between the few convinced Fascists and the few active antifascists', there now lay 'a vast grey area of hungry, ignorant people, of the indifferent, the sceptical, the bored, the larvae'.[10] Rosselli's focus had shifted from Fascism (understood as the 'autobiography of the nation') to a society encompassing a wide range of behaviours that did not identify with Fascist ideology as such but formed the basis of the regime, and would be the precondition for its overthrow. The question at the heart of early twentieth-century culture was that of a partial, incomplete nation-building, and this issue would eventually resurface in Rosselli's analysis.

The adjective 'totalitarian', coined by Giovanni Amendola in 1923, recurred in Rosselli's work from 1934 onwards, as it did in the work of other GL writers, to define Fascism and 'its planned total manipulation of the state and control of the masses'.[11] In the context of the imminent outbreak of the Fascist war in Ethiopia, Rosselli identified an indissoluble link between Fascism and war, alluding both to the European conflict of 1914–18 and to the likely future clash on a continental scale: 'Fascism is war. It is born of it, it feeds on it, it is itself a fact of war, of civil war, and it leads in turn, with almost mechanical inevitability, to war.' Fascism, which was 'inconceivable without a world war', placed 'all the paraphernalia of modern tyranny' at the service of 'the permanent and massive

9   [Carlo Rosselli,] 'La lezione della Sarre', *GL*, 18 January 1935.
10   [Carlo Rosselli,] 'Salto nel 1935', *GL*, 28 December 1934.
11   [Carlo Rosselli,] 'Il vero problema', *GL*, 17 August 1934.

mobilization of society with a view to war.'[12] Rosselli identified the totalitarian regimes or states with the fascist ones, while other clandestine circles or exiles recalled the similarities with the Nazi and Stalinist regimes. In any case, the debate concerning totalitarianism in the 1930s entailed a comparative approach to the new movements and political experiments that emerged from the Great War and that were characterized by illiberal, dictatorial drives, mass mobilization, the use of propaganda and terror, and the strategic pursuit of military expansion.[13]

Rosselli's thinking on totalitarianism was far removed from the essentially static, monolithic kind that would become entrenched with the advent of the Cold War. Rather, he sought to represent the contradictory and changing features of the Fascist socio-political dynamic that had first emerged with the Great War, had radicalized during the war in Africa, and would soon spread around Europe. It is not certain whether the leader of GL was as familiar with the literature on 'total mobilization' by the German writer Ernst Jünger as he was with that on 'total war' by the latter's compatriot, General Erich von Ludendorff. These viewpoints, just like Rosselli's, saw the quest for domination at the national level and the bid for expansion at the international level as being inextricably interlocked. One was considered functional to the other, in a circular relationship in which the total war of 1914–18 had unleashed totalitarian forces that would, in turn, plunge Europe into a new and even more catastrophic total war. As long as Hitler and Mussolini's regimes were free to act, the peace agreements formally signed in 1919–23 were themselves a sham, and the Great War continued to propagate its destabilizing effects.[14]

From the late 1920s onwards, and increasingly in the first half of the 1930s, Mussolini tried to consolidate the regime's popularity and shape a true Fascist 'faith' that would reconcile Catholicism, nationalism, and Fascism; in other words, he attempted to establish a new totalitarian

---

12   Speech by Rosselli to be delivered during a meeting of antifascists, April–September 1935, Fondo Carlo Rosselli, cassetto 1, inserto IV, Biblioteca Nazionale (Florence).

13   See Abbott Gleason, *Totalitarianism: The Inner History of the Cold War*, Oxford: Oxford University Press, 1995; Enzo Traverso (ed.), *Totalitarisme: le 20e siècle en débat*, Paris: Seuil, 2001; Bernard Bruneteau, *Le totalitarisme. Origines d'un concept, genèse d'un débat 1930–1942*, Paris: Cerf, 2011.

14   [Carlo Rosselli,] 'Riflessioni sullo stato d'Europa', *GL*, 29 January 1937.

political religion, based on the national and imperial myths of a 'Greater Italy'. In particular, the 'question of young people', those who had grown up and been educated under the regime, but were expressing unease and a longing for change, required the development of pedagogical strategies to be implemented over the long term.[15] Calosso focused on the remarkable ability of fascist regimes to involve the popular masses and to organize collective rites that revealed their powerful religious dimension. He went on to develop his reflections on fascism as a 'new totalitarian religion' impacting on 'very large numbers of young people from all classes, especially the working class'.[16]

It is not easy to say who Calosso's interlocutors were, let alone what sources of information fuelled his views. Nonetheless, his ideas were foreign to the Marxist tradition, as they tended to substantially play down the political, social, and cultural roots of Fascism while emphasizing its 'reactionary' character. The question was raised in the 1930s of the relationship between political religions and modern totalitarian regimes, mainly on a Christian (Catholic, Protestant, and Orthodox) cultural basis. Nikolay A. Berdyaev, Waldemar Gurian, Jacques Maritain, Don Luigi Sturzo, Paul Tillich, and Eric Voegelin were among the most cogent interpreters of this question.[17] Calosso's thinking, however, was closer to the philosophical current inspired by the ideas of Croce and Gentile, and, at that stage, more by Gentile than by Croce. His analyses were, in part, akin to the reflections and impressions that the young historian Delio Cantimori had drawn from his research in Central Europe and subsequently reported about the German National-Bolshevik, national-revolutionary and National-Socialist currents in the journals *Critica fascista*, *Vita nova*,

---

15 Renzo De Felice, *Mussolini il fascista*, vol. 2, *L'organizzazione dello stato fascista: 1925–1929*, Turin: Einaudi, 1968, 357–60, and Renzo De Felice, *Mussolini il duce*, vol. 1, *Gli anni del consenso: 1929–1936*, Turin: Einaudi, 1974, 25–6. As for the diverse forms of nationalist radicalism and its fascist version, see Emilio Gentile, *La Grande Italia: il mito della nazione nel 20. Secolo*, Rome-Bari: Laterza, 2011.

16 C. [Umberto Calosso], 'Punte vive', *GL*, 20 March 1936.

17 Emilio Gentile, *Le religioni della politica. Fra democrazie e totalitarismi*, Rome-Bari: Laterza, 2001, 69–102; Roger Griffin (ed.), *Fascism, Totalitarianism, and Political Religions*, London: Routledge, 2005. Most recently and importantly see James Chappel, 'The Catholic Origins of Totalitarianism Theory in Interwar Europe', *Modern Intellectual History* 8, no. 3, 2011, 561–90.

Leonardo, Giornale critico della filosofia italiana, and *Studi germanici*, from the late 1920s to the mid-1930s. In many ways, the distance between an antifascist exile like Calosso, unprejudiced though he was, and a Fascist, albeit intellectually restless, scholar like Cantimori was unbridgeable. However, the revolutionary radicalism of Italian Fascism and its European and universal vocation within the context of the new wars of religion were topics for reflection that Calosso could hardly have ignored.[18]

Notably, Calosso's review of Angelo Tasca's important work, *La naissance du fascisme: L'Italie de 1918 à 1922*, published in French in 1938, explored the question of the origins of Italian Fascism, and in doing so established a close link between religion and revolution. The theme addressed by Tasca, who had wound up in the French Socialist Party after leaving the PCd'I, was revolutionary maximalism in Italy after 1918. Without limiting himself to the obvious opposition of 'revolution' to 'reaction', Tasca brought to light the subtle relationship between socialist maximalism and Fascism, which was, at one and at the same time, of both opposition and interrelationship. He summarized this relationship by defining Fascism as a 'posthumous and pre-emptive' counterrevolution. He understood better, and earlier, than others just how postwar Italy was characterized by the dissolution of social ties and the radicalization of political struggles, of which Fascism's seizure of power was a consequence rather than a cause. Tasca's book sparked extensive debate within GL. Calosso, in particular, went even further in his criticism of postwar socialist maximalism. He believed that the struggle against Fascism between 1918 and 1922 had been 'a series of failures in tactical timing', including the mistake of ceding to Mussolini 'the idea of youth, of novelty, of boldness', thereby allowing him to appropriate 'the socialist factor'. Paradoxically, Fascism had taken revolutionary socialism more seriously than vice-versa. According to Calosso, the Socialist Party was characterized by 'an atmosphere of purely verbal maximalism, of abstract sovietism with no literal relationship to Italian reality', while the Fascist squads operated according to the new wartime tactic of 'small, daring groups'. On the other hand, in a spirit of rare non-conformism within socialist and communist antifascist culture, Calosso noted that Fascist recruitment, which

---

18 Delio Cantimori, *Politica e storia contemporanea. Scritti 1927–1942*, ed. Luisa Mangoni, Turin: Einaudi, 1991, and Delio Cantimori, *Il furibondo cavallo ideologico. Scritti sul Novecento*, ed. Francesco Torchiani, Macerata: Quodlibet, 2019.

disregarded all traditional class patterns, 'centred on the peasantry and the working classes from the very beginning'. Consequently, one could not deny 'the popular roots of Fascism'. Instead of charging socialist maximalism with specific political errors in the years 1919–22, Calosso accused it of 'only engaging in politics during a time of religious war'. With a certain bitterness, he ironically observed that the 'reactionary mentality' was nothing more than 'a belated revolutionary theme': Fascism had defeated socialism at the point where religion, revolution, and politics converged and became one.[19]

Crisis of Democracy and of the Nation-State

The constant intellectual fascination with fascism, according to GL, derived from its ability to recall a range of issues key to understanding the political, institutional, social, and cultural situation in Europe after 1914. Moreover, fascism offered the opportunity, and triggered the urgency, for a rethinking of the framework within which nineteenth-century liberalism had been conceived and practiced, in terms of both its constitutional structures and its sources of legitimacy. Lawyers, as well as political scientists, sociologists, and historians, were increasingly concerned with the crisis of the state's authority, the inefficiency of the parliamentary representative system, the fragmentation of political parties, and the paralysis of national governments; in their writings, the dividing line between analytical approach and moralistic attitude, between criticism of existing political systems and rejection of politics as such, often became increasingly difficult to perceive, and not infrequently was fraught with ambiguity. Claims of the 'crisis of democracy' trod the treacherous thin line separating the criticism of democratic governments' instability and the paralysis of parliamentary institutions on the one hand, and the wish for the palingenetic destruction of democracy as such on the other.[20] This 'crisis of democracy' was inseparable from fascism, as pointed out in Max Ascoli's reflections, fostered by his American experience and his conversations with New School sociologists. Yet, far from constituting evidence of national backwardness, fascism was

---

19   Subalpino [Umberto Calosso], 'Tasca vivo', *GL*, 4 November 1938.
20   On interwar democracy as a 'deserted temple', see Mark Mazower, *Dark Continent: Europe's Twentieth Century*, London: Allen Lane, 1998, 1–39.

firmly embedded in the 'crisis in the development of democracies that was particularly pronounced in the postwar world'.[21]

Salvemini had long based his reflections about Italian Fascism on the dichotomy between democracy and dictatorship. The Great War had offered a lasting and profound lesson regarding the reversibility of democratic processes and the susceptibility of mass societies to political movements based on obedience to the leader, on collective emotions, and on the primacy of the exclusive knowledge of a ruling elite. Salvemini astutely recognized the irrational basis of the Fascist regime: 'Dictators need myths, symbols, and ceremonies to regiment, glorify, and frighten the masses and to suppress any attempt at thought'.[22] Chiaromonte, in keeping with these reflections, described the 'myth of the state' as 'the state that disposes not only of bodies but also of consciences; that monitors and prescribes how people are to feel and think; that demands unanimity and absolute obedience'. In this interpretive scheme of things, 'the morphological affinity' between Stalin's and Mussolini's regimes was obvious: 'In Moscow, as in Rome, the oligarchic, centralizing, violently enforced state triumphed temporarily – in a word, in a tyrannical manner'. A long series of teachings and practices had characterized the triumph of the modern state, from Hobbes to Hegel and Comte, and the emergence of the 'myth of the state' was 'the direct result of the habits of militarized government established during the Great War'.[23]

Various members of GL questioned the centralized model of the Italian state that had surfaced as the result of the nation-building process, and which the Fascist regime had subsequently appropriated. Despite the group's professed allegiance to Mazzini, they paradoxically supported the federalist views of Cattaneo and Proudhon. Leone Ginzburg leaned towards a new arrangement combining the 'decentralization' of state powers with the bottom-up transformation of economic production through 'councils': Proudhonian federalism became 'the only liberal form of our time, the formulation and presidium of concrete liberties'. His passion for bottom-up autonomy led to a federalist proposal that undermined the abstract,

21   Letter from Max Ascoli to Carlo Rosselli, 30 December 1931, in Davide Grippa, *Un antifascista tra Italia e Stati Uniti. Democrazia e identità nazionale nel pensiero di Max Ascoli (1898–1947)*, Milan: Franco Angeli, 2009, 97.

22   Gaetano Salvemini, 'Il mito dell'Uomo-Dio', *GL*, 20 July 1934.

23   Gualtiero [Nicola Chiaromonte], 'Lettera di un giovane dall'Italia', *Quaderni di GL* 5, December 1932, 33–4.

centralist construction of state sovereignty with the establishment of local and regional councils, but without questioning the national political space as such. Ginzburg embraced Gobetti's call to choose Cattaneo over Mazzini, but baulked at 'putting the Risorgimento on trial.'[24] Despite the completely different cultural and biographical premises concerned, Lussu's political perspective, focused as it was on regional autonomy, nevertheless tended to converge with Ginzburg's national federalism. In an essay written in March 1933, the Sardinian socialist criticized the Risorgimento for having privileged unity over freedom, centralism over federalism, monarchy over democracy, and for having adopted a political solution to a social issue. According to Lussu, the 'crisis of modern democracy' resulted from the unchallenged rise of state centralism, which had suppressed free, spontaneous popular initiatives and culminated in Fascism. The insurrectional overthrow of Mussolini's regime was thus to lead to a federal republic, which would be based on institutional structures more respectful of local diversity, designed to guarantee observance of the ethical and political principle of self-government. In his view, the region was the 'moral, ethnic, linguistic and social unit best suited to become a political unit' in the organization of 'post-Fascism.'[25]

A more radical reflection was stimulated by the confrontation with the current of social and legal pluralism, which, due to the European and global crises of 1917–23, had reshaped the anarchist and syndicalist revolutionary critique of the state in a new, more refined form. The various theories of pluralism, already outlined in the immediate postwar period, and centred on the relationship between civil society and the state, strongly encouraged the formation of an anti-totalitarian current during the 1930s. Georges Gurvitch, a sociologist and legal philosopher of Russian origin and French adoption, was the most consistent and energetic proponent of the theory of legal pluralism. In L'idée du droit social (1932), he started from a consideration of the spontaneous and disorganized law produced by each community understood as a 'complex moral person'. This 'social law', as he called it, allowed a plurality of

---

24 M. S. [Leone Ginzburg], 'Chiarimenti sul nostro federalismo. Dall'Italia', Quaderni di GL 7, June 1933, 48–56.

25 Tirreno [Emilio Lussu], 'Federalismo', Quaderni di GL 6, March 1933, 7–24 (especially 10).

groups to integrate themselves into a bottom-up, federal, cooperative structure, alternative (and in fact complementary) to the top-down, centralized rule of law and state sovereignty.[26] These positions were shared by Pierre Ganivet (the pseudonym of Achille Dauphin-Meunier), who between 1934 and 1938 directed the journal *L'Homme réel*, a publication inspired by the revolutionary syndicalist tradition. In a text published in both *L'Homme réel* and *Quaderni di GL*, Gurvitch refuted Rousseau's theory of the general will as an abstract category based on the purported identity of private interests with the general interest. Following the productivist conception of Proudhonian origin, Gurvitch defined the general interest as a 'concrete universal' enclosing a network of conflicting, coexistent interests. Far from being identified with the sovereign state, interests could be represented by a variety of more or less spontaneous organizations, including trade unions.[27]

Caffi profoundly internalized Gurvitch's libertarian, federalist, cooperative conceptions. At the same time, drawing on the historical analysis included in *L'idée du droit social*, he connected the experience of Italian Fascism to nineteenth- and twentieth-century political and juridical traditions to explain the 'monstrous omnipotence' of the sovereign state in modern Europe.[28] Rosselli, in turn, adopted Gurvitch's libertarian and anti-state perspective without denying the specificity of Fascist dictatorship. However, his article 'Contro lo Stato', published in September 1934, revealed an ambivalent position. On the one hand, the dictatorship represented a 'logical consequence of etatism' as 'a coercive, frosty, impersonal, intrusive, tyrannical, inhuman association'; on the other hand, the watershed of 1914–18 had changed the nature of the state and mobilized 'an activism that was both frenzied and servile'. Drawing on his personal genealogy of the European revolutionary tradition linking Proudhon, Bakunin, and Marx, Rosselli called for 'social federalism' in place of the 'despotic, centralizing state'.[29]

---

26   Georges Gurvitch, *L'idée du droit social. Notion et système du droit social. Histoire doctrinale depuis le XVIIe siècle jusqu'à la fin du XIXe siècle*, Darmstadt: Scientia Verlag Aalen, 1972. Caffi read the original edition published in Paris: Éditions Sirey, 1932.

27   Georges Gurvitch, 'I sindacati e l'interesse generale', *Quaderni di GL* 10, February 1934, 29–36.

28   Caffi, *La dottrina fascista*, 271, Archivio Tasca.

29   [Carlo Rosselli,] 'Contro lo Stato', *GL*, 21 September 1934.

Rosselli's wavering between his strong criticism of state sovereignty and a specific rejection of Hitler and Mussolini's dictatorial solutions reflected an ambiguity inherent in fascism. On the one hand, the totalitarian projects of fascist regimes drew on a long-standing tradition of statehood, in order to suppress and eliminate any autonomy that civil society may have possessed. On the other hand, fascist activism mobilized the masses to express its rejection of the rule of law and the existing political order, which implied the crisis of any form of state sovereignty. In this sense, Rosselli's libertarian turn risked underestimating the devastating scale of the anti-political dynamics that the Fascist and Nazi regimes had embraced and that threatened civil society and its legal foundations right across Europe. Trentin and Caffi proposed two alternative solutions to the crisis of state sovereignty: the radical reconfiguration of the state through the introduction of national federalism; and the comprehensive reorganization of society through European federalism.

At the margins of this debate, Trentin formulated an original reflection linking the 'crisis of the state' with the 'crisis of democracy'. This reflection revolved once again around the concept of 'autonomy', which had led him to abandon the republican viewpoint of the centralized state. The rethinking of the legal foundations of democracy, inspired by the ideas of Proudhon, was triggered by reflections on the crisis of positive law in postwar Italy and Europe. Legal positivism, which guided the work of Léon Duguit and Hans Kelsen, separated law from morality and institutions from society, turning jurisprudence into a pure logical abstraction. Gurvitch was at least partially closer to Trentin in his thinking, for the opposite reason. In Trentin's view, Fascism was a child of the era ushered in by the Great War, a conflict that had disproportionately expanded state powers while emancipating force from law, thus setting the stage for a severe state sovereignty crisis. Yet, unlike Kelsen and Karl Loewenstein, who examined the failures of the parliamentary systems in Germany and Austria, Trentin did not think in terms of the constitutional right to defend democratic institutions. This was deemed to be ineffective in the face of what the Baltic philosopher Hermann von Keyserling referred to as 'telluric forces', 'movements that rise up from below' and disrupt the political, social, economic, and cultural order of Europe. Without being as complacent as Keyserling about the 'return of the barbarians', Trentin captured the essence of the European crisis in his work *La crise du droit et de l'État*

(1935). The solution to the 'crisis of the modern state' – equated with the 'crisis of democracy' – could only be a revolution capable of creating a new positive law and a federalist order based on the principle of the autonomy of individuals and groups.[30]

Despite their different intellectual backgrounds, Trentin's federalism was, like that of Ginzburg and Lussu, embedded within the national context. Caffi was the first to encourage GL to consider the crisis of the nation-state from the perspective of a radical federalist transformation of Europe. As a young man, Caffi had started appropriating a federalist, libertarian tradition, based on the heritage of Herzen and Proudhon and reshaped by Russian 'populist' and socialist culture. During the war, however, he embraced voluntarism and interventionism, collaborating with the Berne Special Press and Propaganda Bureau for national emancipation within the Austro-Hungarian monarchy, without hesitating to sharply criticize the new Europe of Versailles after 1919. In the second half of the 1920s, Caffi grappled with one of the fundamental problems raised and radicalized by the Great War: the organic connection between international anarchy and absolute state sovereignty. By this time, the Austrian philosopher and politician Richard Coudenhove-Kalergi had organized the 'Paneuropa' movement, with the (often confusing) intention of creating a democratic federal space as an alternative to the United States and the Soviet Union. Efforts to rebuild a stable European order, promoted by French Foreign Minister Aristide Briand, instead sought (unsuccessfully) to establish the institutional conditions for overcoming nation-state sovereignty. Gaston Bergery, known as one of the 'Young Turks' of the French Radical Party, advocated the creation of the 'United States of Europe' that might respond to the challenge of Fascism and Nazism by overcoming the postwar order of Versailles.[31] In the June 1932 number of *Quaderni di GL*, Caffi took up this point again, arguing that forms of further integration at the European level were inevitable, regardless of whether they were achieved by democratic or authoritarian means.[32] However, Caffi's ideas, stemming from Gurvitch's legal pluralism and cooperative federalism,

30   Silvio Trentin, *La crise du droit et de l'État*, Paris: Alcan, 1935.

31   See Peter M. R. Stirk (ed.), *European Unity in Context: The Interwar Period*, London: Pinter Publishers, 1989.

32   Onofrio [Andrea Caffi], 'Il problema europeo', *Quaderni di GL* 3, June 1932, 62.

were in substantial agreement with the notions of non-territorial autonomy and national self-determination on a personal basis elaborated by
Austro-Marxists. Overall, they made it possible to rethink the very concept
of the state and to imagine a polity based on the self-government of individuals and social groups within federalist institutions.[33]

It was not until the spring of 1935 that Rosselli embraced the idea of a
federal Europe, as a radical response to the ever-widening crisis in a continent now threatened by the outbreak of another war. Caffi's reasoning,
however, revealed the ambiguous character of the concept of Europe,
which was compatible with different, often contradictory political projects.
Europeanism offered a cultural ground linking minority currents of
Fascism and antifascism, which, despite their profound differences, were
rooted in a shared awareness of the inefficiency, or at least the political and
social inadequacy, of the nation-state as it was organized at the time. In the
early 1930s, Fascist culture increasingly focused on the decline of nation-
states and the prospect of a new European order.[34] From Giuseppe Bottai's
Critica fascista to Asvero Gravelli's *Anti-Europa*, from Berto Ricci's
L'Universale to Mario Carli and Emilio Settimelli's *Impero*, the purported
goal was to subvert the European order established by the peace conference of Paris, and with this to counter American power and to compete
with the Soviet model. In November 1932, the Italian Royal Academy's
Volta Foundation organized a series of lectures on Europe. Complementing
integral nationalism, the positions adopted by the aforementioned writers
linked imperialism, anti-Slavism, and Europeanism, while evincing a
mixture of sympathy and hostility towards Bolshevism. The most radical
among them (influenced by the Mazzinian legacy) were eager to identify
Fascism with the 'European revolution'. These included Delio Cantimori,
who, at the time, was mainly a contributor to Giuseppe Saitta's *Vita nova*,
and closely scrutinizing the German radical Right.

GL sought to combine political opposition to Mussolini's regime with
its restless desire to capture those cultural spaces then occupied by the

33   Most recently, see Börries Kuzmany, 'Non-Territorial National Autonomy in
Interwar European Minority Protection and Its Habsburg Legacies', in Peter Becker
and Natasha Wheatley (eds), *Remaking Central Europe: The League of Nations and
the Former Habsburg Lands*, New York: Oxford University Press, 2020, 315–43.
34   See Peter M. R. Stirk, *Authoritarian and Nationalist Socialist Conceptions of
Nation, State and Europe*, in Stirk, *European Unity in Context*, 125–48.

more ground-breaking currents of Fascism. Recognition of the need to foreground socio-political questions (and their possible solutions) on a continental scale was one example of this. Another was the search for an alternative take on individualism and collectivism, and on liberalism and communism. The urge to follow this Fascist 'third way' stemmed from an acute awareness of the traumatic crisis of a state faced with (often violent) social conflict during the early postwar period. In this sense, Fascist corporatism was part of a broader attempt to stabilize the organization of economic interests. The myth of corporatism thrived in the sphere of traditionalist Catholicism as it did in that of modern technocracy, and found a multitude of advocates throughout Europe (from Portugal to Romania), particularly in the wake of the 1929 Great Depression.[35] The corporative system, officially introduced in Italy by a law of January 1934, was the result of a long and complicated process that had begun in 1926 with the reorganization of collective bargaining agreements and the redefinition of the role of the Fascist trade union, and that in 1930 saw the creation of the National Council of Corporations. One extreme, yet nebulous idea – that of Ugo Spirito's 'proprietary corporation' (*corporazione proprietaria*) – went so far as to suggest the abolition of private property. This proposal was hotly debated at the Congress of Trade Union and Corporate Studies in Ferrara in May 1932, but was rejected as being too radical. The most prominent Fascist achievement resulting from massive state intervention in the economic sphere, in the aftermath of the Great Depression, was the Istituto per la Ricostruzione Industriale (IRI), constituted in 1933.

Antifascism, however, denounced the gap between the aspirations and the actual achievements of the Fascist corporative system. Salvemini vigorously rejected the Fascists' claim that class conflict in Italy had been resolved and denied that Mussolini had achieved Sorel's revolutionary syndicalist myth.[36] Salvemini discussed matters with the French scholar Louis Rosenstock-Franck, a former student at the École Polytechnique and, subsequently, a graduate in political economics from the University of Lille, where he studied under the supervision of the economist Bernard

---

35   António Costa Pinto (ed.), *Corporativism and Fascism: The Corporatist Wave in Europe*, London: Routledge, 2017.

36   Gaetano Salvemini, 'Capitale e lavoro nell'Italia fascista', *Quaderni di GL* 8, August 1933, 99–127.

Lavergne. Rosenstock-Franck's interest in corporations was sparked by discussions with Giuseppe Bottai and by reading Gino Arias's work *Economia nazionale corporativa* (1929). In his discussions with Salvemini, Nitti, and Tasca, and in his involvement with the 'non-conformist' Catholic milieu of *Esprit*, Rosenstock-Franck put forward the argument that 'the Fascist economy is essentially and exclusively a capitalist economy', hence, no corporate economy existed 'except on paper'.[37]

Vittorio Foa, who combined sympathy for the working class with legal expertise, produced the most original analysis of Fascist economic policies and ideas published in the *Quaderni di GL*. He had started writing for the Fascist journal *I problemi del lavoro*, edited between 1927 and 1940 by Rinaldo Rigola, the first secretary of the General Confederation of Labour. This monthly publication's line was that the integration of trade union action into Fascist institutions sanctioned the end of the liberal practice of non-state intervention in the economic sphere. Intellectuals such as Sergio Panunzio, Agostino Lanzillo, and Angelo Oliviero Olivetti, who were already close to the revolutionary syndicalist currents, had contributed to the formulation of the corporatist idea, whereas the leaders of the Fascist trade unions (such as Edmondo Rossoni) opposed the construction of the legal and institutional system of corporations. In the early 1930s, a new generation of trade union leaders, who were deaf to the libertarian, anti-bureaucratic demands of revolutionary syndicalist culture, helped revive the 'Fascist Left' or 'Left Fascism'. Republican, futurist, nationalist, and anti-clerical sensibilities merged into vibrantly anti-bourgeois, populist, anti-political cultures critical of Mussolini's dictatorship but open to a 'second revolutionary wave'. Examining Fascist legal literature and political propaganda claiming Fascism's emergence 'from the ruins of classical individualist economics', Foa took seriously the 'simple, mistaken conclusions of many ignorant and deluded people' and their 'visionary and dogmatic mental constructions'. In fact, he believed these conclusions to be 'dangerous', because they fed 'empty hopes and often a sterile and senseless opportunism'. At the institutional level, however, Foa was convinced

---

37 'La corporazione nel giudizio di uno straniero' [from an article by Rosenstock-Franck, *Esprit*, 1 January 1934], *Quaderni di GL* 10, February 1934, 13–15. See Louis Rosenstock-Franck, *Il corporativismo e l'economia dell'Italia fascista*, ed. Nicola Tranfaglia, Turin: Bollati Boringhieri, 1990.

that Fascism represented 'the anti-historical, violent, artificial preservation of totally decadent classes': the corporate order of the state, in Foa's
view, was instrumental to a regime 'without popular consensus'. Without
having superseded 'the sacred principles of economic individualism', and
without having achieved a new 'democracy of labour', the construction of
the corporative system – 'always from above, from the state, and never
from below' – sealed the primacy of private interests, which excluded the
concrete participation of the working masses and favoured the entrepre-
neurial classes. The result, he believed, was the paradox of 'an admittedly
liberalist regime, but a controlled one' that had been 'mistaken for a move
towards state socialism'.[38] Foa identified the fundamental ambivalence of
Fascist corporatism, which oscillated between the 'complete repudiation
of all abstentionist doctrines' and the permanence of the 'essential features
of economic individualism, namely the private appropriation of profit,
rent and interest'.[39] From this point of view, etatism and liberalism were by
no means two opposite poles, as the regime's propaganda claimed, but
were instead two inseparable, overlapping faces of Fascism. Yet the critical
arguments against Fascist corporatism did not stop GL from recognizing
its modernity. Agreeing completely with Foa, Rosselli maintained that the
corporative state was 'the technical instrument of modern reaction, a
counterfeit of the free and creative workers' movement for conservative
purposes'. It was precisely through the corporate organization of the state
that 'a mass reaction' was achieved.[40] However, the leader of GL sympathized with criticism of 'real corporatism' by the younger generations who
had grown up under Fascism, in the name of an 'ideal' corporatism.[41]

Rosselli, who was prepared to critically assess and embrace any innovation in the European society and culture of the time, made sure that the
unbiased positions of GL were accompanied by his own antifascist political
project. The members of GL were willing to take seriously the Fascist solutions that, from Europeanism to corporatism, set out to establish a political
and economic system in the face of the general crisis afflicting Europe. Can

38   Emiliano [Vittorio Foa], 'La politica economica del fascismo (dall'Italia)',
Quaderni di GL 8, August 1933, 80–94.
39   Emiliano [Vittorio Foa], 'Genesi e natura delle corporazioni fasciste (dall'I-
talia)', *Quaderni di GL* 10, February 1934, 16–28.
40   'La realtà dello Stato corporativo', *Quaderni di GL* 10, February 1934, 12.
41   [Carlo Rosselli,] 'Salto nel 1935', *GL*, 28 December 1934.

it be said that they, too, pursued the aforementioned 'third way' between liberalism and socialism, individualism and collectivism? This would not seem to be the case. To classify their paths, which were as fluid and heterogeneous as ever, as constituting the pursuit of a 'third way' would be to squeeze them into the overly rigid strictures of existing political ideologies and to ascribe the value of a coherent political alternative to an attitude that was *primarily* critical of the present. The paths into the realm of politics taken by GL's activists were narrow and tortuous. Given their opposition to the Fascist regime, however, they could not avoid critically engaging with the Russian Revolution, the Stalinist regime, and the class perspective.

Class Politics, Revolutionary Myths, Soviet Dictatorship

The communist question played a relatively minor role in GL's early years. Rosselli's group, which sought a democratic revolution, claimed to be completely different from the Italian Communist Party: it eschewed traditional Marxist vocabulary, rejected the prospect of the dictatorship of the proletariat, and polemicized with the 'class against class' line adopted by the Third International. Although a generic myth of the Russian Revolution was a common denominator for all leftist cultures of the time, this did not preclude a rather negative judgement of Stalin's regime and Soviet etatism. Nevertheless, the Great Depression of 1929 and its devastating social and political consequences, in both the United States and Europe, lent the Soviet experiment new appeal. The various socialist cultures represented a very different spectrum of positions, ranging from complete condemnation (by Karl Kautsky) to partial leniency (on the part of Otto Bauer and Friedrich Adler).[42] Kautsky, the leading theoretician of German Social Democracy, had, since 1918, voiced his profound criticism of the Bolshevik dictatorship in the name of the democratic constitutional state. He denied the socialist character of the Soviet Union, despite its collectivization and

---

42 See François Furet, *The Passing of an Illusion: The Idea of Communism in the Twentieth Century*, Chicago: University of Chicago Press, 1999, 62–92, and Israel Getzler, *Ottobre 1917: il dibattito marxista sulla rivoluzione in Russia*, in *Storia del marxismo*, vol. 3, *Il marxismo nell'età della Terza Internazionale*, 1: *Dalla Rivoluzione d'Ottobre alla crisi del '29*, Turin: Einaudi, 1980, 5–51.

industrialization – or rather, precisely because of this shift in direction as a result of mass violence. On the other hand, the leading Austro-Marxists distinguished between criticism of Stalin's regime and the revolutionary potential of Soviet society that had emerged since 1917. Fascinated by the Five-Year Plan, Bauer and Adler trusted that this enormous modernizing endeavour would lead to an adaptation of the socialist structural 'base' to form a democratic political 'superstructure'.[43]

Caffi was the member of GL best suited to offer an informed opinion on the Russian revolutions, Bolshevism, and the Soviet regime. His knowledge of the Russian language and culture, plus his extensive network of relations with Menshevik and Social Revolutionary émigrés in Paris, gave him a vantage point on the Soviet Union. In the years 1917–21, he had been seduced by the myth of radical palingenesis seemingly embodied by revolutionary Russia. Afterwards, he completely changed his mind and developed some very clear ideas, which, in March 1932, he set out in the second number of *Quaderni di GL*. Caffi resolutely denied the myth according to which the Soviet Union, despite its dictatorial degeneration under Stalin, would continue to constitute the testing ground for socialism. Opposed to the pro-Soviet orientation of the left-wing Mensheviks inherited by Ju. O Martov and then developed by Fyodor I. Dan, Caffi was close to the right-wing Mensheviks led by Raphael R. Abramovitch and Boris I. Nikolaevsky, who raised the question of the relationship between socialism and democracy and sharply criticized the Stalinist dictatorship and its economic policy.[44] While acknowledging that the 1917 revolution had been 'a positive, general uprising of the masses of the people', the USSR had become not only 'a state as efficient in the exercise of absolute power as any other state organization in the world', but also 'a grandiose mechanism for the coercion and exploitation of individuals'.[45] Caffi noted the 'obvious affinities [of Stalin's

43   See Mark E. Blum and William Smaldone (eds), *Austro-Marxism: The Ideology of Unity*, vol. 1, *Austro-Marxist Theory and Strategy*, Leiden: Brill, 2015, and vol. 2, *Changing the World: The Politics of Austro-Marxism*, Leiden: Brill, 2017.

44   See Leopold H. Haimson (ed.), *The Mensheviks: From the Revolution of 1917 to the Second World War*, Chicago: University of Chicago Press, 1975, and André Liebich, *From the Other Shore: Russian Social Democracy After 1921*, Cambridge, MA: Harvard University Press, 1997.

45   Onofrio [Andrea Caffi], 'Opinioni sulla Rivoluzione russa', *Quaderni di GL* 2, March 1932, 92.

dictatorship] with the monstrosities of our own epoch' and threw light on their deep mutual relationship and their common roots in the wartime experience. Far from being 'a "counterweight" to the regimes of capitalist reaction' in Europe and the United States, the Soviet Union was 'an element of this reactionary constellation'.[46] Unlike Caffi, who had developed his passion for politics on the basis of Russia's revolutionary traditions and experiences, Rosselli's political opposition to Fascism had gradually reshaped his overall assessment of the 1917 revolutions and the Soviet regime. However, wavering attitudes, even certain contradictions, between ideas of social progress and political dictatorship emerged in Rosselli's article 'Note sulla Russia' published in March 1932. His main evaluative criterion was adherence to the 1917 Revolution, which he understood and celebrated as a single, indeterminate 'bloc': 'Before every consecration of Marxism and every dictatorial atrocity lies the revolution that destroyed autocracy and gave land to the peasants.' At the same time, Rosselli's critical judgement of Stalin's regime was accompanied by a fascination with the planning of the 'collectivist economy' which, 'for all its faults and horrors', nevertheless represented 'the alternative'.[47]

Rosselli's position tended to converge with the thinking of Bauer, Adler, and Dan, who believed that eventual democratization would result not from the reaction to, but from the transformation of, the Soviet system. The revolutionary myth pushed the GL leader to engage with the 1917 revolutions and the Soviet experiment, events that subsequently degenerated into Stalin's dictatorship; while sympathizing with the former, he was highly critical of the latter. At the same time Rosselli was always sceptical, if not openly critical, of Trotsky's positions, despite his admiration for one of the victors of the Russian civil wars. As shown in an interview in Paris in May 1934, their visions were quite different, at times bitterly opposed, in terms of organization of the revolution, relations between the bourgeoisie and the proletariat, and the relationship between antifascism and communism.[48] In an article published on the seventeenth anniversary of the capture of the Winter Palace, Rosselli distinguished between the 'unique memory of October' and 'the epic deeds of the

---

46   Ibid., 99.
47   Curzio [Carlo Rosselli], 'Note sulla Russia', *Quaderni di GL* 2, March 1932, 103–7.
48   Carlo Rosselli, 'Incontro con Trotzski', *GL*, 25 May 1934.

Russian Revolution'. The Bolshevik regime posed a 'challenge' to the 'bourgeois world', but its methods tended to 'go off in a direction contrary to the set goal'.[49] When confronted with Caffi's explicit comparison between the two dictatorships, he took a step back and acknowledged the Soviet Union's right to 'defend itself'. However, he called the extensive, massive campaign of terror that followed the assassination of Leningrad party leader Sergei M. Kirov 'a mistake and proof of weakness': while during the 1918–21 civil wars, violence had been 'necessary', after seventeen years of rule it had become 'abhorrent and highly harmful to the very goals of the revolution'. GL's editors, however, downplayed Caffi's reasoning, rejecting 'any parallel between the Russian dictatorship and the Fascist dictatorship', since the former had emerged 'from the greatest revolution seen in the modern world'.[50]

Soviet mythology, in many ways, tended to deny, ignore, or indeed justify the mass violence of Lenin and Stalin's socio-political experiments, but offered a progressive way out of the cultural pessimism rampant in the 1930s. Regardless of the extent of police repression and the subsequent scale of human losses, the myth of the Soviet, the Leninist example of the revolutionary vanguard, the appeal of state planning, and the terrible enigma of Stalinism continued to spur and sometimes fascinate the non-communist antifascists. However, attitudes towards the Soviet Union changed, and even confusingly overlapped, according to different temporalities and understandings of fascism (and, accordingly, of antifascism). In Rosselli's case, the judgement he offered of the Soviet dictatorship was inseparable from that of the 'Russian Revolution' (despite the ambiguity of equating heterogeneous phenomena). This connection, regardless of its contradictions, offered the basis for a critique of Stalin's regime, or for the possible different development of the Soviet revolution in the West. Trentin and Lussu, the proponents of a socialist shift within GL, instead insisted on a class interpretation of the antifascist revolution and stressed the socialist potential of the Soviet experiment despite Stalin's dictatorship.

Lussu was an important but irregular presence during GL debates, often having to withdraw from political work due to health problems. In his first article for *Quaderni di GL*, published in June 1932, Lussu

---

49   [Carlo Rosselli,] '7 Novembre', *GL*, 9 November 1934.

50   [Carlo Rosselli,] 'Corsivo redazionale', in Andrea [Andrea Caffi], 'Tragedia moscovita', *GL*, 4 January 1935.

established an inseparable link between revolution and freedom, democracy and socialism, when he stated that 'outside of democracy there is no socialism, only permanent terror.'[51] In a context increasingly dominated by class language, Lussu identified the conflict between dictatorship and democracy with that between the bourgeoisie and the working classes. In this sense, he rejected the essential message contained in Rosselli's *Liberal Socialism*, in which the author had affirmed the perfect reciprocity and complementarity of the two concepts. However, like the leader of GL, he acknowledged the need for a dictatorial phase in order to proclaim the democratic revolution of the socialist movement.

In the meantime, Lussu established personal and political relations with Trentin during a stay in Auch (southern France) in the winter of 1933–34.[52] Trentin had been a member of the Republican Party in exile since 1926 and worked with the Lega Italiana per i Diritti dell'Uomo and the Concentrazione antifascista, and in early 1934 took on an important role in Rosselli's group. During this phase, Trentin's political views became more radical, as a result of the decline of his professional and social status: from being a university professor in Italy he was now a printer in exile. Nevertheless, this turning point developed from a reflection inspired by the juridical realism of Giovanni Vacchelli and the French social school led by Maurice Hauriou and Léon Duguit, together with neo-Kantian ethical idealism. Constitutional arrangements were now seen as insufficient to ensure respect for individual rights in the absence of a belief in freedom. Taking the Weimar lesson into account, Trentin became increasingly critical of the 'bourgeois' legal tradition, and aware of the need to create a 'new order' not through law but through the revolutionary overthrow of the existing system.[53] In *Riflessioni sulla crisi e sulla rivoluzione*, written in late 1932, published in 1933, and further developed in other essays during the 1934–35 period, Trentin described the prospect of integral collectivism: 'Only a great expropriating revolution can pave the way for the new order.'[54]

---

51   Tirreno [Emilio Lussu], 'Orientamenti', *Quaderni di GL* 3, June 1932, 46.

52   Emilio Lussu, 'Profilo di Silvio Trentin', in Silvio Trentin, *Scritti inediti: testimonianze, studi*, ed. Paolo Gobetti, Parma: Guanda, 1972, 5–23.

53   Silvio Trentin, 'Popolo e Costituzione', *La Libertà*, September 1932.

54   Silvio Trentin, 'Sugli obiettivi della rivoluzione italiana', *Problemi della rivoluzione italiana*, March 1934, 19.

These reflections were particularly inspired by Austro-Marxist culture, which represented 'an untouched oasis, a little world apart, living on its own ideology' within the Second International. After the bloody suppression of the Vienna Commune, Trentin was shocked by the 'irretrievable failure of the traditional formations' of European socialism, which had inhibited the revolutionary power of the masses with the 'evil virus' of reformism. Since capitalism was a 'regime of war', it could only be 'eradicated by its destruction'. In a position that differed from that of the Paris GL group, and that partially coincided with that of Lussu, he argued for the 'pure class basis' of antifascism, thus regarding the bourgeoisie as a 'historical relic'.[55] This political change of direction corresponded to his strong desire for action. Accordingly, Trentin offered a benevolent, indulgent appraisal of the Soviet Union, inspired in part by Leon Trotsky. The Soviet experiment, which until the early 1930s had been considered a dictatorship on a par with Fascist dictatorship, was now viewed as a 'glimmer of light'. Trentin, however, believed that the 'contingent manifestation' of Stalin's regime did not represent the 'final form of that future regime' which was to resolve the crisis of contemporary society.[56]

Trentin's collectivist perspective, embodied in the idea of 'state capitalism', excluded the bourgeoisie from playing any positive role. On the contrary, Lussu wondered how Trentin believed he could achieve 'such a radical form of immediate socialization in Italy without terror'.[57] Lussu, in turn, pursued a socialism that was both democratic and class-oriented, rejecting revolutionary terror but identifying the bourgeoisie with fascism. He held that 'the only class that fought for and defended democracy' was the working class, even if he included the 'petty bourgeoisie' among that class.[58] Despite their clear differences with Rosselli, Lussu and Trentin were afforded increasing space on the pages of GL's publications. Salvemini,

---

55   Silvio Trentin, 'Bisogna decidersi (aprile 1934)', *Quaderni di GL* 11, June 1934, 99–108.

56   Silvio Trentin, *Riflessioni sulla crisi e sulla rivoluzione*, Marseille: ESIL, 1933, quoted in Giannantonio Paladini, 'Trentin e l'URSS', in *Silvio Trentin e la Francia. Saggi e testimonianze*, Venice: Marsilio, 1991, 138–9.

57   [Emilio Lussu,] 'Riflessioni sulla crisi e sulla rivoluzione', *Quaderni di GL* 7, June 1933, 102–3.

58   Tirreno [Emilio Lussu], 'Discussioni sul nostro movimento: orientamenti', *Quaderni di GL* 10, February 1934, 60.

on the other hand, then living in exile at Harvard and caustically critical of their 'illusion' regarding the 'working class', wrote to Rosselli: 'Revolutions are not made by classes, but by organized parties.'[59]

In the polarized climate at the time of the Popular Front, however, judgement of Soviet communism was considered the inescapable factor differentiating fascists from antifascists; and, even within GL, there were those who not only avoided comparing the dictatorships of Hitler and Mussolini with that of Stalin, but were willing to acknowledge the democratic self-representation of the Soviet Union. From 1932 on, leniency and sympathy towards the Soviet Union (often identified with the 'Russian Revolution') alternated with perplexity, if not condemnation, with regard to Stalin's dictatorship. Later, between 1935 and 1937, at the very time when internal repression under the Soviet regime was on the rise, openly apologetic arguments came to the fore. Calosso was attentive to the thoughts of the famous couple Sidney and Beatrice Webb, founders of Fabianism and advocates of a gradualist, anti-Marxist Labourism. After reflecting at length on industrial democracy, the authors passionately analysed the processes of industrialization and collectivization under Stalin's regime. Significantly, their 1932 work *Soviet Communism. A New Civilization?* saw the title's question mark deleted in the later 1935 edition. Calosso's review of the book, which appeared in February 1936, shared the Webbs' assessment of the democratic nature of the entire Soviet project, which drew more on collective action than on Stalin's leadership. The Communist Party was understood as 'a kind of religious order, a Samurai Order or an Order of Jesuits'; an order operating 'for transcendent reasons, almost like the Church alongside the state': like capitalism, the advent of socialism had been accompanied by a 'religious revolution' based on 'asceticism'.[60]

On the other hand, Trentin did not hide his enthusiasm for the draft constitution approved by a commission chaired by Stalin himself, which was to become the new legal and institutional foundation of the USSR. First, he recognized that the dictatorship of the party had been replaced by the dictatorship of the proletariat, which had achieved the 'creation of a

59   Letter from Gaetano Salvemini to Carlo Rosselli, 23 April 1934, in Carlo Rosselli and Gaetano Salvemini, *Fra le righe: carteggio fra Carlo Rosselli e Gaetano Salvemini*, ed. Elisa Signori, Milan: Franco Angeli, 2009, 214.

60   Umberto Calosso, 'La Russia in un libro dei Webb', *GL*, 7 February 1936.

classless socialist society'. The new Soviet Constitution consecrated 'the final establishment of the socialist state', and enshrined 'the original expressions of the collective life of a country which, through an historically unprecedented revolution, has overtaken the phase of bourgeois democracy for ever, in the fatal bend in the development of Western political institutions'. More importantly, the new Constitution succeeded in 'finally reconciling the need for emancipation, for a violent break with the past, with respect for the immanent demands of Order, that is, of Law, as an indelible guarantee of coexistence'.[61] Trentin was not alone in praising the progressive, democratic character of the new Soviet Constitution, being echoed by, for example, British Labour Party intellectuals such as Harold Laski and the Webbs. The editors of *GL*, however, distanced themselves from the 'enthusiastic judgement' offered by Trentin, who they deemed 'attached excessive importance . . . to the legal formulation' when examining the Constitution.[62]

In the minds of Calosso and Trentin, the Soviet Union thus embodied the coming of socialism – for the first, as the outcome of a religious revolution, for the second, as the result of a legal invention. Both men projected their own cultural and political expectations onto the Soviet experiment; however, the positions of Calosso and Trentin in 1936 did not indicate the ultimate significance of their quest for socialism, or indeed account for the entire spectrum of positions within GL. Dilemmas, doubts, and uncertainties continued to shape the attitudes of GL's members towards the Russian Revolutions and Stalin's Soviet Union; but, at the height of the Popular Fronts' importance, the imperatives of antifascist mobilization and the expressions of anti-Stalinist criticism became increasingly dissonant.

---

61   Silvio Trentin, 'La nuova costituzione russa', *GL*, 3 July 1936; Silvio Trentin, 'La nuova costituzione russa', *GL*, 10 July 1936; Silvio Trentin, 'La nuova costituzione russa', *GL*, 17 July 1936.

62   'Un commento di Silvio Trentin', *GL*, 3 July 1936.

1. The editorial board of *Non mollare*, 1925 (left to the right: Nello Traquandi, Tommaso Ramorino, Carlo Rosselli, Ernesto Rossi, Luigi Emery, Nello Rosselli)

2. The flight of Carlo Rosselli (centre), Emilio Lussu (right), and Francesco Fausto Nitti (left) from the island of Lipari

3. Arrival of Carlo Rosselli, Emilio Lussu, Francesco Fausto
Nitti, Oxilia, at Cap Bon, in southern France, 1929

4. Marion Cave with Nello and Carlo Rosselli on the sea front of Ostenda, 1930

5. Carlo Rosselli walking at the Bois de Boulogne with his son John, 1930

6. Carlo and Nello Rosselli
in France, 1934

7. French historian Elie Halévy,
close friend of Carlo Rosselli

8. Leone Ginzburg

9. Franco Venturi

10. Vittorio Foa

11. Carlo Levi with some peasants during his confinement in Aliano, 1935

12. Silvio Trentin in his farmhouse at Auch, in southern France

13. Silvio Trentin standing in front of his library in Toulouse

14. Andrea Caffi and Nicola
Chiaromonte in Toulouse, 1947

15. Carlo Rosselli
in Spain, 1936

16. Carlo Rosselli with other fighters in Spain, 1936

17. The funeral of Carlo and Nello Rosselli, Paris, 19 June 1937. This is the entrance to the Maison des Syndicats (33 Rue de la Grange aux Belles), where the coffins of the Rosselli brothers were brought and the first part of the funeral ceremony took place. In the foreground Aldo Garosci holds a cushion with the overalls and militia cap used by Carlo Rosselli during the Spanish Civil War.

18. The funeral of Carlo and Nello Rosselli, Paris, 19 June 1937 (left to right: Alberto Cianca, Emilio Lussu, Alberto Tarchiani, and Aldo Garosci)

19–20. The funeral of Carlo and Nello Rosselli, Paris, 19 June 1937

'Non-Conformist' Strategies of Imitation and Competition

Exile proved over time to be a fundamental experience for the reviewing and reshaping of the political and intellectual path taken by GL's members, whether as a result of occasional decisions or through the coercive pressure of the Fascist dictatorship. The antifascist struggle was enriched and inspired by sources from other political cultures, while the distance from Italy offered an epistemological viewpoint from which to develop a critical attitude towards the relationship between present, past, and future. GL did not turn its back on the Risorgimento tradition, but many of its members, through their close relationship and contact with other European cultures (especially French culture), were able to adopt new perspectives that were, in various ways, linked to socialism.[63] Although Rosselli continued to travel frequently to England, in the 1930s he focused less on the Labour Party and on Fabian and Guild developments than he had in the 1920s. It is likely that, in this respect, he shared the 'bitterness of dashed hopes' that Élie Halévy expressed in a London lecture given in April 1934 on the topic of 'Le socialisme et le problème du parlementarisme démocratique'.[64] This was hardly surprising: in 1931, having squandered the trust it had gained in winning the 1929 election, the Labour Party suffered a dramatic setback that was to mark the beginning of a long period of Conservative rule (until 1945). Moreover, 1930s Labourism was characterized by its limited theoretical creativity, starting with its substantial lack of interest in the 'Keynesian revolution'. The one notable exception was Oswald Mosley, who soon left the Labour Party and embarked on a path that was to lead him to a very personal form of 'fascism'. Rosselli's interest in the more unbiased figures of the Labour

---

63 Franco Venturi, 'Carlo Rosselli e la cultura francese', in *Giustizia e Libertà nella lotta antifascista e nella storia d'Italia: Attualità dei fratelli Rosselli a quarant'anni dal loro sacrificio*, Florence: La Nuova Italia, 1978, 163–78, and Edoardo Tortarolo, 'L'esilio della libertà. Franco Venturi e la cultura europea degli anni Trenta', in Luciano Guerci and Giuseppe Ricuperati (eds), *Il coraggio della ragione. Franco Venturi intellettuale e storico cosmopolita*, Turin: Fondazione Einaudi, 1998, 89–114.

64 Élie Halévy, 'Le socialisme et le problème du parlementarisme démocratique', in *L'ère des tyrannies. Études sur le socialisme et la guerre*, Paris: Gallimard, 1990, 201.

movement who searched for new, possible solutions to the crisis (from Stafford Cripps to Mosley) was always secondary.[65]

The leader of GL followed with immense interest the development of French and Belgian socialism during the early 1930s. The Great Depression, despite affecting Western Europe more gradually and less damagingly than Central and Eastern Europe (or perhaps for that reason), forced some minority socialist currents to review their analytical instruments and their political perspectives. In particular, the economic crisis of 1929–31, together with Hitler's seizure of power in 1933, focused attention on and aggravated the question of the middle classes, which had provided the fundamental impetus for Bernstein's revisionism in the late nineteenth century. Contrary to Marx's prediction, contemporary society had not experienced the process of extreme polarization that Marx thought would trigger the decline and eventual disappearance of the middle classes (through their 'proletarianization'). On the contrary, as Bernstein had recognized, the importance of these classes had increased over time and had eventually become a focal point for the proletariat. The middle classes' vacillation between the pursuit of economic advancement and the fear of losing their social status in times of crisis was, in turn, one of the keys to understanding the emergence and success of fascism.

De Man's *planisme*, Marcel Déat's *néo-socialisme*, and the ideas of heterodox socialist and syndicalist minorities aimed to overcome the immobility of political thought and action in relation to the structural changes affecting European society. Setting aside all forms of revolutionary maximalism, these minority currents of Western European socialism sought to assume direct political responsibility in the face of the dynamics of fascistization in Europe. World War I represented a genuine break with the past, leading to the emergence of a new model of state intervention in the economy, in the organization of the means of production, in the mobilization of manpower and in the distribution of resources. The technocratic and organizational trends had identified an exemplary experience in Walther Rathenau's construction of a 'new economy' in Germany, and in Albert Thomas's forms

---

65   Per the political cultures, see G. D. H. Cole, *Storia del pensiero socialista*, vol. 4, *Comunismo e socialdemocrazia, 1914–1931*, Bari: Laterza, 1968, 74–107; for the context, see Robert Skidelsky, *Politicians and the Slump: The Labour Government of 1929–1931*, Basingstoke: Macmillan, 1967.

of union discipline in France. On closer examination, ideas of representation of economic functions and interests echoed a long nineteenth-century tradition of antiliberal contamination: the organic reorganization of communities was a reaction to the dissolution of social ties (*liens sociaux*) initiated by the French Revolution.[66] However, this long tradition was not enough to confirm the hegemony of those in favour of state planning, nationalization, and economic intervention in the 1930s (unlike after 1945), while most of the Section Française de l'Internationale Ouvrière (SFIO) remained loyal to the main categories of Marxism and to the discussion of its ethical revision as suggested by Bernstein.[67]

Néo-socialisme – the current within the SFIO grouped around Déat, Pierre Renaudel, Adrien Marquet, Barthélemy Montagnon, and Paul Marion – sought to provide a political response to the economic and psychological vulnerability of the middle classes who, faced with the crisis of international capitalism and the consequent falling back on autarchic and nationalist strategies, tended to slip into adopting 'fascist' positions. From this point of view, Déat seemed to take the Marxist perspective of the proletarianization of the middle classes much more seriously than Bernstein and to seek a political solution in the 'race' against fascism.[68] The *néo-socialistes* formed a small but vocal minority of the SFIO, and introduced a motion at the July 1933 Congress proposing socialist support for the radical-led government in an 'antifascist' sense. However, the speeches given by Déat, Marquet and Montagnon, accompanied by the slogans 'order, authority, nation', were

66 Jean-Philippe Parrot, *La représentation des intérêts dans le mouvement des idées politiques*, Paris: Presses Universitaires de France, 1974, and Michele Battini, *L'ordine della gerarchia. Contributi progressisti e reazionari alla crisi della democrazia, 1789–1914*, Turin: Bollati Boringhieri, 1995.

67 George Lichtheim, *Marxism in Modern France*, New York: Columbia University Press, 1966, 42–3; Tony Judt, *Le marxisme et la gauche française, 1830–1981*, Paris: Hachette, 1986, 125–69; and Jacques Julliard, *Les Gauches françaises, 1762–2012. Histoire et politique*, Paris: Flammarion, 2012, 483–95. On the context see Julian Jackson, *The Politics of Depression in France, 1932–1936*, Cambridge: Cambridge University Press, 1985; on the long-term legacies, see Philip Nord, *France's New Deal. From the Thirties to the Postwar Era*, Princeton, NJ: Princeton University Press, 2010.

68 Alain Bergounioux, 'Le néo-socialisme. Marcel Déat: réformisme traditionnel ou esprit des années trente', *Revue historique* 260, no. 2, October–December 1978, 389–412.

riddled with ambiguities which the majority, gathered around party leader Léon Blum, promptly branded 'fascist'. After the congress, Rosselli granted Déat a right of reply in the *Quaderni di GL*, in order that he might defend himself against the accusation of 'National Socialist deviationism' that would later be officially given as the reason for the expulsion of the *néos* from the SFIO (in November 1933). Déat's reply, tellingly wondering 'how to bar the road to fascism', drew from the lessons of the German Social Democratic Party's downfall. He identified the need in France to compete with fascism through the 'enthusiastic consensus of the masses'. His interpretation of fascism as 'a kind of revolt of the bourgeoisie threatened by proletarianization and social decadence' led to him targeting the regeneration of the nation and the restoration of the state.[69] Rosselli's willingness to engage with Déat's view drew directly from the lessons learnt from the collapse of the Weimar Republic and German Social Democracy. What impressed him was 'not so much the victory of a National Socialism that was even more brutal and lacking in ideas than Italian Fascism – although much greater and more powerful than the latter – but the immediate submergence of the old democratic, social-democratic, communist world, which we could consider grotesque were it not so infinitely painful'.[70]

The question was: how should national political power be assumed in order to fight fascism without adopting its authoritarian and nationalist slogans? How were the middle classes to be embraced so as to ensure political freedom and social cohesion, while maintaining the pursuit of socialist goals? In three articles published in *La Libertà* in August 1933, Rosselli was quick to share the basic arguments of the *néos*, aimed at countering 'antifascist ideological conservatism'. The point was not to choose between revolution and reform, but to focus on the alternative between 'an intermediate system dominated by reactionary forces' and 'a preparatory system dominated by the forces of renewal'.[71] Salvemini's reaction was quite different. In a letter to Rosselli, he condemned the 'ambiguous formulas' proffered by the *néos* with a number of rhetorical questions: 'Do the left-wing fascists intend to abolish parliamentary institutions with the

---

69   Marcel Déat, 'Come sbarreremo la strada al fascismo', *Quaderni di GL* 8, August 1933, 21–30.

70   [Carlo Rosselli,] 'Italia e Europa', *Quaderni di GL* 7, June 1933.

71   [Carlo Rosselli,] 'Il neo-socialismo francese', *La Libertà*, 17 August 1933.

help of the masses? What do they want to replace? And do they also want to sacrifice personal rights and political freedoms?'[72]

Sharing the concerns expressed by the *néo-socialistes*, the Belgian socialist de Man strove for a 'constructive socialism' that moved beyond Marxism, and he was appointed by the Belgian Workers' Party – Parti Ouvrier Belge (POB) – to head the Bureau d'Études Sociales. His main proposal consisted of the 'Plan du travail', published in the Brussels Socialist newspaper *Le Peuple* in October 1933 and presented at the POB Congress of December 1933. Having overcome the opposing maximum and minimum programmes that typified the Second International, de Man proposed a series of 'structural reforms' that would enable the capitalist system to survive the crisis, find new stability, and win a broader consensus among the middle classes who were increasingly exposed to the effects of the Great Depression. Hence his concept of an 'intermediary system', which quickly became loaded with corporate features.[73]

The *planiste* current spreading through France, particularly after February 1934, was significantly heterogeneous. The weekly *La Vie socialiste*, of the *néo-socialiste* Renaudel, was involved in formulating the *Plan*. De Man, on the other hand, preferred to work with the Révolution constructive group, formed by the historian Georges Lefranc, the economist Robert Marjolin, and the philosopher and anthropologist Claude Lévi-Strauss. This latter group was close to the SFIO and was very keen on the idea of planning and public intervention in the sphere of economic production and distribution.[74] The journal *Combat marxiste*, inspired by Lucien Laurat

72   Letter from Gaetano Salvemini to Carlo Rosselli, 5 August 1933, in Carlo Rosselli and Salvemini, *Fra le righe*, 168.

73   Erik Hansen, 'Hendrik de Man and the Theoretical Foundations of Economic Planning: The Belgian Experience 1933–40', *European Studies Review* 2, 1978, 234–57; John Horne, 'L'idée de nationalisation dans les mouvements ouvriers jusqu'à la deuxième guerre mondiale', in 'Les nationalisations d'après-guerre en Europe occidentale', *Le Mouvement social* 134, January–March 1986, 9–36, and Sheri Berman, *The Primacy of Politics: Social Democracy and the Making of Europe's Twentieth Century*, Cambridge: Cambridge University Press, 2006, 96–124.

74   Georges Lefranc, 'Le courant planiste dans le mouvement ouvrier français (1935–1936)', *Le Mouvement social*: 54, January–March 1966, 69–89; Georges Lefranc, 'Histoire d'un groupe du Parti socialiste SFIO. Révolution constructive (1930–1938)', in *Essais sur les problèmes socialistes et syndicaux*, Paris: Payot, 1970, 169–96; Pierre Rosanvallon, *L'État en France: de 1789 à nos jours*, Paris: Seuil, 1990, 226–42.

(pseudonym of the Austrian economist Otto Maschl), a former communist and later socialist who had published a volume entitled *Économie planée contre économie enchaînée* for the Librairie Valois in 1932, endorsed the dirigiste and decisionist solutions set out in the *Plan*. The engineer Jean Coutrot, the *néo-socialiste* Louis Vallon, and the reformist socialists Jules Moch and Charles Spinasse (members of the *X-Crise* group founded by the École Polytechnique) shared de Man's ideas. Together they contributed to the *Plan* of 9 July 1934, which also saw the involvement of radical cultural figures such as Bertrand de Jouvenel and Jean Zay under the leadership of the writer and philosopher Jules Romains. This initiative, inspired especially by de Jouvenel and his call for a 'direct economy', heralded a state reform that brought together both anti-parliamentary and technocratic outlooks. In the Confédération Générale du Travail (CGT), too, the spirit, if not the doctrine, of de Man began to prevail, thanks to René Belin. Blum's SFIO, on the other hand, condemned *planisme* in the belief that it represented a form of stabilization of the capitalist system that would persist, hence blocking the socialist transition from the 'exercise of power' to the 'conquest of power'. In September 1934, de Man's arguments were given an airing on a particularly illustrious stage, namely the 'Décades de Pontigny', an annual symposium held in a Cistercian abbey in Burgundy under the direction of Paul Dejardins. Tasca, Rosselli, and Chiaromonte attended the event, as did Gurvitch, Laurat, Voitinsky, de Jouvenel, and the trade unionists Robert Lacoste and Édouard Dolléans.[75]

The moving away from Marxism, the need to go beyond purely negative antifascism through implementation of a positive, constructive programme, and the competition with fascism for the approval of the bourgeoisie from an anti-capitalist point of view, inevitably fascinated Rosselli. GL promptly acknowledged the importance of the POB adopting the *Plan*, noting its similarities with the GL's 'Schema di programma'. These included: the shared 'structural reforms' in terms of the socialization of credit and of monopoly industries, and the mixing of public and private economic sectors. Nevertheless, Rosselli reiterated his own fundamental principle: 'Partial socialization is a guarantee of freedom, universal socialization is a cause of slavery'.[76]

75   François Chaubet, *Paul Dejardins et les Décades de Pontigny*, Villeneuve-d'Ascq: Presses Universitaires du Septentrion, 2000.
76   'Socialismo e socializzazione', *GL*, 8 February 1934.

The figure who fascinated (and also disquieted) these socialist circles, more than Marx, was Saint-Simon. The great early nineteenth-century thinker from Geneva had reflected on the impact of the French Revolution on European society and had developed a new philosophy of history, imbued with religiosity and designed to establish a communal sense to the dissolution of post-revolutionary *liens sociaux*. Starting from his analysis of Saint-Simon, to whom he had devoted a pioneering study in 1924 together with Bouglé, Halévy developed his idea of the ambivalences and ambiguities of socialism.[77] Bouglé, in his historical and sociological work *Socialismes français*, recalled the importance of Saint-Simonianism to the efforts made to reorganize society after the 1789 Revolution, and to resolve the serious social problems caused by liberal individualism. Déat's socio-logical studies also drew inspiration from Saint-Simon, as Déat called for the replacement of the 'government of men' with the 'administration of things'.[78] Rosselli, much as he shared the need for a two-sector economy as advocated by both de Man and Déat, inclined more towards the positions of Halévy and Bouglé. He regarded with suspicion the Saint-Simonian reduction of government to the 'administration of things', which he consid-ered to be 'the road leading to dictatorship in the name of maximum production'.[79]

Néo-socialistes and *planistes* helped usher in a cultural change within GL that was to lay the foundation of the welfare state and public inter-vention in postwar Europe. However, the willingness to compete with fascism in the 1930s exposed the more creative, restless figures and currents among the antifascist front to the temptation of shifting away from clear opposition to a more or less covert, unwitting fascination. As in a mirror image, both contrary and yet identical, antifascism ran the

---

77   Célestin Bouglé and Élie Halévy, *Doctrine de Saint-Simon*, Paris: Rivière, 1924. Many issues were taken up in his lectures, collected in Élie Halévy, *Histoire du socialisme européen*, Paris: Gallimard, 1948; on the problems of this edition, see Michele Battini, *Utopia e tirannide. Scavi nell'archivio Halévy*, Turin: Bollati Boringhieri, 2011, 36–88. On the long shadow of Saint-Simon over French socialism, see Julliard, *Les Gauches françaises*, 578–613.

78   Marcel Déat, *Perspectives socialistes*, Paris: Librairie Valois, 1930.

79   Carlo Rosselli, 'Discussione sul federalismo e l'autonomia', *GL*, 27 December 1935.

risk of overlapping, conflating or identifying with its professed enemy.[80] Rosselli and other representatives of GL, however, never lost sight of that profound link between ethics and politics, and to some extent between moralism and anti-moralism. Despite his openness to the demands of Déat and de Man, Rosselli remained convinced that it was the moral crisis that dissolved social bonds and drove dictatorial solutions. The 'race' against fascism necessarily had to take place on the political playing field established by fascism itself; and so, it was necessary to move to another terrain in order to rethink the meaning of politics and respond to the 'crisis of civilization'.

Crisis of Civilization

Writers and thinkers of the 1930s were often plagued by a sense of spiritual and cultural decadence that emerged with the rise of mass society and was exacerbated by the wartime catastrophe of 1914–18. In tune with this literature, which, in many ways, questioned the nineteenth-century myth of progress, Rosselli shared the idea of the crisis of European civilization. Fascism and Nazism became the ultimate result of a 'moral crisis' that had unfolded on three levels – 'democracy reduced to pure form, socialism reduced to pure economy, freedom reduced to mere instrument' – and affected not only capitalist society but 'society, pure and simple'. Hence Rosselli's desire for a total palingenesis and his call for a new humanism, as expressed in his article 'Italy and Europe', published in the June 1933 number of *Quaderni di GL*:

> An antifascism that does not want to end up a shadow of its former self
> must be aware of this crisis, of its ideal inadequacy, in order to rethink
> its very foundations through its actions. Until now, we have built on
> sand. We now need to look for rock. And to find it, we must have the
> courage to question all of our positions, all of our half-truths, our very

---

80 See Zeev Sternhell, *Neither Right nor Left: Fascist Ideology in France*, Princeton, NJ: Princeton University Press, 1986, 195–312; for a point of view that can be shared more readily than Sternhell's, see Philippe Burrin, 'Le fascisme français', in *Fascisme, nazisme, autoritarisme*, Paris: Éditions du Seuil, 2000, 247–66.

programme, if necessary to lay the foundations for a new civilization, a new Man.[81]

The opposition between fascism and antifascism was here expressed in language taken directly from the Sermon on the Mount. Calosso, in turn, warned GL to move away from the sphere of politics (in the party-political sense) in this issue of *Quaderni di GL*, laying claim to the 'realm' of 'antipolitics' and proclaiming the need for 'powerful, suggestive, new' ideas.[82] He argued that GL needed to learn, from Fascism, how to utilize the mythological and symbolic sphere to engage the masses in the pursuit of a new social and political order. By so doing he was endorsing a cultural tradition stretching from Giambattista Vico to Giovanni Gentile, that encountered Georges Sorel as well as Charles Péguy along the way.[83]

The GL leaders' French exile allowed them to observe more closely a society and culture increasingly plagued by the sense of the decline of its former greatness.[84] However, the common obsession with decadence did not exclude an urge for innovation and experimentation, which motivated the 'non-conformist' currents, both 'realist' and 'spiritualist'. In the late 1920s and the first half of the 1930s, many small groups, circles and journals existed, ranging from *Jeune Droite* to *Ordre Nouveau*, and from *Esprit* to *Plan*. The 'realists' (such as Jean Luchaire, Georges Valois, Bertrand de Jouvenel, Gaston Riou) mainly advocated economic modernization, reform of the state, and the unification of Europe. The 'spiritualists' (such as Robert Aron, Arnaud Dandieu, Thierry Maulnier, Jean-Pierre Maxence, Jean de Fabrègue, Emmanuel Mounier, and Georges Izard) denounced the 'crisis of civilization' and called for a new humanism based on the primacy of the 'spirit'. Alongside Mounier's personalism, these currents were joined

---

81   [Carlo Rosselli,] 'Italia e Europa', *Quaderni di GL* 7, June 1933, 4.

82   Letter from Umberto Calosso to Carlo Rosselli, 26 July 1933, in Archivio Giustizia e Libertà, Sezione I, Scatola I, Fascicolo I, Sottofascicolo 23, Istituto Storico Toscano della Resistenza e dell'Età Contemporanea (Florence).

83   On the critical importance of the appeal of the mythical and symbolic dimension for purposes of antifascist mobilization, see Anson Rabinbach, 'George Mosse and the Culture of Antifascism', *German Politics and Society* 18, no. 4, Winter 2000, 30–45.

84   Eugen Weber, *The Hollow Years: France in the 1930s*, New York: Norton, 1994.

by representatives of Catholic spiritualist and neo-Thomist culture, such
as Jean Wahl, Jacques Maritain, Étienne Gilson, and Gabriel Marcel. This
French 'non-conformist' culture transcended the classic dichotomy
between Left and Right, and often shared a non-political, or even anti-
political, stance which, in turn, transcended the opposition between
fascism and antifascism. Certain *ni droite ni gauche* ambiguities – far from
being fascist per se – were nevertheless susceptible to fascist impregnation,
that is, to the fascination of Mussolini's Italy and Hitler's Germany.[85]

In its creative quest for a new socio-cultural order, GL converged
towards the French 'non-conformist' circles comprising 'spiritualists'
rather than 'realists'. At the time, Rosselli conducted an all-encompassing
survey of French culture, including figures such as Alfred Fabre-Luce, 'the
prototype pro-fascist dandy', and Ramon Fernandez, 'a writer who, in the
name of poetics, calls for a pragmatic, highly concrete, realist politics; he
basically calls for fascism'. The leader of GL referred to the reflections of
Jean Schlumberger, editor of the *Nouvelle Revue Française*, thus touching
on a non-political longing for the reshaping of politics.[86] Nevertheless, he
sympathized with Mounier's position, polemicizing against politicians
who were 'too purely political, concerned only with external means and
methods, the seizure of power and the preservation or reform of institutions', while attacking 'democracy itself, which is becoming increasingly
totalitarian and tyrannical'. Despite being 'anything but a politician',
Mounier, an advocate of personalist thought, outlined the importance of a
'new politics'.[87] Rosselli considered the magazine *Esprit*, founded by
Mounier in 1932, as 'the expression of one of the most lively and original

---

85   Olivier Dard, *Le rendez-vous manqué des relèves des années 30*, Paris: Presses
Universitaires de France, 2002. Standard works on these themes are Jean Touchard,
'L'esprit des années trente: une tentative de renouvellement de la pensée française', in
Tendances politiques dans la vie française depuis 1789, Paris: Hachette, 1960, 89–120;
Jean-Louis Loubet del Bayle, *Les non-conformistes des années 30. Une tentative de
renouvellement de la pensée politique française*, Paris: Éditions du Seuil, 1969;
Sternhell, *Neither Right nor Left*. For a recent, different reading see Stuart H. Jones,
'Catholic Intellectuals and the Invention of Pluralism in France', *Modern Intellectual
History* 18, 2021, 497–519, with special attention to Gurvitch's influence on Maritain
and Mounier.

86   [Carlo Rosselli,] 'Stampa amica e nemica. Letterati e politica in Francia', *GL*,
15 February 1935.

87   [Carlo Rosselli,] 'Stampa amica e nemica. Impolitica', *GL*, 15 February 1935.

revivalist movements in a France that wrongly considers itself decrepit', and admired its 'moral zeal', 'irreverence', and 'extreme determination in regard to social issues'.[88]

A 'culture of crisis' emerged in the wake of World War I and the Russian Revolutions, whose representatives included Benedetto Croce, Guglielmo Ferrero, José Ortega y Gasset, Paul Valéry, Julien Benda, Stefan Zweig, Ernst Curtius, and Thomas Mann. They perceived the crisis of Europe as a sign of the impending collapse of the world as they knew it. The extreme example of the literature on the subject was Oswald Spengler's *The Decline of the West* (1918–23), which offered a cyclical vision of the history of civilizations and warned that the result of the present crisis of civilization would be a terrible new form of Caesarism. This cultural trend, however, cohered around a distaste for mass society, dismay at the decline of 'aristocratic' individualism, and an obsession with moral decadence, while it lay the ground for a 'spiritual' refoundation of liberalism.[89] Caffi's reflections were embedded in European crisis literature, but were driven by deeply religious, anti-deterministic hopes for a new humanism. In a letter to Rosselli, Caffi refused to give in to 'apocalyptic pessimism', although he was very disconcerted by the 'effects of the catastrophe' that had been the Great War; he claimed that this had disfigured 'the great nineteenth-century humanitarian tradition'. The 'immense reconstruction effort' needed 'life to be breathed into it by a religion like that which built the Acropolis or the Gothic cathedrals'.[90]

Fascism combined radical cultural pessimism with a no less consistent voluntarism that linked the fate of civilization to that of the 'young generation'. Since 1928, the conservative and conformist tendencies of Mussolini's regime had often been publicly questioned, for example in Giuseppe Bottai's magazine *Critica fascista*, where the 'youth question' had begun to emerge (and be discussed). Fascist education played out on two distinct

---

88   [Carlo Rosselli,] 'Stampa amica e nemica. Leggere *Esprit*', *GL*, 10 May 1935.

89   In general, see Karl D. Bracher, *The Age of Ideologies: A History of Political Thought in the Twentieth Century*, New York: St. Martin's Press, 1984, but the standard reference is Henry Stuart Hughes, *Consciousness and Society: The Reorientation of European Social Thought, 1890–1930*, New Brunswick, NJ: Transaction Publishers, 2008.

90   Letter from Andrea Caffi to Carlo Rosselli, 29 April 1929, in Alberto Castelli, 'Il socialismo liberale di Andrea Caffi', *Storia in Lombardia* 2, 1996, 151–2.

but interconnected levels, with integration into the national community as a function of the construction of a 'new Fascist civilization' destined to project itself onto the European and global stage to meet the challenges of the postwar period. This gave rise to a debate about 'Rome and Moscow' as well as 'Rome or Moscow': the competition between the Fascist and Bolshevik models did not preclude the imitation of one by the other, and vice-versa.

Caffi, a keen reader of Fascist publications, recognized the legitimacy of the revolutionary demands of Italian Fascism and Soviet Communism, but rejected their solutions, which implied a passive, uncritical acceptance of the authoritarian regimes in Rome and Moscow. In an article published in the December 1932 number of *Quaderni di GL*, Caffi sought to understand the 'ideas and "moods" of the younger militants' of the Fascist National Party, accepting that there were also 'convinced' fascists, despite what he perceived as their 'confusion'.[91] Rosselli saw the ambiguities of crisis culture through his political opposition to Fascism, while Caffi tried to avoid the dramatic alternative of cultural pessimism or political voluntarism. In this respect, Chiaromonte found himself in perfect accord with Caffi, whom he first met in Paris in May 1932 and with whom he established a close personal and intellectual relationship.[92] As a result of his anti-historicist education and certain irrationalist tendencies, Chiaromonte understood Fascism, Nazism, and Stalinist Communism as radical responses to the keen awareness of the crisis in Europe. In turn, Caffi's ideas heightened Rosselli's awareness of that European crisis and his insight into the need for a 'new humanism' of a socialist, secular, libertarian kind that would offer an alternative to Marxist and Christian traditions. In a series of three articles published in August 1934, Caffi attributed the crisis of postwar Europe to a form of 'nihilism' stemming not from persistent 'intellectual concerns', but from the contingent cycle of wars and revolutions during the period

---

91   [Andrea Caffi,] 'Attraverso le riviste fasciste', *Quaderni di GL* 5, December 1932, 55, 59.

92   See Andrea Caffi and Nicola Chiaromonte, *'Cosa sperare?' Il carteggio tra Andrea Caffi e Nicola Chiaromonte: Un dialogo sulla rivoluzione (1932–1955)*, ed. Marco Bresciani, Naples: ESI, 2012, and Marco Bresciani, 'Socialism, Antifascism and Anti-Totalitarianism: The Intellectual Dialogue (and Discord) between Andrea Caffi and Nicola Chiaromonte', *History of European Ideas* 40, no. 7, 2014, 984–1003.

1914–18.[93] He pointed to the willingness of a traumatized society to embrace the aggressively anti-political messages of totalitarian movements and regimes. The most dynamic youth groups in Europe in the 1920s and 1930s, rebelling against the 'remnants of broken religions and shipwrecked faiths', were indeed in search of 'absolute truth'. According to Caffi, they could only be approached by adopting forms of religious renewal capable of restoring the foundations of the social and political order. This 'interpretation, as sharp as it [was] generous, of the drama of the new European generation' inspired Rosselli to write his important essay 'Allargare gli orizzonti', which was published in August 1934. GL's leader, working relentlessly to politicize non-political, or even anti-political, attitudes, accepted the challenge of making antifascism 'a strong and pure thought' aiming at the 'moral and intellectual conquest of the new world'.[94]

Between 1932 and 1934, GL fought over the cultural space occupied by Fascism. More than that, it scoured the cultural spaces that tended towards Fascism throughout Europe in an effort to establish a 'different' revolutionary perspective. Without ever losing sight of its own antifascism, GL came to terms with Fascist culture the better to fight it. Subtly non-political or decidedly anti-political attitudes and moods, encapsulated in the perception of the 'crisis of democracy' and in the self-representation of a 'spiritual aristocracy', circulated in French 'non-conformist' circles as well as in the works on the crisis of European civilization, which also contributed to legitimizing fascist experiments. However, GL wished to embrace a critically anti-deterministic position with regard to these disquieting, fluctuating intellectual trends and build on their potential in terms of a new liberalism, socialism, and humanism. A special contribution towards this was made by the transnational circulation of ideas and cultural contamination deriving from the exiles' experiences in the 1930s. It was only by taking this detour, which radically challenged the existing relationship between politics and culture, that the ruling classes of the post-Fascist future could be formed. In this sense, GL adopted the approach of cultural intervention in early twentieth-century politics, while fundamentally adapting that model to meet the challenges represented by Hitler and Mussolini's regimes.

93 A. C. [Andrea Caffi], 'Nuova generazione', *GL*, 17 August 1934.
94 [Carlo Rosselli,] 'Allargare gli orizzonti', *GL*, 24 August 1934.

3
Time for Action?

A 'European Civil War'

When Rosselli arrived in Paris in the summer of 1929, he was sure that his stay abroad was only temporary, that the Fascist regime was about to fall, and that the activists of GL would soon return home to build a new Italy. However, the active struggle against Fascism turned out to be far more complex and all-embracing, as a political and intellectual experiment, than the technical organization of conspiracy had been. In the years that followed, although he did not completely lose hope, his exile increasingly took the form of a one-way journey, which was to leave deep scars. In the autumn of 1933, Carlo wrote to his mother Amelia that his life was 'restricted to a single level' with an increasingly 'one-way focus':

> We are now uprooted and at the storm's mercy; and even when the storm has passed, we will have a hard time putting down roots again, or we will put them down again more by convention and illusion than by any real bonding capacity.[1]

---

1 Letter from Carlo to Amelia Rosselli, 8 November 1933, in *Epistolario familiare. Carlo, Nello Rosselli e la madre (1914–1937)*, Milan: SugarCo, 1979, 550.

These words intimately convey the discouragement experienced by an exile who held his deracination to be the essential feature of his existence. At the same time, one can sense the gloomy political scenario increasingly marked by Hitler's shadow falling over Europe. In November 1933, after Germany had withdrawn from the League of Nations and begun to implement its policy of brutal revisionism, Rosselli published a famous editorial entitled 'La guerra che torna', in which he declared that 'the illusion of peace' was over. The Nazi seizure of power had once again relegated peace to its usual place in history: 'a negative and precarious condition, a parenthesis between two wars, a war, as Clausewitz said, that continues under changed circumstances'. Faced with the prospect of the return of war, Rosselli called for 'preventive intervention'; at the same time, it was a matter of transforming the international war into civil war and social revolution.[2]

Rosselli's attitude towards war could not be equated with that of the internationalist socialist traditions, steeped in nineteenth-century philanthropic pacifism, which in his eyes had been irrevocably crushed in the summer of 1914. Nor, indeed, could it be equated with the 'struggle for peace' of the Third International, which had labelled all the great powers as imperialist. The fragmented geopolitical and economic order of post-1918 Europe seemed to stabilize in the second half of the 1920s. With the world economic crisis of 1929–31, the rise to power of National Socialism, and the chain of international tensions that followed, there was a seismic shift that made the possibility of renewed war in Europe a reality. International socialist forces, however, were anxious to avoid another arms race at all costs, and consequently they staunchly defended an increasingly precarious status quo. The establishment of Hitler's new totalitarian regime in Germany, and the first steps taken by National Socialist foreign policy, aimed to undermine the order instituted by the Treaty of Versailles; as such, international socialism saw no justification for abandoning its pacifist programme of general disarmament and the arbitration of disputes (particularly regarding the German problem). In the meantime, however, more irreverent minority currents within Belgian and French socialism, epitomized by de Man and Renaudel, had begun to raise the question of national defence.

---

2   [Carlo Rosselli,] 'La guerra che torna', *Quaderni di GL* 9, November 1933, 1–8.

Rosselli was quick to recognize the dramatic break represented by National Socialism's seizure of power in Germany, and also to acknowledge the connection between the dynamics of continental fascistization and the possibility of a new European war.[3] As early as June 1933, National Socialism was denounced as an 'Anti-Europe' intent on an 'ideological war', if not on 'war tout court'. The analysis of Europe's political and social collapse, depicted as a 'moral crisis', led to the embrace of antifascism as a 'cause of civilization and Europe', and the 'vanguard of a new Europe'.[4] Rosselli now favoured the ideological conflict between fascism and antifascism as the key to interpreting postwar Europe; at the same time, however, he drew on the legacy of interventionism and the longer tradition of democratic nationalism. By combining the perspective outlined by Lenin during World War I and Mazzini's legacy, Rosselli argued that revolution would result from the transformation of the impending war between states into a civil war. His idea of a 'European civil war' between 'a European, socialist party' and 'national, fascist, nationalist parties' pointed to the total conflict between rival conceptions of the individual, society, and civilization that transcended national boundaries and undermined state sovereignties. In the face of what he perceived as a civilizational crisis that had destroyed the values of the nineteenth century, paved the way towards, or already unleashed, violence on an unprecedented scale, and led to social breakdown and national revolutions, Rosselli called for a 'new religion of the European nation'.[5]

Unpredictable events contributed to strengthen the illiberal and authoritarian trends in the governments in Western and Central Europe

---

3   This was first noticed by Nicola Tranfaglia, 'Carlo Rosselli e l'antifascismo', in *Giustizia e Libertà nella lotta antifascista e nella storia d'Italia: Attualità dei fratelli Rosselli a quarant'anni dal loro sacrificio*, Florence: La Nuova Italia, 1978, 186–211.

4   [Carlo Rosselli,] 'Italia e Europa', *Quaderni di GL* 7, June 1933, 7.

5   [Carlo Rosselli,] 'Appunti riguardanti una critica al fascismo e il progetto di una nuova organizzazione d'Italia e dell'Europa', 1934, Fondo Carlo Rosselli, cassetto 1, inserto IV, fascicolo 22, Biblioteca Nazionale (Florence). For different understandings of the 'European civil war', see Ernest Nolte, *Nazionalsocialismo e bolscevismo: la guerra civile europea, 1914–1945*, Florence: Sansoni, 1988; Claudio Pavone, 'La seconda guerra mondiale: una guerra civile europea?', in Gabriele Ranzato (ed.), *Guerre fratricide. Le guerre civili in età contemporanea*, Turin: Bollati Boringhieri, 1994, 86–128; Claudio Pavone, *A Civil War: A History of Italian Resistance*, London: Verso, 2014 (1991), 362–73; Enzo Traverso, *Fire and Blood: The European Civil War, 1914–1945*, London: Verso, 2016.

and to mark mutually enforcing stages in the polarization of European politics and society. During 1934, the storming of the National Assembly in Paris by an array of rightist *ligues* and the following leftist rallies and strikes (6–12 February), the armed opposition and subsequent suppression of Austrian Social Democrats by Dollfuss's dictatorial government in Vienna (12–16 February), and the miners' uprising bloodily repressed in the Asturias region as the starting point of Spain's *bienio negro* (5–18 October), stirred the perception of increasingly overlapping temporalities in the ideological conflict between fascism and antifascism on the European scale. At the same time, antifascists saw the revolts of the Viennese and Asturian workers as a revival of the myth of the Paris Commune of 1871. Then, in 1935 and 1936, the erosion of the post-1919 geopolitical order became clearly apparent, suggesting that a new international conflict was likely. It was only then that Rosselli openly embraced the idea of a new, federal Europe. After German rearmament resumed, in open violation of the existing peace treaties, the leader of GL was certain that a 'massive duel' was underway between 'pure Fascism' and 'old Europe', with the latter tied to 'ideas of conservation and formal democracy'. Since the goal of Fascism was to 'subvert Europe in order to dominate it by sword and fire', the 'unification of Europe' could only be achieved by forceful means.[6] More precisely, Rosselli believed that Fascism, with its plans for military expansion on the European continent and around the Mediterranean, was a major threat to national sovereignty. Therefore, to oppose the growing influence of Hitler and Mussolini's experiments, Rosselli became one of the most coherent advocates of a united, federal Europe opposed to all fascisms: for him, 'making Europe' had to be the essential goal of antifascism. A European assembly, elected by the peoples of Europe, needed to be urgently convened, tasked with adopting a European federal constitution, appointing the first European government, reducing the burden of national borders and customs regulations, organizing an army to defend the new Europe, and promoting the United States of Europe. However, it became increasingly likely that this new Europe could only come about through another catastrophic war.[7]

---

6   [Carlo Rosselli,] 'Come vince il fascismo', *GL*, 22 March 1935.
7   [Carlo Rosselli,] 'Europeismo o fascismo', *GL*, 17 May 1935.

By the mid-1930s, politics seemed torn apart by a 'European civil war' (in Rosselli's sense), but on closer examination, the two camps of 'fascism' and 'antifascism' were themselves rent by profound differences, not to say clear rifts. In April 1935, Caffi strongly criticized those antifascists who attributed the European crisis to the political conflict between democracy and fascism. Even more clearly than in 1932, he posited a very close relationship between the absolute sovereignty of modern nation-states on the one hand, and the danger of new, catastrophic wars on the other. He denied, or perhaps disregarded, the different nature of political institutions as authoritarian or democratic, 'fascist' or 'antifascist': 'What drives Europe to war is not fascism, but the division of Europe into sovereign states. The territorial divisions, the "corridors", the national minorities, the economic ruin caused by customs barriers – all this was not invented or created by fascism.'[8]

While Rosselli believed that the danger of a new European war stemmed from the specific link between the Great War and Fascism, in Caffi's view, any such war was inextricably linked to the formation of nation-states and their claims to exclusive identity and absolute sovereignty, radicalized by the breakdown of the former Russian, Ottoman, Habsburg, and German empires. While, in Rosselli's opinion, European federalism represented a radical response to the challenge posed by Fascism and Nazism, Caffi considered it to be the only viable way of eliminating the threat of nationalism. Over the course of his lengthy trajectory, the Russian-born intellectual had learnt from political cultures that did not fit the model of the French nation-state. As early as 1919, he had criticized the policies adopted by the victors of World War I and had called for a federal reorganization of the formerly imperial territories, themselves reluctant to be divided into homogeneous political entities with fixed national borders. Caffi was confronted with issues and perspectives that coincided with the federalist thinking of many Central and Eastern European intellectuals; such ideas were tied to imperial experiences, and as such could not be represented purely in terms of Right and Left.[9] In 1935, Caffi held that the only possible

---

8   Andrea [Andrea Caffi], 'Semplici riflessioni sulla situazione europea', *GL*, 19 April 1935.

9   See Holly Case, 'The Strange Politics of Federative Ideas in East-Central Europe', in 'New Directions in Legal and Constitutional History', special issue, *Journal of Modern History* 85, no. 4, December 2013, 833–66.

response to the international crisis remained that of a 'European revolution' against the modern nation-state, which he believed had favoured the spread of fascism and its inevitable drive towards centralization and nationalization.

From mid-1934 on, the growing threat of Nazi Germany required a substantial (albeit gradual and mostly instrumental) review of the Soviet Union's foreign policy; at this point the USSR moved closer to the European security system, joined the League of Nations, and launched its new Popular Front policy in favour of 'peace, bread, and democracy'. At the same time, the need to contain the spread of fascism, which had been mobilizing the masses since February 1934, especially in France, had led to a change in the Comintern's line at the Seventh Congress, held in July–August 1935. The leadership of the Third International, represented by Georgi M. Dimitrov and Togliatti and encouraged by Stalin, proclaimed the suspension of revolutionary catastrophism, dropped the previous line of 'class against class', and opened the door to possible political agreements of the Communist Parties with Socialists, radicals, and democrats.[10] The 'struggle for peace' approach, directed against imperialism in all capitalist countries, was replaced by one in which fascism, especially 'German fascism', constituted the principal enemy representing the greatest danger of war. The Comintern's new attitude attracted important currents and figures from international socialism, including the Austro-Marxist Otto Bauer, the Menshevik Fyodor Dan, and the French socialists Jean Zyromski and Marceau Pivert. However, some of the opponents of fascism, who were not ready to give up their freedom of thought, continued to pose serious questions. When Victor Serge, a Belgian-born Russian revolutionary and opponent of Stalin's regime who had been deported to the Urals in 1933, was released in the spring of 1936, Rosselli wondered: 'No internal danger justifies this senseless repression. Should we form a front to fight fascism? How can we block its path when there are so many concentration camps behind our own lines?'[11]

10   On communists and antifascism, see Silvio Pons, *The Global Revolution: A History of International Communism, 1917–1991*, New York: Oxford University Press, 2014, 75–91.

11   [Carlo Rosselli,] 'Stampa amica e nemica', *GL*, 12 June 1936. This was an indirect quotation from a letter of Victor Serge, written on the eve of André Gide's journey to the Soviet Union in May 1936 (Victor Serge, *Memoirs of a Revolutionary*, New York: New York Review of Books, 2012, 397).

These questions came increasingly to the fore during the Popular Front era. In May 1934, the Concentrazione antifascista disbanded, while GL's problematic relationship with other émigré organizations re-emerged when the Socialist and Communist Parties signed an action pact the following August. Giving up on its polemics against 'social fascism', the PCd'I attempted to justify the new antifascist approach by appropriating a national vocabulary and symbolism, invoking the need for an 'Italian revolution'. In this new context, both the purported link with the Risorgimento tradition, and Rosselli's definition of a 'European civil war' in terms of a radical antagonism between fascism and antifascism, constituted the cornerstones of his political actions, aimed at accrediting GL with its role in the strategy of the Italian Popular Front. GL welcomed the recognition of individual parties' autonomy and of the importance of the 'bourgeois liberties' affirmed at the Seventh Congress of the Comintern. However, it objected that the PCd'I, while willing to make 'all political and tactical concessions', wanted to 'take advantage of the revolutionary crisis to impose its own dictatorship through the dictatorship of the proletariat'.[12]

During the Fascist mobilization for war in Ethiopia, a series of meetings were held to explore the possibility of a settlement between the Italian Communists and GL. However, the new communist tactic of legal action under the regime, which resulted in the political discourse on 'national reconciliation' and notably Togliatti's appeal to the 'brothers in black shirts', met with Rosselli's firm opposition. This approach was, in fact, a long way off GL's own position. GL considered mass operations conducted from within Fascist organizations to be 'political suicide'; it believed that the fight against Fascism should be the prerogative of an 'enthusiastic and intelligent minority'.[13] However, the impossibility of reaching an agreement with the Italian Communists did not prevent Rosselli from sympathizing with the French Popular Front, led by Léon Blum and supported by radicals, socialists, and communists alike. Blum, the head of the SFIO, was the most influential and astute interpreter of the attempt to restore a revolutionary but anti-Leninist dimension to socialism by distinguishing between the 'exercise' of power and the 'conquest' of power. Blum was an opponent of the gauchistes Pivert and Zyromski, the leaders of the Bataille socialiste current until 1935; these then

---

12 'Il VII Congresso dell'Internazionale comunista', GL, 9 August 1935.
13 [Carlo Rosselli,] 'Non è l'ora di ripiegare gli ideali', GL, 24 July 1936.

parted ways, with Pivert founding the Gauche révolutionnaire. Pivert, aligned with the Fédération Socialiste de la Seine, criticized Blum's political government and its compromises with the 'bourgeoisie', but was ready to justify the social actions that emerged from the Front's electoral victory in June 1936. According to his motto , 'everything is possible.' While Zyromski was more interested in foreign policy, softening his opposition to Blum in the name of the antifascist alliance with the Soviet Union, Pivert focused on domestic policy and vigorously advocated an antifascist revolutionary line.[14]

These positions found resonance in those antifascist emigration circles that were most sensitive to the profound transformations underway in their host European liberal democracies, starting with the French Third Republic. However sceptical he was of the Trotskyist sympathies of the SFIO left-wing currents, Rosselli inclined towards a 'movement-oriented' version of the Popular Front, and had lost much of his confidence in parliamentary institutions. In May 1936, at the height of a wave of mass social movements in France following the electoral victory of the Popular Front, Rosselli, who feared the 'defensive' character of the Popular Front strategy, doubted that the Blum government would be able to carry out those 'structural reforms without which any attempt at transformation would fail, due to the internal balance of the capitalist regime and the inertia of a heavy coalition majority'. In Rosselli's eyes, however, 'the initiative of the masses' prevented – or would have prevented – the new government from immediately running aground 'on the shoals of parliamentarism'. Announcing the Matignon agreements on a series of important social reforms, promoted by the CGT and its leader Léon Jouhaux and stipulated with the Blum government on 8 June, Rosselli spoke of a 'victory for the French proletariat'. In his eyes and those of his comrades, France was the home of revolution and democracy, and had once again come to embody 'the supreme conflict'.[15]

This tortuous trajectory revealed the difficulties and criticalities of parliamentary systems and democratic governments in France and Western Europe, raising the question of whether it was a crisis of democracy itself. On

14   André Thirion, *Révolutionnaires sans révolution*, Paris: Laffont, 1972, and, more generally, Jacques Julliard, *Les Gauches françaises, 1762–2012. Histoire et politique*, Paris: Flammarion, 2012, 613–53.

15   [Carlo Rosselli,] 'Speranze di Francia', *GL*, 5 June 1936. For the context, see Julian Jackson, *The Popular Front in France: Defending Democracy, 1934–1938*, Cambridge: Cambridge University Press, 1988.

the one hand, the myth of the Popular Front, associated with a long European revolutionary tradition, led Rosselli to imagine for a moment that the opposition between fascists and antifascists might play out its decisive battle in France. On the other hand, GL felt that the Blum government, under pressure from massive popular movements, should be more concerned with domestic politics than with foreign policy – with reforming the French workers' conditions, rather than with fighting Europe's various fascisms. However, the outbreak of the Spanish Civil War led to the prompt reformulation of the priorities of France (and other countries), and revealed that there were no domestic solutions to what Rosselli perceived as the 'European civil war'.

'Which Italy'?

Rosselli's national democratic roots had enabled him and his comrades-in-arms not only to draw lessons from the socialist defeat of 1920–22 but, more importantly, to understand the reasons for the victory of Fascism. Only a national, all-embracing form of socialism could repair the rifts created by World War I and by the movement that was to become a regime, by appropriating the political and symbolic heritage of that war. The debate over the Risorgimento's legacy and its relationship to Fascist Italy had begun in the mid-1920s. While the idealist philosopher Giovanni Gentile viewed Fascism as the 'fulfilment' of nineteenth-century liberalism, the historiographical debate had become polarized, with on the one side the version offered by Gioacchino Volpe's *Italia in cammino. L'ultimo cinquantennio* (1927), and on the other that of Benedetto Croce's *Storia d'Italia dal 1871 al 1915*. Volpe believed that Fascism was the realization of the Italian nation-building process, which, thanks to Mussolini, condensed the activism and energies of the nation; Croce, for his part, viewed Fascism as a serious aberration in the process of affirmation of the liberal state started by Cavour. Another interpretation was given by Nello Rosselli in his work *Mazzini e Bakunin* (1927): this shed unprecedented light on the severe social and economic plight of large sections of Italy's industrial workers and peasants that the Risorgimento had not succeeded in mobilizing and integrating into the new state.[16]

---

16   For the dispute over the Risorgimento see Claudio Pavone, 'Le idee della Resistenza. Antifascisti e fascisti di fronte alla tradizione del Risorgimento', *Passato e*

Calosso continued to maintain that GL had to learn from Italian Fascism when it came to activating the irrational and symbolic spheres in order to appeal to the masses. Antifascism was inevitably located in, and conditioned by, the world shaped by Fascism. Thus it was urgent to 'address the Fascist mentality of young people', but the question was, how? Calosso looked to the fact that the watershed of the Great War had opened up a 'religious horizon' that would impact and upset 'the roots of Man'. A way out of this radical crisis could only be found through a patriotism understood as the 'religion of modern Man'.[17] It was thus more urgent than ever to return to Mazzini's ideas, to challenge Mussolini's concept of the 'primacy of the Italians', and to wrest from Fascism the symbolic and mythological repertoire of nationalism. In order to win the decisive propaganda war, it was necessary to overcome the 'contempt for symbols, for flags, for elementary and fascinating words', stemming from the 'inability to overthrow the enemy's positions and ally with youth'.[18] Like Calosso, Rosselli did not demur from dealing with the question of national tradition competing with Fascist culture, but he went further than Calosso, by seeking to clarify their opposing political implications.

> Fascism speaks in the name of the nation. We also speak of the nation, as an actual reality; of a free nation, not an instrument of the state, but a nation that opens itself to Europe and the world. Fascism glorifies Italy and being Italian. We too glorify these things. But which Italy and which Italianness are we talking about?[19]

These questions posed by Rosselli were the prelude to a debate in March 1935 triggered once again by Caffi, who rejected the official myth of the Risorgimento that was so present in antifascist democratic and republican

---

Presente 7, January–February 1959, 850–918, in *Alle origini della Repubblica*, Turin: Bollati Boringhieri, 1995, 3–69; Roberto Vivarelli, 'Tra storia e politica: appunti sulla formazione di Franco Venturi negli anni dell'esilio (1931–1940)', in Luciano Guerci and Giuseppe Ricuperati (eds), *Il coraggio della ragione. Franco Venturi intellettuale e storico cosmopolita*, Turin: Fondazione Einaudi, 1998, 73–7.

17   Umberto Calosso, 'Ballata delle donne giovani', *GL*, 15 June 1934.

18   U. C. [Umberto Calosso], 'Una strada strabiliante (con relativa morale)', *GL*, 6 July 1934.

19   [Carlo Rosselli,] 'Classismo e antifascismo', *GL*, 25 January 1935.

propaganda. Although his grandfather Ippolito Caffi, a painter with Garibaldine sympathies (but cosmopolitan ambitions), had been killed at the Battle of Lissa (1866), Andrea Caffi had harboured a certain distrust of the national democratic tradition since his youth. GL's antifascism was to stand in sharp contrast to the 'glorious dead of the Risorgimento', for the future lay in a federal Europe to be built by cosmopolitan elites. Echoing Gobetti's idea of Fascism as the 'autobiography of the nation', Caffi argued that the Risorgimento constituted 'an episode in European history of merely secondary, provincial import'. He declared it 'a tamed, deviant movement seized upon by ambiguous profiteers', and had led to Fascism 'as its (by no means unexpected) outcome'.[20] Following the studies of Nello Rosselli, who recalled the pioneering role of the Russian revolutionary Mikhail A. Bakunin in the Italian Risorgimento movement, Caffi argued against a process of state-building that ignored the workers' and peasants' material conditions as well as their need for social reforms and provisions. Despite the widespread rural poverty observed during the mid-nineteenth century and the growing hardships of the urban working class, the leaders of the Risorgimento (with the exception of Pisacane) had privileged the national question over the social question. Caffi basically drew on the thinking of Herzen and Proudhon, who had seen the discourse of 'nation' as the basis for an authoritarian, hierarchical political order, and who had developed a whole series of critical arguments against the Italian Risorgimento.

While Caffi disputed the legitimacy and usefulness of the Risorgimento's appeal to a movement that aimed to establish a new European federal order, Venturi invoked history to affirm the complete compatibility of nationhood and Europe, of patriotism and cosmopolitanism within a revolutionary political perspective. The real target of Venturi's polemic was the nationalist and Fascist emphasis on the indigenous originality of the state-building and nation-building process in Italy. According to the young historian from Turin, it was plain to see 'how much was truly European' about the Risorgimento, 'how much of it concerned purely local problems and how much the spirit of freedom that characterized the nineteenth century'. This passionate defence of the national tradition echoed Adolfo Omodeo's polemic against Gobetti and his *Risorgimento senza eroi*,

---

20   Andrea [Andrea Caffi], 'Discussione sul Risorgimento', *GL*, 10 May 1935.

and also Croce's definition of the Risorgimento as a 'masterpiece of European liberalism' in his work *History of Europe*. The voice of the historian was mixed with that of the fighter as Venturi tried to find once again, 'in the men of the Risorgimento' and in the 'spirit that drove them on', the spur for the fight against Fascism.[21]

Venturi's historical take on the events of the Risorgimento, which countered Caffi's criticism, was firmly rejected by Chiaromonte. He believed that 'liberal historiography', to which he ascribed Venturi's reflections, failed to understand 'the weaknesses of the last century'. Chiaromonte deemed nationalism to be a permanent feature of contemporary politics and an essential aspect of Fascism, thus implying the prospect of further European wars and calling for a severance of the correlation between national democratic tradition and revolutionary antifascism. He was more inclined towards the cosmopolitan critique of nationalism than to the European implementation of federalism; he took an even more radical approach than Caffi, believing that the nationalist movements had distorted and suppressed 'the ideal of political freedom'.[22] While Chiaromonte denied that there was any real difference between patriotism and nationalism, Venturi believed that the 'sense of nationality' was kept alive 'by freeing it from all ties to the state, the mystical, nationalist, imperialist tradition, and the Mazzinian illusion of primacy'. He tried to separate 'the idea of the nation' from the 'racist conception of the nation' that had taken hold as a result of 'current nationalisms'.[23]

The tension generated by this controversy prompted Rosselli to intervene, and in concurrence with Caffi he 'opposed any generic Risorgimento sentiment'. GL's leader was certain of the political sense of a discussion concerning the relationship of the Italian revolutionary movement to the national tradition. Significant in this regard was his total rejection of the alleged failure of post-Risorgimento Italy, following the approach already defined by Gobetti: 'The relationship between the Italian unification and the rise of Fascism', Rosselli acknowledged, 'was one, if not of filiation, then of progressive degeneration, which, contrary to what Croce believes, compels us not to draw a line under Italian history in the year 1914, but to

---

21   Gianfranchi [Franco Venturi], 'Sul Risorgimento italiano', *GL*, 5 April 1935.

22   Luciano [Nicola Chiaromonte], 'Sul Risorgimento', *GL*, 19 April 1935.

23   Gianfranchi [Franco Venturi], 'Replica di Gianfranchi', *GL*, 3 May 1935.

extend that history, without too many obstacles until the Fascist March on Rome and beyond.' Rosselli, however, tended to distinguish between 'two Risorgimentos' – the 'moderate' and the 'popular'. The latter, understood as the 'self-redemption of the people not from the bondage of others, but from their own, moral, political, economic bondage', combined 'the problem of independent national sovereignty' with that of 'social freedom'.[24]

In his contribution concluding the debate, Calosso stressed the importance of revolutionary nationalism, or the need to provide an answer to both the social question and the national question through the organic concept of 'the people' (*popolo*). While sharing Rosselli's political line, he decided to participate in Venturi's cultural battle to appropriate, from the philosopher Giovanni Gentile, the interpretation of Mazzini as the 'soul of the Italian Risorgimento' and 'prophet of the young nations of Europe'. Calosso's point of departure was his belief that, far from being an 'unimportant historical event' to be explained in class terms, 'European fascism' had, in fact, dramatically changed the nature of political struggle: paradoxically, any future revolution – even an antifascist revolution – would be a form of 'dissident fascism' or a 'fascism in revolt'.[25] Though certainly an ironic, even provocative, definition, it nevertheless emphasized the radical novelty of Fascism and the consequent impossibility of any return to a pre-Fascist world.

The controversy over the legacy of the Risorgimento broke out at a time when preparations for the Ethiopian War were underway. From the outset, Fascism had pursued a project that was both nationalist and imperialist, aimed at extending the boundaries of the Italian nation-state to a far greater imperial space spanning the Adriatic, Central and Balkan Europe, and the entire Mediterranean. According to Rosselli, however, the war in Abyssinia would provoke a severe weakening of Fascist Italy, pave the way to the German annexation of Austria, and lead to a 'total outbreak' on a European scale.[26] In considering the war in Ethiopia not only a 'fascist war', but also a 'colonial war', Rosselli's group occupied a somewhat

---

24   Curzio [Carlo Rosselli], 'Discussione sul Risorgimento', *GL*, 26 April 1935.

25   [Umberto Calosso,] 'Palinodia mazziniana', *GL*, 24 May 1935. Togliatti accused GL of being 'a *dissident Fascist* movement' (Palmiro Togliatti, 'Caldara e gli altri', *La Voce Operaia*, June 1934, in *Opere 1929–1935*, vol. 3, part 2, ed. Ernesto Ragionieri, Rome: Editori Riuniti, 1973, 392).

26   [Carlo Rosselli,] 'Nuovo crimine?', *GL*, 15 February 1935.

singular position in the Italian political emigration, while ever more connections and potential tensions between antifascism and anti-imperialism emerged with regard to the colonial oppression of the Western Great Powers.[27] The acknowledgment of fascism as an international threat after Hitler's ascent to power certainly did not encourage a critical attitude towards Western democracies' imperialism in British and French Left public opinions and political forces, and the former more often than not silenced the latter, from the mid-1930s onwards.[28] However, the war in Ethiopia, which began with the Italian attack in October 1935 and culminated with the proclamation of the Empire in May 1936, catalysed widespread antifascist and anti-imperialist movements all over the world and provided the ground on which GL tried to address both fascism and imperialism, testing the identity of antifascism and anti-imperialism.[29] According to Calosso and Venturi, Mussolini's empire-building was an illegitimate operation doomed to failure, as it was a product of ruthless political project instead of a slow, organic historical process like in the case of the Roman or British empires; contrary to Fascist expectations, this claim for Italian imperial greatness would prove a source of social and economic decadence. Calosso and Venturi, alongside Rosselli, thus opposed the idea of an antifascist nation to the colonizing Fascist Empire.[30]

Starting from a colonial setting, the Fascist war in Abyssinia affected the post-1919 international order and challenged the British Empire in the Mediterranean Sea. However, Rosselli mistakenly interpreted it as a turning point in Italy itself, pushing Mussolini's regime towards the final crisis

27   [Carlo Rosselli,] 'Perché siamo contro la guerra d'Africa', *GL*, 8 March 1935.

28   See Tom Buchanan, ' "The Dark Millions in the Colonies Are Unavenged": Anti-Fascism and Anti-Imperialism in the 1930s', in 'Transnational Anti-Fascism: Agents, Networks, Circulations', special issue, *Contemporary European History* 25, no. 4, November 2016, 645–65.

29   See Joseph Fronczak, 'Local People's Global Politics: A Transnational History of the "Hands Off Ethiopia Movement" of 1935', *Diplomatic History* 39, no. 2, 2015, 245–74; especially Joseph Fronczak, *Everything Is Possible: Antifascism and the Left in the Age of Fascism*, New Haven, CT: Yale University Press, 2023, 142–74; and many contributions in Kasper Braskén, Nigel Copsey, and David J. Featherstone (eds), *Anti-Fascism in Global Perspective: Transnational Networks, Exile Communities, Radical Internationalism*, London: Routledge, 2020.

30   [Umberto Calosso,] 'Contro l'impero, per la nazione. La legge degli imperi', and Gianfranchi [Franco Venturi], 'Quindici secoli', *GL*, 15 May 1935.

and paving the way for a revolutionary antifascist action. Up until then, different, albeit complementary, forms of antifascism had coexisted within GL. In the spring of 1935, under the pressure of ongoing events, these different approaches and currents began to clash, creating a rift in the unity of GL which soon brought about a major rupture. In fact, the main concerns of Rosselli's group were closely linked to the international dynamic that the Abyssinian War had unleashed between the autumn of 1935 and the spring of 1936, and that the Spanish Civil War would catalyse in the summer of 1936. Yet, before looking at revolutionary Barcelona, we must first return to Fascist Italy, where Mussolini's regime suppressed the remaining groups participating in the GL conspiracy.

'Conspiracy in Broad Daylight' (Turin)

In the early 1930s, the Fascist regime appeared more stable and popular than ever. Unlike the Italian exiles, none of the conspirators operating inside Italy could imagine that its downfall was imminent. Above all, the close network of police controls radically limited the opportunities for the establishment of underground groups. Nevertheless, spies, informants, and public security emissaries, who had infiltrated both clandestine circles and émigré groups, tended to acknowledge the threat from GL and to flag up its 'terrorist' potential, usually accompanied by fanciful ideas about plots and attacks. Such infiltrators often succeeded in gaining the trust of GL members and in penetrating their circles in both Paris and Turin. Through their reports to OVRA, they helped weaken and eradicate its networks. In this sense, spies such as René Odin ('Togo') and Dino Segre ('Pitigrilli', also a successful author of racy novels), played a key role.[31]

After the dismemberment of the Milan group in October 1930, the Turin unit remained the most important of GL's groups operating in Italy, although it developed somewhat independently from the Paris leadership. As we have already seen, culture in the city of Turin flowered to an extraordinary degree in the immediate postwar period and was subsequently stifled by the repressive, illiberal grip of Fascism. The enduring

---

31   Mario Giovana, *Giustizia e Libertà in Italia: storia di una cospirazione antifascista, 1929–1937*, Turin: Bollati Boringhieri, 2005.

tradition of Gobetti together with the regular presence of Croce continued to nourish a lively debate, however, despite the ever-shrinking spaces
available for such. Among the most active cultural initiatives in Turin at
the time was the magazine *Cultura*. Its editor was an eccentric, versatile
figure, Arrigo Cajumi, a journalist and critic of French literature who was
close to Gobetti and contributed to Luigi Salvatorelli's national daily, *La
Stampa*. Women like Ada Marchesini, Gobetti's wife and a translator of
Russian and English literature, and Barbara Allason, a translator and
critic of German literature, also played a prominent role in Turin's GL
groups.[32] The key meeting points for the city's antifascists were Gobetti's
apartment in the city centre (in Antonio Fabro Street) and Allason's country house in the surrounding hills (at Pecetto Torinese). Sometimes Croce
turned up, or his friends from Gobetti's milieu, such as Carlo Levi and
Leone Ginzburg, met there.[33]

Ginzburg's perspective was based on his realistic grasp of the balance of
power between Fascism and its opponents, and its relationship to the
dictatorship's penetration of everyday life, as demonstrated by the PNF
membership campaign, conducted on the occasion of the tenth anniversary of the March on Rome. His article 'Viatico ai nuovi fascisti', published
in March 1933 in the *Quaderni di GL*, offered both a personal testimony
and a close analysis of the social reality of Fascism. From this emerged his
ethical conception of antifascism and its task within Italian society:

> One must have spent the last few years in Italy, or in close contact with
> those who remained there, to no longer distinguish charity (which does
> not exclude intransigence) from judgments on collective morality . . .
> We, who have chosen more difficult paths and want to work on behalf of
> everyone, are entitled to express great compassion for those who have
> seized us, and the duty to help them as much as we can.

---

32   Giovanni De Luna, *Donne in oggetto. L'antifascismo nella società italiana
(1922–1939)*, Turin: Bollati Boringhieri, 1995; Patrizia Gabrielli, *Tempio di virilità.
L'antifascismo, il genere, la storia*, Milan: Franco Angeli, 2008; and Noemi Crain-
Merz, *L'illusione della parità. Donne e questione femminile in Giustizia e Libertà e nel
Partito d'Azione*, Milan: Franco Angeli, 2013.
33   Barbara Allason, *Memorie di un'antifascista, 1919–1940*, Turin: Spoon River,
2005 (1946).

The new members of the National Fascist Party, especially young people, after their 'initial, grudgingly accepted compromise', should not have been driven to 'desire and promote further such compromises in order to obscure the memory of the first', but they should 'prevent themselves from being contaminated as far as possible'. Precisely because many such new recruits had joined for reasons of pure survival, without any real ideological conviction, it was GL's task to help them 'redeem a forced attachment, preserve their own personalities, and deepen their revolutionary consciousness through meditation, study, and clandestine activity'.[34] Ginzburg believed that political work under the dictatorship required 'more than immediate action, the preparation of ideas and cadres', since Fascism had 'penetrated very deeply into Italian life . . . and poisoned everything'.[35] He thus rejected the communist tactic of 'entryism', that is, the infiltration of the regime's mass organizations in order to achieve immediate or partial goals. It was not a question of implementing a 'dual channel' policy (one legal, the other illegal), and certainly not of choosing, in a sectarian manner, conspiratorial isolation from the surrounding society. Rather, Ginzburg laid out a different range of actions, designed to deplete popular support for Fascism and to cultivate the political consciousness of individuals and small groups. This perspective, which saw the transition to clandestine action as the most challenging and consequential moment, reflected an awareness of existing power relations and, at the same time, an effort to undermine those relations from within, through a slow and patient process of cultural transformation.[36]

In an obituary for his uncle Claudio Treves (1933), Carlo Levi confessed that he had not come 'to politics by nature, but almost reluctantly, as a matter of duty', unlike those who had made politics 'their total life experience'.[37] In a similar way, Ginzburg approached politics 'almost reluctantly'. As recorded

34 M. S. [Leone Ginzburg], 'Viatico ai nuovi fascisti', *Quaderni di GL* 6, March 1933, 4–6. For an insightful commentary, see Vittorio Foa and Carlo Ginzburg, *Un dialogo*, Milan: Feltrinelli, 2003, 71–2.

35 M. S. [Leone Ginzburg], 'Ipotecare il futuro (dall'Italia)', *Quaderni di GL* 10, February 1934, 75–6.

36 For a more articulated analysis, see Marco Bresciani, 'Quasi a malincuore. Leone Ginzburg e Cesare Pavese, dalla dittatura fascista alla guerra civile', *Contemporanea* 1, January–March 2023, 31–59.

37 [Carlo Levi,] 'In morte di Claudio Treves', *Quaderni di GL* 7, 1933, 1.

by Carlo Levi himself, he combined the intransigence required by the struggle against the Fascist regime with a 'highly sensitive temperament'; he expressed 'common sense and a desire for normality, for composed freedom, which did not preclude the possibility of storms ahead'.[38] These traits of his personality seemed to mirror the 'keen sensibility' of the Russian writer Vsevolod M. Garshin, whom Ginzburg wrote about in an article published in 1930 in *La Cultura*: 'No one is sadder than those who truly feel the beauty of a serene life, when faced with the sufferings that seek to disturb that life'.[39] This combination of ethics and aesthetics, however, was inspired above all by Ginzburg's love for the 'deep humanity' of Leo Tolstoy, who in *War and Peace* had raised the dilemma of those who pursue both happiness and justice.[40] Rather than totally investing himself in the political sphere, Ginzburg's decision to operate clandestinely thus reaffirmed the everyday rights of the personal and social sphere, which had been violated and distorted by history and politics. Hence his ambivalent attitude towards politics, which he perceived as a passion for action and freedom and, at the same time, as an organized technique of governing and delegating. As he put it:

> Politics is not always such an essential activity (at least the politics of government); it can in fact be delegated when, due to the coexistence of autonomous institutions, it is only a technique, the administration of affairs. However, these institutions are the result of a struggle that has established its own equilibrium, and they can implement internal change. Certain problems lose their meaning (as in individual morality) and become mere administration when in practice they have been resolved; when freedom has become a common, habitual heritage, this or that position of the government is of little importance. One is freed from politics by politics itself.[41]

This project of freeing himself 'from politics through politics' revealed in a paradoxical form the tensions between different conceptions of politics in

38   [Carlo Levi,] 'Leone Ginzburg', *GL*, 16 November 1934.

39   [Leone Ginzburg,] 'Vsevolod Garšin', *La Cultura* 4, 1930, 268–77.

40   [Leone Ginzburg,] 'Celebrazione fattiva di Lev Tolstoj', *Il Baretti* 12, 1928, 57–8.

41   M. S. [Leone Ginzburg], 'Il concetto di autonomia nel programma di G. L.', *Quaderni di GL* 4, 1932, 7.

this dictatorial context. Not incidentally, Ginzburg had embarked on a unique path linking politics to philology, history, and literature, through clandestine operations. Following the line set out by Gobetti, albeit developing it according to his own abilities, Ginzburg specialized in the history and criticism of Russian literature, and worked with publishing houses such as Alfredo Polledro's Slavia and Frassinelli's Biblioteca Europea, as well as with Cajumi's magazine *Cultura*. Together with other high-school graduates of the Liceo Classico D'Azeglio (like his friend, the poet and writer Cesare Pavese), he played a key role in the founding of Giulio Einaudi's publishing house on 15 November 1933.[42] In the meantime, he had been appointed as a professor and taught a course on Pushkin before renouncing this post in January 1934, when taking an oath to the Fascist regime became obligatory. His decision to side with the antifascist cause, which he had already made in secret, was now public.

Prompted to take up the political struggle against the Fascist dictatorship and convinced that the regime was not about to fall, the members of the Turin group of GL tried to avoid any direct confrontation that would inevitably lead to their being checkmated. Political conspiracy was thus channelled through a long-term form of underground cultural action, whose antifascist implications frequently escaped the very 'bourgeois' society to which many GL members belonged. A vivid snapshot of this situation is offered in Natalia Ginzburg's *Family Lexicon* (1963), with its simple, ironic language of childhood memory. In describing the state of mind of her father, the renowned professor of anatomy and histology, Giuseppe Levi, Natalia Ginzburg sheds light on a widespread belief held in Turin (as well as Italian) society at that time:

> He didn't believe there were any conspirators in the new, younger generation, and if he had suspected that there were, he would have thought them crazy. In his opinion, there was nothing, absolutely nothing to be done about fascism.[43]

---

42   Luisa Mangoni, *Pensare i libri. La casa editrice Einaudi dagli anni Trenta agli anni Sessanta*, Turin: Bollati Boringhieri, 1999.

43   Natalia Ginzburg, *Family Lexicon*, New York: New York Review of Books, 2017 (1963), 81.

One of these 'crazy' young people, Leone Ginzburg, began to frequent Giuseppe Levi's house and befriended two of his children, Mario and Natalia. It was Leone Ginzburg who introduced Mario Levi, then marketing director of the Olivetti Factory in Ivrea (close to Turin), to GL. As we read in *Family Lexicon*, her brother's decision to join the GL group was something of a surprise:

> My father was, however, thrilled to have a conspirator for a son. He hadn't expected it. He'd never thought of Mario as an antifascist. Mario used to constantly contradict him in all their arguments and he used to speak badly of the socialists once so beloved by my mother and father. He used to say that Turati was hugely naive and made mistake after mistake. And whenever my father heard him say this, even though he said it himself, he was mortally offended.
>
> 'He's a fascist!' my father would say to my mother. 'At heart, he's a fascist!'
>
> Now he could no longer say this. Now Mario had become famous for his political exile.[44]

In her usual, spare but vivid language, Natalia described the generational conflict that pervaded certain upper-class Turin families, in which political opposition *seemed* to be blurred (or even absent altogether) compared to the cultural rift among family members. On the one hand stood fathers who were liberal or socialist, nationalist or decidedly Fascist, but who, in any case, had adapted to the requirements of the regime; on the other, sons who could no longer bear the climate of mass conformism under the dictatorship, and so tended towards a new form of political engagement that was more indeterminate and unprejudiced. This is where GL came into play: it was capable of picking up on the language of the above-mentioned generational conflict and using it to encourage clandestine action against the regime. Both Giuseppe and Mario disputed the errors of the older generation of socialists epitomized by Turati; but to his father's ears, young Mario spoke the same language, and had the same mentality, as the Fascists. The language of youth as such sounded 'Fascist' to the ears of Giuseppe: it was only the conscious decision to emigrate that dispelled his suspicions regarding Mario. To be sure, Mario had been operating underground for some time before he had to flee in March 1934.

---

44   Ibid., 93–4.

The political police's reports described him as Ginzburg's intermediary, passing on information and material from Paris to Turin.

After arriving in the French capital, Mario Levi began to work intensively within GL, and grew particularly close to Caffi, Chiaromonte, and Renzo Giua, who were increasingly critical of Rosselli's political line. In October 1934, Mario Levi delivered a report to Rosselli demolishing the exclusively political image that the émigrés had of the conspiracy in Italy. First, in reference to the Turin GL members, he explained that 'the ties that unite these elements are not political, but cultural affinities, friendships, shared repulsions, and also some rather general desire to get a better understanding of the situation'; he went on to record the 'political indeterminacy' of those workers who formally joined clandestine communist formations.[45] This led to Mario Levi's distrust of political parties, whose inevitably centralist and authoritarian structure limited, and sometimes prevented, the free exchange of ideas: GL should therefore be a 'point of attraction' rather than an organization.[46] Levi was particularly fascinated by Caffi; it was he who transmitted to Levi Proudhon's predilection for small groups operating on the fringes of large organizations (starting with the state and industrial cartels). Only in this way could the essential prerequisite for liberalism be established: 'a common language shared by all classes'.[47]

The first of the two raids that led to the dismantling of GL's Turin network was the consequence of something that had happened elsewhere. On 11 March 1934, Mario Levi and Sion Segre Amar were stopped by border officials on one of their trips between Italy and Switzerland, suspected of being smugglers. When copies of *Quaderni di GL* were discovered in their car, Levi threw himself into the Tresa River and managed to escape, while Amar was arrested. On 13 March 1934, fourteen people were arrested in Turin on the strength of Pitigrilli's denunciation, including Leone Ginzburg, Barbara Allason, Giuseppe Levi, and Riccardo Levi. Carlo Levi was stopped in

---

45   Selva [Mario Levi], *Memoriale*, typescript, October 1934, sent in a letter to Carlo Rosselli, October 1934, in Paolo Bagnoli, *Rosselli, Gobetti e la rivoluzione democratica*, Florence: La Nuova Italia, 1996, 73–6.

46   Letter from Mario Levi to Andrea Caffi, 18 June [no year], in Fondazione Alfred Lewin, Biblioteca Gino Bianco, Fondo Andrea Caffi, Corrispondenza, Lettere di Mario Levi (1936–1937 e 1944–1947), Forlì.

47   Letter from Mario Levi to Andrea Caffi, 13 September 1936, in Biblioteca Gino Bianco, Fondo Andrea Caffi.

Alassio on 13 March, released, and given an official warning in May. Only Leone Ginzburg and Sion Segre were remanded in custody and sentenced: Ginzburg, after a brief period of detention at Regina Coeli Prison, was transferred to Civitavecchia Prison and sentenced to two years. About twenty days after the arrests, the Stefani news agency published a clearly antisemitic statement proclaiming the Jewish origins of many of the arrested antifascists, probably with the intention of sounding out the public's reaction.[48] With the arrest of Carlo Levi and Ginzburg, Foa became a leader of the Turin group. Foa had been influenced by the liberal-democratic, national-patriotic, yet pacifist attitudes of his family. Thanks to Ginzburg, whom he had met at the Liceo Classico D'Azeglio, he began writing for *Quaderni di GL* and joined the band of conspirators. During his law studies, his reading of Oriani and Pareto, Einaudi and Salvemini, Gobetti and Ruffini had led the very young law student to a 'liberal' and 'Jacobin' understanding of politics, which quickly superseded the Giolittian intellectual legacy of his father – to take an interest in the working class, but to disregard the great historical and ideological debates concerning socialism and communism.[49]

On 15 May 1935, in a second, bigger raid triggered by Pitigrilli's denunciations, forty-one Piedmontese intellectuals were arrested. These included Foa, Mila, Michele Giua, Augusto Monti, Carlo Levi, Franco Antonicelli, and Cesare Pavese, while Norberto Bobbio and Giulio Einaudi were also arrested and interrogated. The latter were shortly released, whereas Foa and Giua were sentenced to fifteen years in prison, and Mila and Monti to seven and five years respectively. Pavese was interned in the southern Italian village of Brancaleone Calabro for three years, but returned to Turin in late 1936. Carlo Levi was interned in the province of Matera,

---

48   Joel Blatt, 'The Battle of Turin: Carlo Rosselli, Giustizia e Libertà, OVRA and the Origins of Mussolini's Antisemitic Campaign', *Journal of Modern Italian Studies* 1, no. 1, 1995, 22–57, to be read alongside the critical, shareable considerations of Carlo Ginzburg, 'Quegli arresti del 1934 a Torino: Chiara Colombini, Carlo Ginzburg', *Doppiozero*, 19 December 2014, doppiozero.com. More generally, see Luisa Mangoni, 'Ebraismo e antifascismo', *Studi storici* 47, no. 1, January–March 2006, 65–79, and Alberto Cavaglion, 'Ebrei e antifascismo', in Marcello Flores, Simon Levis Sullam, Anne-Marie Matard-Bonucci, and Enzo Traverso (eds), *Storia della Shoah in Italia. Vicende, memorie, rappresentazioni*, vol. 1, Turin: Utet, 2010, 170–92.

49   Vittorio Foa, *Il cavallo e la torre. Riflessioni su una vita*, Turin: Einaudi, 1991, 23–45.

initially at Grassano (until September) and then in Aliano (until May 1936), at which point he was pardoned in the surge of Fascist jubilation following the conquest of Ethiopia and the proclamation of the Empire. Leone Ginzburg left Civitavecchia prison in March 1936, while subsequent to the raids of March 1934 and May 1935 the main members of the Turin group of conspirators were either imprisoned, interned, or forced to do more prudent intellectual and editorial work, as in the case of Ginzburg. The latter, together with Pavese, resumed his philological and organizational duties at the Einaudi publishing house.

To what extent can the GL conspiracy be classified as political opposition? Certainly, the production and distribution of political propaganda material was considered illegal by the Fascist authorities. Moreover, in their eyes, every act of non-conformist action was charged with an implicit political meaning. For those who chose to conspire, however, such as Levi and Ginzburg, things were more complicated: politics represented the gravest problem of their time, before it offered a *possible* way out. Both Levi and Ginzburg had arrived reluctantly at active political commitment. And yet their underground network allowed them and other GL activists in Turin to establish an autonomous space in which to redefine the meaning of politics. This space coincided first and foremost with their own intellectual freedom, which rejected mass conformism and was in turn the precondition for the future regaining of political freedom. In fact, the recurrent non-political tendencies and aversion to (party-) political action reflected the resurfacing of a deeper layer which, via Gobetti, was fed by early twentieth-century culture.

Different Time Frames

It may seem paradoxical, but exactly what GL was, and particularly what it was supposed to be, is anything but obvious. Unsurprisingly, the nature of militant engagement within Rosselli's group, the organization's forms of action and its political perspectives, and the relationship between politics and culture were constantly the subject of debate and argument, and it was this that ultimately undermined the unity of the group itself. The group's leading figures were faced with a series of alternatives and dilemmas arising from the challenges posed by Hitler and Mussolini's regimes and the rapid, unpredictable changes in those regimes. So, what was GL exactly, and what did it purport to be? Was it an underground vanguard of freedom fighters? A conspiratorial minority prepared to take terrorist action? A new revolutionary political party appealing to the masses? Or an intellectuals' club, a circle of philosophers, an underground world of rebels, persecuted dissidents, and heretics?

From the very beginning, Rosselli described GL as a group of 'men experienced in the illegal struggle, accustomed to risk and sacrifice, ready to go to prison and take up arms'.[50] He recognized the 'crucial function of a disciplined and armed minority' tasked with fighting Mussolini's regime, and aware of the 'inevitability of a provisional dictatorship' that was to guide the difficult transition from Fascism to democracy.[51] Despite his incessant arguments with the communists and their plans for a dictatorship of the proletariat, from 1934 onwards the leader of GL began to look with growing interest at Bolshevism as an example of a revolution that had managed to 'become reality'. Nevertheless, he was aware that the Italian revolution would not develop according to a predetermined pattern, but along 'unpredictable lines'.[52] According to the report of one spy, Rosselli wanted to become 'a second Lenin', and all the works of the Russian revolutionary, which Rosselli studied 'assiduously', were kept in the living room of his house on the place du Panthéon in the heart of Paris' fifth *arrondissement*.[53] Regardless of the possible exaggerations of this report, Rosselli's starting point was the 'inert' and 'amorphous' character of the masses under the Fascist regime: this situation would only change with the advent of crisis, an inevitable crisis that GL could accelerate without provoking it. In this sense, he echoed the conviction 'also held by Lenin' that, in the revolutionary period, 'the task of the revolutionary minority, forged in the

---

50   [Carlo Rosselli,] 'I presupposti della lotta rivoluzionaria', *La Libertà*, 6 October 1932.

51   [Carlo Rosselli,] 'Un nuovo movimento italiano', article for a review of German political exiles, undated (end 1933 or early 1934), in Carlo Rosselli, *Scritti dell'esilio*, vol. 1, *Giustizia e Libertà e la Concentrazione antifascista 1929–1934*, ed. Carlo Casucci, Turin: Einaudi, 1988, 273.

52   [Carlo Rosselli,] 'Premesse alla discussione sulla tattica rivoluzionaria', *GL*, 29 June 1934.

53   See Confidential Report, 29 June 1934, Ministero Interni, Direzione Generale Pubblica Sicurezza, Divisione Polizia Politica, fascicolo personale Carlo Rosselli, busta 78, Archivio Centrale dello Stato (Rome).

period of illegal struggle, [was] essential.'[54] Rosselli thus reread Lenin through the eyes of Sorel: on the one hand, he considered history as an open-ended, plural process; on the other, he highlighted the role of the active minority, the determined, audacious vanguard, the revolutionary elite, without accepting its transformation into a political party along Bolshevik lines. In this respect, Rosselli fully agreed with the position that Lussu had been urging since February 1934 with regard to Lenin's example. In 'revolutionary times', compared to the 'quiet years of transition' that had characterized prewar Europe, 'not only an elite of intellectuals, but the entire socialist vanguard' needed to abandon 'humanitarian phraseology' and adopt 'a psychology of war and not of peace'. Indeed, as Bakunin used to say, 'to rise up, man must have the devil in his body.'[55]

Awareness of the rupture separating ordinary and extraordinary times, the drive towards conspiratorial organization, and the definition of the revolutionary avant-garde model, led to discussions directly concerning the relationship between politics and culture and between intellectual responsibility and (public or clandestine) action. In certain letters sent from Italy and published in the *Quaderni di GL* between 1932 and 1934, Chiaromonte expressed his dissatisfaction with the political line taken by Rosselli's group: a libertarian antifascism aiming to fight tyranny needed to 'educate the elites'.[56] It was on precisely this 'need' for the intellectual's political commitment that Franco Venturi focused in his first article, published in the *Quaderni di GL* in November 1933. Coming from an exceptional family and cultural background, at a young age Venturi had begun to reconsider the role of intellectuals and their ability to effect change in politics, institutions, and society. This very young man enrolled in the Sorbonne's Faculty of Literature, where he followed courses in eighteenth-century French and European history taught by scholars like Paul Hazard and Daniel Mornet.[57] Focusing on the significance of the events in

54   [Carlo Rosselli,] 'G.L. e le masse', *GL*, 20 July 1934.

55   Tirreno [Emilio Lussu], 'Discussioni sul nostro movimento. Orientamenti', *Quaderni di GL* 10, February 1934, 69–70.

56   Sincero [Nicola Chiaromonte], 'Per un movimento internazionale libertario (dall'Italia)', *Quaderni di GL* 8, August 1933, 15.

57   Michael Confino, 'Introduzione: La Russia di Franco Venturi', in Antonello Venturi (ed.), *Franco Venturi e la Russia. Con documenti inediti*, Milan: Feltrinelli, 2006, XV–XXXIX.

Spain that had led to the transition from a monarchy to a republic in the spring of 1931, Venturi not only insisted on the 'general fact of the participation of intellectuals in politics (especially important in the turbulent moments of renewal)', but also on 'the preponderance of intellectual minorities in triggering the crisis'. The Spanish Revolution of 1931, which had enabled the establishment of a republican regime, represented in Venturi's view the model of a 'revolution of the ruling elites'.[58]

In this debate, Caffi echoed Chiaromonte's position, but drew on a cultural and existential context of very different scope. Caffi affirmed the need to re-establish the primacy of cultural development, by disentangling the close (typically Mazzinian) bond that GL had created between thought and action, between theoretical and practical moments. Different, yet convergent, cultural legacies had contributed towards establishing this position: the nineteenth-century Russian intellectual tradition, particularly that personified by the later works of Herzen, dealing with the dilemmas and aporias of revolutionary action (in the wake of the Nechayev–Bakunin affair, which was also to be a source of inspiration for Fyodor Dostoevsky's *The Devils*); the critical, 'aristocratic' reflections of Tocqueville and Burckhardt, who had raised the problem of revolution, democracy, and modern state formation; Croce and Halévy's thoughts on the nature of the crisis that had engulfed Europe in 1914–18 through the highly destructive dynamics of war and revolution. Noting the general refusal to 'restore society to a normal order without a more or less long, more or less harsh "passage" via dictatorship', Caffi rhetorically asked: 'What "myth" other than that of violence can be invoked, if "action", materially speaking, is given a kind of moral primacy over thought?' According to Caffi, this question gained rhetorical force insofar as 'war and the resulting violent solutions' had been the defining experiences of European society since 1914. He argued that the fundamental difference between working to transform the cultural preconditions of a socio-political order, and struggling to overthrow power, lay in the 'necessarily different time frames'. Accordingly, Caffi acknowledged that the elite played a significant role, accomplishing a 'grandiose endeavour of intellectual preparation', but considered it 'unlikely' that the same

---

58 Gianfranchi [Franco Venturi], 'Nuova Spagna', *Quaderni di GL* 9, November 1933, 22.

elite could 'take over the leadership of an ongoing insurgency'.[59] While the intellectual elite planned for the long term, professional revolution-aries or conspirators were impatient to achieve their political goals in the shortest time possible. Thus, rather than the transformation of GL into a political party, as mooted by Lussu and rejected by Rosselli and Venturi, Caffi seemed to fear a transformation of the revolutionary antifascist group into a *minorité agissante*, along the lines foreseen by Sorel and which had subsequently inspired Lenin and Mussolini. Commenting on Caffi's position, Garosci stressed the importance of doing politics – 'all politics, complete with its attendant dangers, fears, and necessities'. Questioning the 'separation of tasks' between the intellectual elite and the revolutionary vanguard, he acknowledged the legitimacy of free discussion, but without denying the necessity of 'sectarianism'. The belief that there was a 'salvation' that could only be found outside of Fascist Italy was, in Garosci's mind, 'a forceful act, an act of conspiracy' implying an 'organizational action' but it did not, for this reason, negate 'the disin-terested nature of culture'.[60]

On the one hand, recognizing different time frames in the antifascist revolution as proposed by Caffi meant to prioritize long-term intellectual responsibility over short-term political commitment. On the other hand, establishing the primacy of politics as invoked by Garosci appeared more an attempt to impose a minimum of internal discipline within the group than an instrument to speed up the revolutionary struggle against the Fascist dictatorship. As a matter of fact, the dilemmas between, and inter-twining of, politics and culture that characterized GL to varying degrees played out on a level largely distinct from the communists' conception of politics. Rosselli and his comrades sought to understand the enemy, to learn from it, the better to fight it. The communists aimed above all to oppose the enemy – an enemy defined in varying ways according to Soviet foreign policy lines at the time. In a self-critical key that preluded the formation of the Popular Front in October 1934, Togliatti argued: 'Our party has not fully or promptly understood that the establishment of a

---

59   A. C. [Andrea Caffi], 'In margine a due lettere dall'Italia', *Quaderni di GL* 11, June 1934, 68–9, 71.

60   Magrini [Aldo Garosci], 'Nota' to A. C. [Andrea Caffi], 'A proposito di due lettere dall'Italia', *Quaderni di GL* 11, June 1934, 79–80.

totalitarian Fascist dictatorship does not require the communist vanguard to limit the scope of its political actions, but to expand that scope, to "do politics" boldly and without giving any respite to the enemy, to pursue and fight it at all levels.'[61]

Faced with a dictatorship that aspired primarily to 'last' (as the Duce put it), the temporal dimension became the key element of GL's oppositional strategy. In this sense, Fascism shaped the temporalities and trajectories of revolutionary antifascism. Was priority to be given to the immediate goals of political struggle, or to the broader goals of social and cultural renewal? By what organizational and intellectual means could these goals be achieved, and what possible contradictions might arise? Was violence a useful and legitimate means by which to accelerate the historical process and build a new social and political order? To what extent did feverish militant activity consume any space available to individual privacy, thus sapping the roots of GL's project of emancipation? Each member of GL tried in different ways to combine tense bursts of political action and patient spells of intellectual reflection, short-term efforts for organizing the antifascist struggle and long-term elaborations for renewing Italian and European culture and society. By the second half of 1935, however, Rosselli felt that the preparations for and outbreak of the Ethiopian War had ushered in a new, dynamic cycle in which action took absolute precedence and short periods prevailed over long periods. The decision to go to war was an effect rather than a cause of a crisis that, according to the leader of GL, thwarted Mussolini's ambition to 'last'. In a situation of accelerating crisis, it was necessary to transform the war of position into a war of movement, to 'anticipate the time', to choose between the 'Fascist war' and the 'concrete and active struggle for its crushing, that is, for total subversion'.[62]

61   Ercoli [Palmiro Togliatti], 'Où est la force du fascisme italien?', *L'Internationale communiste* 19, 5 October 1934, 1265, in Paolo Spriano, *Storia del Partito comunista italiano*, vol. 2, *Gli anni della clandestinità*, Turin: Einaudi, 1969, 412. This attitude was theorized in a different political context by Vladimir I. Lenin, 'Learning from the Enemy', 28 November 1905, in *Lenin's Collected Works*, vol. 10, Moscow: Progress Publishers, 1965, 60–1. More generally, on Italian Communists and antifascism see Silvio Pons, *I comunisti italiani e gli altri. Visioni e legami internazionali nel mondo del Novecento*, Turin: Einaudi, 2021, 38–82.

62   [Carlo Rosselli,] 'Tre passi avanti e nessun passo indietro. Prospettive e compiti dell'antifascismo', *GL*, 13 September 1935.

Therefore, it is not surprising to find that Rosselli, for whom the Bolshevik example epitomized the 'decisive function exercised by a minority of disciplined, united revolutionaries', thought Lenin to be a 'great master of tactics'. On the eve of the Ethiopian War, the language of GL changed radically. An example of this can be seen in the 'Manifesto agli Italiani', written by Rosselli and Calosso and presented at the movement's First Congress, held in Paris on 11–12 September 1935. The chronic inability of the Mussolini regime to meet the expectations it had generated, and thus to trigger an 'apparent dynamism', was the cause of its political and social failure. It was necessary to start with 'a slate clean of all past values and institutions', to unleash the revolution 'against the ever-present spirit of compromise', and to create the conditions for the 'total liberation of humanity': in this regard, GL looked to the Russian revolutionary example, but without losing sight of the 'unique features of the West and of Italy'.[63] The significance of the 'Manifesto' became clear at the end of 1935, when an editorial stated:

> Italy cannot heal without radical treatment. Italy will not be saved without a revolution that sweeps away the structure of the old society. What do we want? Very few, but important, things. First of all, we want freedom. All forms of freedom, and if need be, in the beginning, with all due respect to the gentlemen tourists, we also accept licenses. We have been vegetating for thirteen years in the most suffocating of prisons. When we get out, we will raze this prison, this damn prison, to the ground. We will need to destroy the totalitarian state's leaders, institutions, roots. The problem of freedom is linked to the problem of justice. There will probably be a great many reprisals. But that is not the important thing. What matters is that those responsible pay; that the rulers, the powerful, realize that their final reckoning is coming; and that those who sow Fascism reap social revolution.[64]

Lussu, who had persistently advocated the revolutionary socialist line and had therefore distanced himself from the line taken by GL's Paris leadership, partly identified with the new positions taken by GL, which he saw as the

---

63 'Manifesto agli italiani. Manifesto lanciato dal I Convegno di "Giustizia e Libertà", Parigi, 11–12 settembre 1935', *GL*, 20 September 1935.

64 [Carlo Rosselli,] 'Che cosa vogliamo', *GL*, 6 December 1935.

result of his own influence. In a letter dated January 1935 with which he resigned from the group's executive committee, he described the proletariat – 'the class most oppressed politically and most exploited economically by Fascism' – as the only revolutionary antifascist force: 'There can be no substantial antifascism outside of the proletariat.'[65] However, Lussu approved of the 'Manifesto agli Italiani', and its emphasis on the role of the proletariat as a key social actor in the antifascist revolution. Lussu's withdrawal from political activity was the result not only of his disagreement with GL, but also of health issues that saw him admitted to the Calvadel Kurhaus, a centre for the treatment of lung diseases situated in the Swiss mountains. However, before being hospitalized for surgery, he managed to complete his work *La teoria dell'insurrezione*, which was published in 1936. This volume, which aimed to recapitulate his reflections on the history and strategy of revolution, contained a comparison with the Bolshevik Revolution, which he considered to be 'the only insurrection of our time led by a political and military vanguard that proved victorious.'[66] Lussu made it clear that violence was 'an indispensable means of political struggle in certain exceptional moments', but this did not entail consent to any forms of terrorism or tyrannicide. For him, the most important theoretician of revolutionary action was still Lenin, with his fundamental principle: 'A revolutionary movement does not wait for the spontaneous popular uprising, but tries to provoke and accelerate it. And, what is essential, it leads it, politically and militarily.'[67]

The 'Manifesto agli Italiani' was strongly objected to by Salvemini, in exile at Harvard. In a letter to Rosselli alluding to Lussu, he noted that the more the members of GL felt 'impotent', the more they turned to 'extremism' and renounced the 'clear ideas' and language that could help young people in Italy 'find their way'. He bitterly concluded:

What frightens me about you is the confusion of your ideas. You are neither liberal nor dictatorial. You have jumbled the two approaches together and so nothing is clear. When you come to Italy tomorrow,

---

65 'La situazione italiana e l'antifascismo all'estero. (Una lettera di Emilio Lussu)', *GL*, 1 March 1935. The letter dated back to 17 January 1935.

66 Emilio Lussu, *Per l'Italia dall'esilio*, ed. Manlio Brigaglia, Cagliari: Edizione Della Torre, 1976, 127.

67 Ibid., 160.

you will get yourselves killed on the first street corner without know-
ing why.[68]

But the 'great crisis' had already commenced, Rosselli replied, and therefore GL's actions were aimed at 'releasing the forces, creating a dynamic
situation'. He claimed to be still loyal to the 1932 programme, according to
which 'fundamental reforms must be achieved immediately, in the midst
of the revolution, without waiting for answers from the members of the
Constituent Assembly'. Rosselli asked:

> When did you ever think that reforms of this magnitude, especially in a
> country like Italy, could be carried out while preserving the existing
> order? When did you ever think that it would be possible to punish
> those responsible, to eliminate the plague, while respecting legality and
> freedom from the beginning? Our programme was a programme of
> revolution, not only political but also social revolution. And so it has
> remained.[69]

Faced with the perceived looming crisis of the Fascist regime, Rosselli
sensed that the time for action had come. Until then, politics and culture,
thought and action, had been separate but complementary aspects of GL's
project. The new primacy of politics, which served to create a space for
action in the incipient period of the Popular Front, led Rosselli to emphasize the social dimension of antifascism, to appeal to the proletariat as the
chosen agent of revolution, and to evoke even brutal insurrectional methods in the name of the radical transformation of Fascist Italy. This message,
unprecedented more in tone than in content, shifted the emphasis from
the goals of revolution to the means thereof. It was not so much the result
of Rosselli's conversion as the expression of a general radicalization of the
national and European situation, which seemed to be heading towards
catastrophe. Rosselli, however, overestimated the magnitude of the

---

68   Letter from Gaetano Salvemini to Carlo Rosselli, 29 September 1935, in
Carlo Rosselli and Gaetano Salvemini, *Fra le righe: carteggio fra Carlo Rosselli e
Gaetano Salvemini*, ed. Elisa Signori, Milan: Franco Angeli, 2009, 253.

69   Letter from Carlo Rosselli to Gaetano Salvemini, 15 October 1935, quoted in
Roberto Vivarelli, 'Carlo Rosselli e Gaetano Salvemini', in *Giustizia e Libertà nella
lotta antifascista*, 94.

ongoing crisis, which, rather than ending the Fascist regime, actually saw its popularity reach new heights: on 3 May 1936, Mussolini proclaimed the Italian Empire before rejoicing crowds.

Rosselli's newly militant tone prompted a sectarian, hierarchical view of the group's internal structure, with Rosselli assigned the role of undisputed leader; this provoked the dissent of the so-called 'renewers' – Caffi, Chiaromonte, Mario Levi, and Renzo Giua. Despite their age differences, the 'renewers' all rallied around Caffi, who in turn maintained personal and intellectual ties with the Russian anti-Bolshevik, Social Democratic, and Social Revolutionary émigrés through the writer and journalist Mikhail A. Osorgin, his wife Tatiana A. Osorgina-Bakunina (great-granddaughter of Bakunin), the literary critic Marc L. Slonim, and the economist Vladimir S. Voitinsky.[70] It was Caffi himself who, during discussions within GL in 1934 and 1935, had raised the main questions regarding the meaning of antifascism, the value of the Risorgimento tradition, and the evaluation of the Soviet experiment. In July 1935, Caffi and Rosselli tried to pacify relations within the group and clarify their respective positions. Their disagreement had grown to the point where it now involved personal matters as well: these included Rosselli's claim to a 'virile' socialism, which was in open opposition to Caffi's homosexuality and was to contribute to a dramatic break between the two. In a farewell letter to Rosselli, Caffi underscored the general dimension of the European crisis and expressed the need to 'subordinate politics to certain broader spiritual values, and to frame political action in an overarching vision of social action': 'the germ of a true religion' lay in socialist humanism.[71]

The group of 'renewers' gathered around Caffi once again raised the question of the definition of politics and its organizational implications for GL. This question was all the more urgent given the situation of wholesale polarization, and Rosselli responded to it by progressively politicizing his own line. With a reflection of Platonic origin, Chiaromonte affirmed the need to make politics a 'not only more profound, but also more complex,

---

70   For a more detailed analysis of Caffi's connections to Russian anti-Bolshevik emigration, see Marco Bresciani, *La rivoluzione perduta. Andrea Caffi nell'Europa del Novecento*, Bologna: Il Mulino, 2009, 178–90.

71   Letter from Andrea Caffi to Carlo Rosselli, 22 July (1935), in Alberto Castelli, 'Il socialismo liberale di Andrea Caffi', *Storia in Lombardia* 2, 1996, 160–1, 163.

principle of law', that is, a 'bond of a religious nature, that is, of an absolute and irreducible character'. It was, therefore, necessary 'to be, and to want to be, entirely outside of the state' and 'to think outside of politics'.[72] As in other circumstances, Garosci took the floor to defend the line of GL without denying his own libertarian tendencies, to accuse Chiaromonte of 'a constant subtle misunderstanding, confusing politics with political superficiality'. Fascism, like any 'perfect tyranny', had resulted in 'the decisive, complete reduction of politics to violence, and thus of the state to a pure and perfect mechanism of power'. It was possible to be 'against' the state, but not 'outside' the state.[73] From Garosci's point of view, in opposing Fascism it was necessary to use the very understanding of politics as force, whereas, in Chiaromonte's mind, this had to be avoided in order to rule out its reiteration in the antifascist sphere. However, what was at stake here was not so much the question of adopting a particular position in regard to Fascism or politics, but that of defining intellectual responsibility itself: this was the focus of the first International Congress of Writers for the Defence of Culture, held in Paris from 21 to 25 June 1935. A considerable number of important figures from European culture were present at the event, including André Breton, Louis Aragon, André Malraux, Henri Barbusse, Bertolt Brecht, Heinrich Mann, Ilya G. Ehrenburg, Boris L. Pasternak, Isaak E. Babel, Robert Musil, and Max Brod. The communists were instrumental in organizing the Congress, as part of the antifascist initiatives paving the way for the establishment of the Popular Front. However, far from being a mere sounding board for Soviet propaganda, the Congress was the occasion for heated and lively debates, as well as uncritical, eulogistic speeches.[74] Salvemini took the floor and gave a speech as passionate as it was controversial, comparing Mussolini's Italy and Hitler's Germany with Stalin's Soviet Union and denouncing the case of Victor Serge. Chiaromonte, for his part, merely followed the proceedings, not only listening to the speeches

---

72   Luciano [Nicola Chiaromonte], 'La riforma socialista ovvero alla ricerca della vera questione', *GL*, 15 March 1935.

73   Magrini [Aldo Garosci], 'Risposta a Luciano', *GL*, 22 March 1935.

74   See François Furet, *The Passing of an Illusion: The Idea of Communism in the Twentieth Century*, Chicago: University of Chicago Press, 1999, 285–7, alongside a more nuanced analysis in *Pour la défense de la culture. Les textes du Congrès international des écrivains, Paris, juin 1935*, ed. Sandra Teroni and Wolfgang Klein, Dijon: Éditions Universitaires de Dijon, 2005.

from among the audience but also deciphering the messages being trans-mitted behind the scenes. In his opinion, the communists were justifying the 'need for dogmatism' as a 'necessity of war', thus making it an 'intellec-tual position': this 'abstract' and 'dangerous' sophistry inevitably led to the 'justification of military obedience', whereby communism ultimately iden-tified itself with fascism.[75]

Chiaromonte's previous reflections on intellectual responsibility were reiterated, albeit in a different form, in his final argument with GL. His 'Sincere Declaration', sent to GL's central leadership, stated that the prep-aration for the future by a 'revolutionary' movement constituted a 'complex, silent, patient and tenacious task', the execution of which could not be improvised. Action, he said, presupposed 'consistent, clear think-ing accompanied by continuous critical reflection', along with 'spontane-ous activity in the social setting' it was to act within; while activism as an end in itself would, ultimately, replicate the basic direction of the Fascists' 1919 programme. The goal of a revolutionary antifascist group could not be limited to 'the mere overthrow of Fascism' but entailed 'the beginning of a real transformation of Italian society'. Chiaromonte demanded that his 'Sincere Declaration' be made public. The leadership of GL responded with an unequivocal call to order, at the same time showing a certain willingness to engage in dialogue. In a letter dated January 1936, Chiaromonte, Mario Levi, and Renzo Giua announced that they were leaving the group.[76]

The 'crisis of the renewers' represented a fundamental clash between different views on political commitment and intellectual responsibility. This problem, which stemmed from the early twentieth-century debates and subsequently fuelled the post-1918 crisis, resurfaced in the mid-1930s in the form of the clash between Fascism and antifascism. GL always maintained an ambivalent relationship with politics: the 1935 'crisis of the renewers' reflected this ambivalence. The following year, the Spanish Civil War – a decisive moment in what Rosselli referred to as a 'European Civil

---

75   Luciano [Nicola Chiaromonte], 'Il congresso internazionale degli scrittori. II. L'umanismo', *GL*, 19 July 1935.

76   Luciano [Nicola Chiaromonte], 'Franca spiegazione', in a letter to the Committee of GL, 21 December 1935, in Bagnoli, *Rosselli, Gobetti e la rivoluzione democratica*, 92–8.

War' – further politicized this grouping within GL. At that time, learning from the enemy meant more than ever going to its preferred terrain – the battleground.

Spain: An International Battleground

A wave of political violence and social unrest fuelled previous polarization and shattered Spain following the electoral victory of the Popular Front in February 1936. On the 18 July, some generals of the Spanish army, including General Francisco Franco, attempted to violently overthrow the country's liberal and parliamentary institutions, but failed, unleashing a popular uprising both in the main towns and in the countryside. After initial hesitation, the Republican government decided to arm the volunteer militias of the various political parties and trade union federations that had resisted the *coup d'état*, even if this exacerbated the chaotic fragmentation of powers and the widespread proliferation of counter-powers.[77] The local and European roots of the Spanish Civil War were closely intertwined, insofar as long-term issues and conflicts within Spain acquired renewed significance due to the active role of Fascist Italy and Nazi Germany in encouraging the attempted military coup in the mid-1930s. The immediate support for the rebel Spanish army from Mussolini's Italy and Hitler's Germany made the importance of the conflict between fascism and democracy clear to all the supporters of the republic.[78] At the same time, the new scenario of war made it possible to resolve the serious moral and political dilemmas of practical antifascist commitment and prompted an exceptional surge of international mobilization. The Spanish Civil War saw a revival of transnational armed volunteerism as the highest expression of radical political solidarity, one that had spanned the entire nineteenth century

77   See, among others, Helen Graham, *The Spanish Republic at War, 1936–1939*, Cambridge: Cambridge University Press, 2002; Gabriele Ranzato, *L'eclissi della democrazia. La guerra civile spagnola e le sue origini, 1931–1939*, Turin: Bollati Boringhieri, 2004; Paul Preston, *The Spanish Civil War: Reaction, Revolution, and Revenge*, rev. ed., New York: Norton 2007.

78   John F. Coverdale, *The Italian Intervention in the Spanish Civil War*, Princeton, NJ: Princeton University Press, 1975.

and had characterized its various revolutionary cycles, up to World War I and the postwar crisis.[79]

At the end of July 1936, little more than a week after the coup by the generals rebelling against the parliamentary republic, and in the midst of the popular uprising that now shook the whole of Spain, Rosselli called the 'civil war of the Spanish proletariat' the 'war of all antifascism'.[80] The conflict in Spain offered Rosselli the first real opportunity to take up arms against Fascism. At a meeting held in early August at the house of the writer Malraux, then close to the communists, in the presence of Chiaromonte and the Soviet journalist Ehrenburg, the GL leader decided to participate in the conflict. While the former members of GL, Giua and Chiaromonte, reached Spain by separate routes, Calosso was already on a lecture tour in Barcelona at the time the civil war broke out. In a series of letters to GL, he called for intervention in favour of the Republic. Trentin made his Librairie de Languedoc, in the Toulouse hinterland, a logistical hub for volunteers. Garosci went to Spain in early August to explore the possibility of coordinated initiatives with the Confederación Nacional del Trabajo–Federación Anarquista Ibérica (CNT–FAI), the anarcho-syndi-calist organization with a strong presence on the committee of antifascist militias that had taken power in Catalonia. On 17 August, an Italian section was formally established and incorporated into the Ascaso International Column, led by Buenaventura Durruti. However, relations between GL and Catalonia's revolutionary, libertarian, and anarchist movements were far from easy.[81] The immediate experience of revolution-ary Catalonia visibly represented the utopic achievement of a complete overthrow of traditional authorities. The streets of Barcelona, where

---

79 See Nir Arielli, 'Getting There: Enlistment Considerations and the Recruitment Networks of the International Brigades during the Spanish Civil War', in Nir Arielli and Bruce Collins (eds), *Transnational Soldiers: Foreign Military Enlistment in the Modern Era*, Basingstoke: Palgrave Macmillan, 2013, 219–32; and more broadly Nir Arielli, *From Byron to bin Laden: A History of Foreign War Volunteers*, Cambridge, MA: Harvard University Press, 2018 (especially 115–16, for Rosselli). For the complex moral dimension of this armed volunteerism, see Adam Hochschild, *Spain in Our Hearts: Americans in the Spanish Civil War, 1936–1939*, Boston: H. M. Harcourt, 2016.

80 [Carlo Rosselli,] 'Il dovere dei rivoluzionari', *GL*, 31 July 1936.

81 Enrico Acciai, *Antifascismo, volontariato e guerra civile in Spagna. La sezione italiana della Colonna Ascaso*, Milan: Unicopli, 2016.

Rosselli had arrived from Paris in mid-August, teemed with armed trade unionists and workers; theatres and public transportation were free; committees of all kinds gave everyone a chance to speak and vote on the issues of the day; new forms of production and distribution of goods were tested. On the evening of 19 August, a group of about 130 volunteers, including Rosselli and some twenty activists from GL, moved from the Catalan capital to a military camp in the small village of Vicién on the Aragonese plateau. Carlo wrote to his wife Marion:

> The revolution is the greatest epic of modern times, and it cannot end in another reaction or another outburst. A new world is being born, also for us, and it is a great privilege to be able to contribute in some way to its birth.[82]

The baptism of fire occurred at the end of August. The first armed conflict between the Italian section of the Durruti Column and the nationalist troops took place on a bare hill, ironically renamed Monte Pelato, that marked a strategic junction between Zaragoza and Huesca. Mario Angeloni, republican activist and military leader of GL, was one of those who fell in battle. Rosselli obviously rejected the idea of the 'romantic and decadent cult of blood sacrifice' that animated fascist ideology. However, he also affirmed that 'in certain historical, psychological situations, when everything, even the memory of past struggles, seems lost', 'the total sacrifice of the physical person, and not just one, but thousands upon thousands' operated as a trigger capable of mobilizing people's consciences.[83] This cult of sacrifice, which forged the myth of the war experience, resurfaced from time to time within the GL group. Despite being profoundly rooted in European Romanticism, this idea was a rhetorical device oriented towards social progress and anchored in the Enlightenment project of antifascist revolution.[84]

---

82   Letter from Carlo to Marion Rosselli, in Carlo Rosselli, *Dall'esilio. Lettere alla moglie, 1929-1937*, ed. Costanzo Casucci, Florence: Passigli, 1997, 220-1.

83   [Carlo Rosselli,] 'Per l'unità dell'antifascismo italiano', *GL*, 22 January 1937.

84   See Antonio Bechelloni, ' "E' difficile prendere sul serio questa guerra": la Spagna di Rosselli e altre Spagne del '36-'37', in Antonio Bechelloni (ed.), *Carlo e Nello Rosselli e l'antifascismo europeo*, Milan: Franco Angeli, 2001, 153-71. On the Myth of War Experience and volunteers in the Spanish Civil War, see George L.

While Italian military divisions and the Nazi Condor Legion poured into Spain, the French and British governments opted for a policy of non-intervention that in fact favoured the nationalist forces. Beginning in September, the Soviet Union offered massive direct political and military support, which in return meant the possibility of greater control over the fragmented republican front. At the same time, freedom fighters from all over the world were flocking to Spain, and the communists began to incorporate them into the International Brigades. In this dramatic situation, the differences over how exactly to resist the troops of the putschist generals deepened: on the one hand, there was the indivisibility between antifascist war and popular revolution, as preached by the anarchists, libertarians, and revolutionary syndicalists; on the other hand, the priority of the antifascist war, as supported by liberal republicans, socialists of various extraction, and communists (with Soviet backing). The contrast between revolution and counterrevolution in Rosselli's lightning-fast succession of positions did not prevent him oscillating between the reasons for revolution and the reasons for war, the more so as time went on. In the autumn of 1936, the major clashes were concentrated around Madrid, in central Spain, while the Catalan and Aragonese fronts remained relatively quiet. Until then Rosselli's 'liberal federalist socialism', also identified with 'libertarian communism', was closely in line with the anarchist views of his friend Camillo Berneri. Catalonia had become the hotbed of 'a new form of social democracy, a theoretical-practical synthesis of the Russian experience with the heritage of the West'. 'A new world has blossomed, a whole people has tasted the fruits of freedom not only at the rallies but also in the workshops, in the fields and at the front.'[85] In his speech 'Oggi in Spagna, domani in Italia', delivered on Ràdio Barcelona on 13 November 1936, Carlo Rosselli considered that a 'new order' had emerged in Spain, an order based 'on freedom and social justice': 'no dictatorship, no barrack economy, no denial of the cultural values of the West, but the reconciliation of the boldest social

---

Mosse, *Fallen Soldiers: Reshaping the Memory of the World Wars*, New York: Oxford University Press, 1990, 189–95.

85   [Carlo Rosselli,] 'Catalogna baluardo della rivoluzione', *GL*, 6 November 1936.

reforms with freedom'.[86] Arguments between GL's activists and the Durruti Column's anarcho-syndicalists became increasingly violent, prompting Rosselli to leave Spain on 6 December 1936. In February 1937, when he had already left Spain, in a letter to an anarchist friend Rosselli called for 'greater discipline and restraint' and criticized those who 'absurdly' thought they could 'distinguish the problems of the war from those of the revolution, as if a great revolutionary upheaval were not taking place in Spain and the civil war were not by its very nature a proletarian war'.[87]

The Spanish Civil War, while polarizing the European political forces and public opinions between fascism and antifascism, as well as revolution and counterrevolution, catalysed an unprecedented intellectual mobilization. Buoyed on the Iberian peninsula by their libertarian, socialist or communist passion, writers and essayists such as George Orwell, Stephen Spender, Simone Weil, Franz Borkenau, or Arthur Koestler were soon disillusioned, no matter their antifascism, by a reality far more ambiguous and violent than they had imagined.[88] Nicola Chiaromonte, for example, had enthusiastically rushed to Madrid to defend the Spanish Republic as part of the air squadron organized by Malraux. Having recently left GL, he still intended to demonstrate his willingness to act. Soon, however, he left Spain, disappointed by the transformation of the popular revolutionary struggle into an organized state war that was losing its initially spontaneous and creative momentum.[89] Garosci, one of the men closest to Rosselli participating in the

86   [Carlo Rosselli,] 'Oggi in Spagna, domani in Italia', GL, 27 November 1936. 'Today in Spain, tomorrow in Italy' was to become a slogan of the Italian Resistance from 1943 on. For the references to the Spanish experience during the 1943–45 period, see Pavone, A Civil War.

87   Letter from Carlo Rosselli to Alberto Meschi, 14 February 1937, in Paolo Spriano, Storia del partito comunista italiano, vol. 3, I fronti popolari, Stalin, la guerra, Turin: Einaudi, 1970, 138.

88   For the cultural mobilization in the Spanish Civil War and its ambivalent impact, see Aldo Garosci, Gli intellettuali e la guerra di Spagna, Turin: Einaudi, 1959, and James Wilkinson, 'Truth and Delusion: European Intellectuals in Search of the Spanish Civil War', Salmagundi 76/77, Fall 1987/Winter 1988, 3–52.

89   Cesare Panizza, Nicola Chiaromonte. Una biografia, Rome: Donzelli, 2017, 136–46. For a first-hand account of his Spanish experience, see Nicola Chiaromonte, 'Spain: The War', Atlantic Monthly, March 1937, 359–64.

Spanish Civil War, followed a similar arc, albeit within GL. At first he felt convinced that, rather than 'a political struggle that is more or less violent, more or less fierce, but with the forms and manners and precautions of a political struggle', this was a war 'between good and evil, between irreconcilable and religiously opposed principles'.[90] For Garosci, however, the experience marked a radical break that led him to drastically change his view of revolutionary action. The epic of the antifascist war was now accompanied by an awareness of the tragic reality of total war, which he judged 'with a certain pessimism and rigour'. Although he still believed in the ultimate victory of the Spanish Republic, he now acknowledged the 'great fatigue and lack of confidence' of the antifascist fighters, as well as the 'great confusion . . . due to the shortage of supplies and a certain administrative disorder'.[91] The latter phrase is from a report by a spy interested in confirming the split in the group; nevertheless, it is not unlikely that Garosci had a lively argument with Rosselli following the former's return from Barcelona in the spring of 1937.

As a matter of fact, the early months of the Spanish Civil War were characterized by greater levels of chaotic and plebeian violence than Rosselli suggested at first, and the destructive dimension of the revolution far outweighed its constructive aspects. Admittedly, the workers' and peasants' committees confiscated all kinds of property and experimented with forms of total collectivization of industry and land. More broadly, the dissolution of state authorities and the dislocation of social relations led to the political and military confrontation turning into a war of all against all, which indiscriminately affected Spain's civilian population and religious orders. While the various currents of antifascism loudly denounced Francoism's mass violence and repressive measures, most of them concealed or simply ignored the reality of summary executions and murders in republican-controlled areas. During the spring of 1937, the leader of GL got to use unusually aggressive language to justify any form of violence from an antifascist point of view: 'It is useless calling for

---

90   Magrini [Aldo Garosci], 'Guerra di sterminio e rivoluzione costruttiva', GL, 18 September 1936.
91   Confidential Report, 20 April 1937, Ministero degli Interni, Direzione Generale Pubblica Sicurezza, Divisione Polizia Politica, fascicolo personale Carlo Rosselli, busta 78, Archivio Centrale dello Stato (Rome).

civility in struggle. We live in a cruel age. To win, or even just to survive, you must fight. Humanity will be saved today by facing the devil in his own setting, the fascist hell.'[92]

The international communist organization seemed (and often was) the only force prepared to actively fight fascism in Europe. Of course, its direct undertaking to fight Franco's nationalist forces in Spain was in line with the Soviet Union's foreign policy, which aimed to keep the new war threat from Nazi Germany as far away as possible in both time and space. This was all the truer at a stage when Stalin had finally decided to deal with the opposition within his party and impose absolute rule through the systematic use of terror. The political polarization sparked by the Spanish Civil War, however, tended to distort in a lenient direction the judgement of Stalin's regime, which celebrated the first Moscow trial of sixteen party defendants (including Lev B. Zinoviev and Grigory E. Kamenev) in August 1936. Out of political expediency, GL refrained from openly condemning Stalin's repressive policies in the heat of its fight against the military rebels and their fascist supporters in Catalonia and Aragon.[93] But it was impossible to remain silent when the second trial came around, involving seventeen more people (including Karl B. Radek and Georgy L. Pyatakov), who were indicted the following January. Lussu protested at the shooting of 'innocent revolutionaries': 'A regime, unopposed and uncontrolled for so long, has brought the greatest popular revolution of modern times down to this.'[94]

Although Lussu had no sympathy for Trotskyism, his interpretation of events was in keeping with Trotsky's *The Revolution Betrayed*, first published in Victor Serge's French translation in October 1936. Both spoke of a 'dictatorial degeneration' that had wrought no significant change in the social character of the state that arose from the Bolshevik Revolution. However, while Trotsky intended this as an indictment of Stalin, in Lussu's mind it was a gesture of indulgence towards the Soviet Union. Their differences thus remained irreconcilable. Unlike Trotsky, firmly wedded to the idea of the conflict between revolution and counterrevolution, Lussu was

---

92 [Carlo Rosselli,] 'Primo Maggio', *GL*, 30 April 1937.

93 'Il processo di Mosca', *GL*, 28 August 1936.

94 Fen. [Emilio Lussu], 'Commenti. Il nuovo processo di Mosca', *GL*, 29 January 1937.

convinced that the key dilemma in Europe at that time was the opposition between fascism and antifascism. Prominent figures from the world of international socialism, including Kautsky and Adler, spoke out against the Moscow trials. Others, such as Bauer, tended to downplay the scope and significance of those trials in order to preserve antifascist unity, including communists. Blum, for his part, remained silent on the matter for a considerable time, while the French socialist press printed only the official Soviet reports.[95]

In a context where a drastic decision was becoming increasingly urgent, Rosselli's wavering and yielding to the Soviet experiment and the Stalinist regime kept coming up. He met with Victor Serge several times to discuss what was happening in the USSR.[96] His writings increasingly identified anti-communism with fascism, which he believed was ever more ingrained in the bourgeoisie. Rosselli believed that the 'crusade of fascism against Bolshevism' concealed 'the fundamental instrument for the subversion of Europe; the grandiose, psychological and social preparations – more than any diplomatic arrangements – for another war in Europe': the 'anti-communist crusade' implied 'the rediscovery of historical materialism and class struggle in foreign policy'. In his perception of the conflict between fascism and antifascism, Rosselli superimposed the image of an 'international social war' on that of a 'European civil war', indeed replacing the latter with the former. He thus identified anti-communism as the common root of both the aggressiveness of the fascist regimes and the weakness of Western democracies.[97] On the other hand, he linked this simplified view of international events, dictated by the increasing polarization of European politics, to a notion of the events of 1917 as constituting 'an attempt at total liberation that extended to all classes and all human relations' and 'an act of will by a class that destroyed in order to build'. Since then, Rosselli believed that the 'Russian Revolution' had ushered in 'a new civilization' vis-à-vis which the West had to move 'in its own way', as Stalin's

95   Lilly Marcou (ed.), *L'URSS vue de gauche*, Paris: Presses Universitaires de France, 1982, 141–2.

96   Serge, *Memoirs of a Revolutionary*, 397. Serge and Rosselli met in the spring of 1937: see Victor Serge, *Retour à l'Ouest. Chroniques (juin 1936–mai 1940)*, ed. Anthony Glinoer, Marseille: Agone, 2010, 91.

97   [Carlo Rosselli,] 'La crociata antisovietica', *GL*, 26 February 1937.

dictatorship was 'deplorable' but also 'ephemeral'.[98] This was a surprising position for Rosselli to take, as until then he had rejected all forms of determinism. The now simple condemnation of Stalin's regime and its terrorist practices was combined with a firm belief in the existence of a variety of paths to achieving socialism. Rosselli's ideas predominantly echoed Bauer's thinking, which continued to posit the provisional character of the Stalinist dictatorship and the socialist character of the Soviet project.

The fragmentation of local powers constituted a persistent source of political instability for the Spanish Republican government led by Indalecio Prieto and for its largely ineffective military strategy. In early May, the government, including liberal democrats, both revolutionary and reformist socialists, and communists, decided to crush the Trotskyist, anarcho-syndicalist, and libertarian forces (such as the Partido Obrero de Unificación Marxista, or POUM) that had made Catalonia their stronghold.[99] An important role was played by the Spanish Communist Party, under the command of the Soviet forces operating in Spain. The tragic resolution of internal tensions within the Republic – involving the kidnap and murder of the independent communist Andrés Nin (a leader of the POUM) and of the anarchist Camillo Berneri (close to GL) – took place within the context of an indiscriminate campaign of repression against 'Trotskyism', waged by Stalin both in the Soviet Union and abroad. The case for war efficiency seemed to favour the supporters of the Republican government, including the communists, rather than the revolutionary syndicalists, libertarians, and anarchists. However, what appeared to be two ideologically irreconcilable perspectives – either revolution or war – turned out in practice to be a spectrum of differently understood options of political, social, and military governance that only the violence of the first days of May resolved. Rosselli regretfully understood the Republican strategy of centralization and the communist policy of repression. The

---

98   [Carlo Rosselli,] 'Primo Maggio', *GL*, 30 April 1937.

99   On the complex meanings and implications of the Barcelona May Days, see Graham, *The Spanish Republic at War*, 254–315; and the most recent (and more sympathetic) work by Danny Evans, *Revolution and the State: Anarchism and the Spanish Civil War, 1936–1939*, London: Routledge, 2018, and Evans, 'In and Against the State: The Making and Unmaking of the Barcelona May Days (1937)', *European History Quarterly* 52, no. 3, 2022, 485–505.

non-intervention of the British and French governments, which had left the Soviet Union on its own at international level to fight against the perpetrators of the military coup, had, he thought, severely curtailed the alternatives available to the antifascists. He conceded that Soviet intervention in Spain 'moved beyond what was just and necessary', but deemed it to constitute the political, military, and diplomatic prerequisite for Republican resistance: 'Despite all its mistakes, setbacks, and disappointments, Spain remains the battleground between fascism and antifascism.'[100] The leader of GL openly advocated the 'subordination of all political and civil life to warfare'. The only goal now was 'the problem of victory in the antifascist war', and the only criterion of antifascism was 'the will to cooperate towards achieving victory'.[101] Notwithstanding, he was quick to pay tribute to his friend Berneri, the smiling and uncompromising anarchist 'drawn into the bloody maelstrom of a brief yet cruel civil war made part of the other, larger war'. But he remained silent on the question of the responsibility and consequences of this civil-war-within-the-Civil-War that had shattered antifascist unity. In his view, this was not the time to oppose the communists and their methods, which from Barcelona to Moscow had been shaped by Stalinist terror, but to fight against fascism.[102]

In broader terms, the ascendant phase of the Popular Fronts increasingly intermingled with major conflicts on the international arena, namely, the war in Abyssinia (October 1935–June 1936) and the Spanish Civil War (July 1936–March 1939). This tense situation provided a fertile ground for individuals' (eventually armed) intervention in the name of antifascism, especially against Fascist Italy and Nazi Germany in Spain. We can better understand the development of Rosselli's actions and thinking between 1935 and 1937 by considering his fluctuating, contradictory ideas on class and nationhood, on the Risorgimento's democratic traditions and Europe's socialist perspectives, and on revolutionary activism and Popular Front politics. This series of moves and countermoves, the reactions to specific contingencies, were framed within a context that was increasingly characterized by the need to create a new political space within existing power relations (in France, in Spain, among the Italian antifascist émigré community). Six levels can be distinguished in

---

100   [Carlo Rosselli,] 'Crisi in Spagna', GL, 21 May 1937.
101   [Carlo Rosselli,] 'Mediazione impossibile', GL, 28 May 1937.
102   [Carlo Rosselli,] 'Camillo Berneri', GL, 14 May 1937.

Rosselli's complex development, which were alternative or complementary to one another depending on the changing circumstances:

1. A federalist, pro-European orientation as a possible outcome of the future European war provoked by Hitler and Mussolini's regimes (spring–summer 1935);
2. A justification of the democratic tradition of the Risorgimento, in view of the impending collapse of the Fascist regime within the context of the war in Africa (spring–autumn 1935);
3. A more fiery, violent revolutionary tone that emerged with the Fascist war in Ethiopia (autumn 1935) and re-emerged with the civil war in Spain, especially following the polarization of the heterogeneous forces fighting the military rebels and their Fascist and Nazi supporters (spring 1937);
4. A bottom-up interpretation of the Popular Front in the wake of the mass social movements in France, and a subsequent severe criticism of the Blum government (spring 1936);
5. An anti-statist and libertarian, if not anarchist, perspective adopted during his participation in the Spanish Civil War (summer–autumn 1936);
6. A more clearly class-based vision open to redefining the relations between the proletariat and antifascism, together with a more lenient attitude towards the Soviet experience, and an acceptance, albeit hesitant, of the policies of the Republican government of the Spanish Popular Front (winter–spring 1937).

The continuous development and diverse combination of these different levels were brutally cut short by Rosselli's assassination in the vicinity of Bagnoles-de-l'Orne on 9 June 1937.

It is likely that the public initiatives Rosselli had taken since the Ethiopian War had increased the hostility of the Fascist authorities. GL's military involvement in the Spanish Civil War with a view to exporting the insurrectionary model to Italy, relayed in reports submitted by the Italian military service and political police informants in Paris, were of concern to the government in Rome. Furthermore, GL's propaganda campaign the previous March eulogized the greatness and importance of the victory of the International Brigades, including the Garibaldi Battalion, over the Fascist legionnaires in Guadalajara: the clash between Italians on Spanish soil appeared to prefigure, in Rosselli's eyes, the impending showdown with the Fascist regime in Italy. It was in this precise situation that Mussolini's murderous intent emerged, with the complicity of French far-right terrorism. The Comité Secret d'Action Révolutionnaire (CSAR), nicknamed Cagoule, pursued an alliance of France with Fascist Italy and Nazi Germany through a network of international contacts. Under the command of Eugène Deloncle, an engineer who had been wounded and awarded several medals during the Great War, and who was a radical nationalist close to Action Française, the CSAR prepared Carlo Rosselli's assassination as part of a campaign designed to undermine not only the Popular Front government but also the democratic institutions of the Third Republic itself.[103]

In May 1937, the leader of GL was increasingly in the sights of Fascist spies and French terrorists. At the end of that month, unaware of the impending danger, he travelled to Normandy to recover from wounds inflicted in Spain. Carlo's sudden departure from Paris sped up the criminal plan, despite the fact that his brother Nello turned up unexpectedly in Bagnoles-de-l'Orne in early June. The meticulously prepared ambush took place in the evening of 9 June, as the Rosselli brothers' car was travelling past the château de Couterne. The CSAR terrorists stopped the car on the pretext of an accident, then killed both brothers using revolvers and knives. The bodies of Carlo and Nello were only discovered in the nearby woods some two days later.[104]

The news of their death was received with great sadness among the Italian antifascist émigrés and France's Left politicians. Their funeral, accompanied by the strains of Beethoven's seventh symphony (a work particularly dear to Carlo), was attended by over 100,000 people in Paris.

103 Chris Millington, *The Invention of Terrorism in France (1904–1939)*, Stanford, CA: Stanford University Press, 2023 (with references to the murder of the 'Roselli' brothers at page 142).

104 Mimmo Franzinelli, *Il delitto Rosselli. 9 giugno 1937: anatomia di un omicidio politico*, Milan: Mondadori, 2007.

4
Shades of Socialism

Rosselli's Legacy: What Form of Socialism in an Age of Tyranny?

No one can say where the inexhaustible energy and creative intelligence of the still quite young Carlo Rosselli might have taken him and his group. However, in the months before his assassination, which were marked by the bitter aftermath of his participation in the Spanish Civil War, Rosselli delivered a series of five challenging articles to GL, in which he reiterated the meaning of his political experience and introduced the idea of the 'unification of the Italian proletariat'. In doing so, he had two goals: the first was to re-establish the substantial unity of the Italian Left and thus overcome the 1921 splitting of socialists and communists; the second was to renew the Left's political culture on the basis of the lessons learnt from the Fascists' victory in 1922. Indeed, Fascism – which was not only 'a violent class reaction' but also 'the shipwreck of all classes and all values' – had revealed the structural limits of both socialist and communist culture.[1] In this situation, GL represented 'the first European movement that was thoroughly antifascist', because it identified Fascism as being 'the central fact, the tremendous novelty of our time'. Hence 'the unprejudiced, almost

---

1   [Carlo Rosselli,] 'Per l'unificazione politica del proletariato italiano. I. Sguardo d'insieme', *GL*, 19 March 1937.

experimental character' of its actions, as well as its 'intellectual restlessness', which emphasized its 'proletarian character'.[2]

In Rosselli's late thinking, the identification of the fascism/antifascism dichotomy with the bourgeoisie/proletariat one became increasingly important. The leader of GL put aside his reflections on the middle classes' oscillation between socialism and Fascism, no longer criticizing class categories as he had in the past: he now examined them from within, and introduced new nuances of meaning. His clear inclination to identify GL's enemy at the social level did not prevent him from continuing to acknowledge the primacy of politics. In his mind, it was Fascism, which he increasingly identified with the bourgeoisie, that forced GL into formulating a new language of class war. While, up until then, Rosselli had advocated the need for a new political perspective, he now defined a broad, unified social subject in order to establish GL as the innovative pole of attraction and hybridization of the Left:

> In socialism we see the conceptual strength underlying the entire workers' movement, the substance of any true democracy, the religion of the century. Communism represents the first historical application of socialism, the myth (unfortunately very jaded by now), but above all the most energetic revolutionary force. In libertarianism, we see the element of utopia, of the dream, of the overwhelming, yet crude and primitive, religion of Man.

Rosselli's initiative could be summarized as the project to found a 'Single Party of the Proletariat' (synonymous with the 'Single Party of Antifascism'), which had already been suggested by Lussu.[3] Instead of conceiving a political party of the 'socialist proletariat' like Lussu, however, the leader of GL wanted to create 'a broad social force, a kind of anticipation of future society, a social microcosm, with its militant organization, but also with a broad, vibrant intellectual life'.[4] Not surprisingly, their last meeting,

---

2 [Carlo Rosselli,] 'Per l'unificazione politica del proletariato italiano. V. "Giustizia e Libertà"', *GL*, 14 May 1937.

3 Letter from Emilio Lussu to Carlo Rosselli [Clavadel], 18 May [1936], in Emilio Lussu, *Tutte le opere*, vol. 2, *L'esilio antifascista, 1927–1943: storia e milizia*, ed. Manlio Brigaglia, Cagliari: CUEC, 2010, 181.

4 [Carlo Rosselli,] 'Per l'unificazione del proletariato italiano. V. "Giustizia e Libertà"', *GL*, 14 May 1937.

which took place at the end of May 1937, was the occasion for a heated exchange of views, during which their differences regarding relations with the communists and Soviet Communism became evident.[5]

While prompting GL to play a prominent role within the Popular Fronts, Rosselli sought to once more legitimize the unity of the socialist, communist, and libertarian groups at a time when the divisions separating them in Catalonia were becoming disruptive. On closer examination, the head of GL seems to have underestimated the continuing vitality of the Soviet myth, which had been renewed by the antifascist struggle and the Spanish Civil War: his own positions in April–May 1937 were eloquent proof of this. On the other hand, Rosselli seems to have overlooked the communists' claims of left-wing hegemony, and their unwillingness to cut ties with the Third International and the Soviet Union. In any case, in the spring of 1937, a communist delegation and a GL delegation, led respectively by Ruggero Grieco and Rosselli, met to try to reach an agreement. After the armed intervention of the Republican government, with full communist support, aimed at suppressing the internal opposition from revolutionary syndicalists and libertarians in Catalonia, the negotiations were suspended, resulting in a series of misunderstandings and mutual recriminations.

The political biography of Carlo Rosselli has been often considered under the sign of growing radicalization towards Leftist, pro-communist positions. This interpretation tends to neglect the unpredictable tortuosity of Rosselli's path depending on changing political circumstances. However, within the context of the GL group's history, Rosselli's 1937 series of articles 'Per l'unificazione del proletariato italiano' do not appear as the culmination of a trajectory that was suddenly interrupted, but, rather, as the starting point for a lively debate that would continue to animate and divide GL. While Lussu and Trentin were largely (but not completely) in agreement with Rosselli's later thinking, the other members, who until then had aimed to establish their own way forward, grappled with the Rossellian legacy and the complex and contradictory meaning of his political and intellectual experience. This debate was related to the urgent reorganization of GL imposed by the assassination of its leader in June 1937, after which the reins were taken over by a group that included Lussu, Garosci,

---

5   Emilio Lussu, *Essere a sinistra: democrazia, autonomia e socialismo in cinquant'anni di lotte*, ed. Collettivo Emilio Lussu di Cagliari, Milan: Mazzotta, 1976, 38.

Venturi, and Calosso. Following Rosselli's death, Lussu once again played an important role in GL. Embracing Lussu's outlook, the group now referred to itself as a 'movement of socialist unification'. The perspective of the late leader was taken up by Trentin, who shared Rosselli's 'concern for unity, for the unity of the proletarian family'. The series of articles 'Per l'unificazione del proletariato italiano', intended as a 'contribution to direct action by which to lay the foundations of a single great Italian socialist party', contained 'his last message, his political testament'.[6]

Garosci, on the other hand, saw in Rosselli the 'link between the old anti-fascism of political habit and the radical, insurrectionary, apocalyptic mind-set of youth'. Only through his embodiment of the relationship between 'the concerns of culture and the anxiety of action', according to Garosci, would it have been possible to unite 'the fragments of the scattered proletarian parties and the vast mass that emerged from the political traditions of Italian youth'.[7] By tying the prospect of the 'unification of the proletariat' to Rosselli's inimitable qualities, Garosci implicitly dismissed any such prospect now that he was gone. While Trentin declared his loyalty to the project that Rosselli developed in his later years, namely that of the 'political unification of the proletariat', Garosci identified more with Rosselli's *Liberal Socialism*. Though agreeing with the need to understand national problems also from the proletarian point of view, Garosci baulked at perceiving 'the entire complexity of national social life simply in terms of the great factory proletariat'. He believed the class perspective to be 'anti-historical and tyrannical', and one that ultimately legitimized 'the government of a party and a sect'. Garosci invoked Rosselli's humanist reflections, which 'rejected the militarist conception of socialism and rightly saw in egalitarianism a human appeal to justice, the goal as an ideal immanent in every achievement'. Rosselli's conception of 'legal and organizational pluralism' should be the inclusive driver of socialism, integrating the proletariat into the middle classes and addressing the 'present collapse of human values'.[8]

These themes lay at the heart of GL's Paris Conference, during which the group's ideological charter was adopted on 11 and 12 May 1938. Its

---

6　Silvio Trentin, 'L'ostacolo', *GL*, 18 June 1937.

7　Magrini [Aldo Garosci], 'Il Capo', *GL*, 18 June 1937.

8　Magrini [Aldo Garosci], 'Classi medie, partiti borghesi e socialismo', *GL*, January 1938.

main objective was 'a federalist form of collectivism'. The new labelling of GL as a 'socialist movement' triggered a lively debate centred around the key concepts of Rosselli's late thoughts. It was Venturi who supplied greater historical depth to this debate: after focusing on the connection between revolution and nation, from 1936 to 1937 he turned to the problem of the historical development of socialism and communism, with their 'ideational' differences, and reiterated the need to open up to 'the proletarian movement as a whole'.[9] The young scholar was interested in a series of works published by the Éditions sociales internationales, directed by the sociologist Georges Friedmann and devoted to *Socialisme et Culture*, which advanced a 'compromise between a "Soviet-type" culture and the French humanist tradition' while attempting to 'link France's present struggles with Europe's past free cultural tradition'. Between 1929 and 1934, the group centred around the *Revue Marxiste* – Norbert Guterman, Georges Friedmann, Henri Lefebvre, Pierre Morhange, Paul Nizan, and Georges Politzer – was instrumental in renewing French Marxism and elaborating a new model of unity between theory and practice. The rediscovery in 1933 of Marx's *Economic and Philosophic Manuscripts of 1844*, a work that represented the revival of the early Marx's libertarian message and its separation from later positivist layers, gave new momentum to Marxist revisionism.[10] The Russian philosopher Alexandre Kojève's seminars, devoted to Hegel's *Phenomenology of Spirit* and held at the École Pratique des Hautes Études between 1933 and 1939, were also influential in this regard. They were attended by France's leading cultural figures, such as the sociologist Raymond Aron, the surrealist writer Raymond Queneau, and the philosophers Éric Weil and Maurice Merleau-Ponty.[11] Meanwhile Venturi, developing a fascination for the pre-Marxist socialism of Fourier and Pierre Leroux, argued for shifting the debate on the question of dialectical materialism from philosophy to history, overcoming the Marxian

9   Subalpino [Umberto Calosso], 'Risposta a Lussu e Vasco', *GL*, 14 October 1938.

10   See George Lichtheim, *Marxism in Modern France*, New York: Columbia University Press, 1966, 86–9.

11   Alexandre Kojève, *Introduction to the Reading of Hegel: Lectures on the 'Phenomenology of Spirit'*, compiled by Raymond Queneau, ed. Allan Bloom, Ithaca, NY: Cornell University Press, 1980.

distinction between utopia and science and responding to 'the various moral, psychological, and human needs' which, if neglected, would fuel fascism. It was primarily through Jean Jaurès that Venturi found 'a kind of act of faith in the universe, in its immeasurable possibilities', which had informed the 'materialism' of the Enlightenment and would go on to inspire French socialism.[12]

In October 1936, the publication of André Gide's *Retour de l'URSS* reignited the Parisian debate, already inflamed by the Popular Front and the Spanish Civil War. The French writer, a notorious non-conformist, had been driven by faith in the progressive character of the Soviet Union. However, following the disappointments of his trip to Moscow in June–July 1936, he denounced the lies and mass conformism concealing the tyrannical nature of the Stalinist regime. Although GL debated the virtues of Gide's book, Venturi decided to take a different tack when he travelled to Leningrad in January–February 1937 for research purposes. Instead of describing and criticizing the official line adopted by the Communist Party of the Soviet Union, his 'Note dalla Russia' attempted an approximation – 'beyond all orthodoxy' – to the 'new society, the culture, the life born of the Revolution'. Venturi imagined that in 1917 the 'Russian people' had moved 'like a great tide that left its mark on everything'.[13] Despite disregarding the repressive brutality of Stalin's dictatorship, in 1937 the young scholar acknowledged the profound metamorphosis of Russian Marxism and its relationship to Soviet society. The return to the writings of Pushkin, the rediscovery of the Russian classics, the cult of national-patriotic folklore that had resurfaced from 'beneath the skin of superficial dogmatism' represented 'a process of organic absorption of Marxism and thus of elimination of the worthless elements'. These were not 'exclusively reactionary recurrences', although Venturi did not rule out the possibility that they might 'gel into a pernicious, retrograde form of nationalism'.[14] This revealed Venturi's somewhat ambiguous enthusiasm for the 'closed

---

12   Gianfranchi [Franco Venturi], 'Inventario. Felicien Challaye, *Jaurès*', *GL*, 1936.

13   Gianfranchi [Franco Venturi], 'Le strade di Leningrado', *GL*, 15 January 1937. See Andrea Graziosi, 'Nazione, socialismo e cosmopolitismo. L'Unione Sovietica nell'evoluzione di Franco Venturi', in Antonello Venturi (ed.), *Franco Venturi e la Russia. Con documenti inediti*, Milan: Feltrinelli, 2006, 131–65.

14   Gianfranchi [Franco Venturi], 'La cultura delle masse', *GL*, 22 January 1937.

world' of Russia that had achieved the revolution, albeit 'in an extremely crude and simple form'.[15]

Unlike Venturi, Lussu looked more to Austro-Marxism than to French Marxism. In his work *Between Two World Wars: Capitalism, Socialism, and Democracy*, published in exile in Brno in 1936, the major Austro-Marxist theorist Otto Bauer praised the progressive function of the Soviet Union in the context of the simultaneous, multiple crises witnessed in capitalist Europe, and asserted the revolutionary character of the coming antifascist war. While the struggle against fascism had forced Europe's social-democratic parties to go underground, the explosive differences between the socialist 'base' and the dictatorial state had led the Soviet Union down the path of democratization, Bauer argued. This analysis resulted in the proposal of an 'integral socialism' (*integraler Sozialismus*) that would bring together the two internationals and reunite Western social democracy with Soviet Communism. In line with the Austro-Marxists, Lussu adopted a strict class-based approach, and held that the Fascist regime had completely 'quashed' the bourgeoisie, while the only 'democratic revolution' would be a 'socialist revolution'.[16] Accordingly, he emphasized the common goal of socialism and communism, both of which aspired to 'a collectivist society' where, 'through the socialization of the means of production and exchange', private property would be abolished. GL, an 'Italian and European movement of Marxist revision', had therefore to re-establish the cornerstones of 'traditional socialism'.[17]

In the 1930s, Lussu's reflections on socialism and democracy, like Bauer's, became inseparable from his analysis of the Soviet experience. By this time, Lussu could hardly overlook the Third Moscow Trial held in March 1938, involving twenty-one defendants including Nikolai I. Bukharin. In Lussu's articles on the political and constitutional development of the USSR, he constantly veered between critical remarks and apologetic outbursts. He raised a series of disconcerting questions regarding the nature of the defendants' confessions and the heterogeneity of the

15   Gianfranchi [Franco Venturi], 'L'URSS e gli altri', *GL*, 5 February 1937.

16   Tirreno [Emilio Lussu], 'Esperienze e insegnamenti dell'azione clandestina in Italia con Rosselli', *GL*, 10 June 1938.

17   Tirreno [Emilio Lussu], 'Note polemiche e considerazioni politiche', *GL*, 2 September 1938.

accused, some of whom were subsequently sentenced to death though they could certainly not be defined as 'Trotskyists'. Nevertheless, he could not fail to mention – beyond the 'terrible bitterness' of the struggle for 'a heritage, that of pure Leninist tradition' – the 'broader experience of an existing, living communist society, with its negative and positive sides'. Although it was an 'absolute integral dictatorship', Lussu believed that the USSR had 'laid the foundation for a future democracy'. His rejection of the claim that Fascist and Bolshevik dictatorships were comparable was based on the impossibility of 'equating the dictatorship of the exploiters with the dictatorship of the exploited'.[18] He considered the Moscow trials not an internal affair, but an international one, since 'the fate of the world proletariat' was tied to the Stalinist regime. Finally, echoing the classic analogy between Jacobinism and Bolshevism, Lussu conceded that Stalin, 'for all his faults', represented 'the Soviet revolution' – albeit in the role of Robespierre, rather than that of Napoleon Bonaparte.[19]

In 1937–38, the Soviet Union appeared to be, and in fact was, the only geopolitical pole around which a broad antifascist alliance could be formed in Europe. Despite harbouring strong reservations about Stalin's dictatorship, GL could not help but combine its project of revolutionary antifascist action (whether or not such action involved a formal agreement with the communists) with a pro-Soviet stance. However, the group's ideas about the relationship between the 'Russian Revolution', the Soviet Union, and the Stalinist regime, and between socialism, communism, and democracy increasingly diverged. Lussu and Trentin argued that these concepts, despite their dissimilarity, formed part of a continuum. Garosci and Venturi, in many ways inspired by the French historian Halévy, thought otherwise. The dialogue between Rosselli and Halévy had intensified during the latter phase of their lives (both died in 1937), despite their growing differences on the prospect of revolution and the assessment of socialism in Europe. In his lecture on 'L'ère des tyrannies' delivered at the Société Française de Philosophie (Paris) on 28 November 1936, Halévy expressed some perplexity over the likelihood of a 'liberal socialism' that 'aimed to speak the language of both Gladstone and Lenin at one and the

---

18   F. [Emilio Lussu], 'Il plebiscito nella Repubblica Sovietica', *GL*, 24 December 1937.

19   F. [Emilio Lussu], 'Il processo di Mosca', *GL*, 11 March 1938.

same time'.[20] Accordingly, he started with a general outline of the history of European socialism in order to decipher the main features of the post-1914 era, which, he held, was characterized by Bolshevik, Fascist, and Nazi tyranny.[21] This meditation on the era of tyranny suggested that socialism was characterized by a contradiction between an authoritarian, organizational drive and a liberating, democratic trend. At the same time, the lecture also pointed to the inclusion of the fascist enemy in the same socialist family to which GL felt it belonged (while indicating the critical differences between the two). Fascism here took on two meanings. In the broadest sense, it was a method (common to both Lenin and Mussolini) by which 'a group of armed men animated by a common faith decided to be the state': fascism was thus identified with 'Sovietism'. In a more specific sense, fascism was 'a kind of counter-socialism' (or 'corporatism') that Halévy was prepared to take 'more seriously than was generally the case in antifascist circles'. However, the French historian underlined the fundamental difference between the tyrannies in question: unlike the powers in Moscow, those in Berlin and Rome were promising a new war that would lead to the 'generalization of tyranny'.[22]

This lecture was published posthumously in 1938 in the essay collection of the same name, L'ère des tyrannies. Garosci's review of Halévy's work acknowledged its importance by retracing his analysis of 'the problem of the origins of the totalitarian states that seem to characterize the modern epoch'. Garosci pointed out that 'socialist authoritarianism' was the product of 'aspiring to a final stage of humanity', while at the same time the result of 'bringing the entire complex historical world down to economics'.[23] Garosci reproached Halévy for conflating history and politics, and

---

20   Élie Halévy, 'L'ère des tyrannies', in L'ère des tyrannies. Études sur le socialisme et la guerre, Paris: Gallimard, 1990, 246–7. For a more detailed analysis, see Marco Bresciani, 'Socialismo, antifascismo e tirannie. Note sull'amicizia tra Carlo Rosselli e Élie Halévy', Studi storici 53, no. 3, 2012, 615–44.

21   See Michele Battini, Utopia e tirannide. Scavi nell'archivio Halévy, Turin: Bollati Boringhieri, 2011, and Marco Bresciani, 'Entre curiosité et anxiété: Élie Halévy, la politique et l'histoire', in Vincent Duclert and Marie Scot (eds), Œuvres complètes de Élie Halévy. Etudes, Paris: Les Belles Lettres, 2018, 111–27.

22   Halévy, 'L'ère des tyrannies', 215, 227, 245–6.

23   Mag. [Aldo Garosci], 'Inventario. Alle origini ideali del socialismo', GL, 4 March 1938.

theory and reality, in his 1936 lecture; however, Garosci's own approach was no less politically charged. Indeed, the history of European socialism had been characterized by its inherent ambivalence between emancipation and organization – a persistent ambivalence that was once again challenging the very definition of politics at that time. Following Halévy's historical understanding, Garosci recognized the main feature of GL as being its 'rejection of proletarian totalitarianism', its 'denial of finalism' and its 'socialism that is not merely federalist but also pluralist'.[24] While granting that GL thus ran the risk of 'operating on a non-political and metapolitical level', he argued that the crisis of European society called for a 'return to the ideal sources of politics'.[25] These were very different words from those of 1934–35. Back then, Garosci had argued bitterly with Caffi and Chiaromonte, claiming the primacy of political action along the lines of Rosselli, and prompting the 'gang' to resign from GL in early 1936. The traumatic Spanish experience, the death of GL's leader, the debate on socialism and its ambivalences, and the reflection on tyrannies encouraged by Halévy had moved Garosci in a completely different direction.

The critical debate on Marxism together with the pursuit of a 'different' socialism were closely interwoven with the question of the political and social character of the Soviet Union and its relationship to the European revolutionary tradition. In the cultural climate of the Popular Fronts, Venturi had embedded the said pursuit of a new socialism in the national ground, drawing inspiration from Rosselli, who had taken his cue from the socialist defeat of 1919–22. After his stay in Leningrad in late 1936 and early 1937, the young historian from Turin critically engaged with communism, repeatedly making a connection with his studies of the eighteenth century. Venturi made the acquaintance of certain 'heretical' communists, such as the French-Lithuanian revolutionary Charles Rappoport and the French sociologist Georges Friedmann; he read and reviewed some of the most important works of anti-Stalinist literature by ex-communists circulating in Paris at the time, such as Ante Ciliga's *The Russian Enigma*, Yvon's *L'URSS telle qu'elle est*,

---

24   A. Magrini [Aldo Garosci], 'La carta ideologica di "Giustizia e Libertà" ', *Problemi della rivoluzione italiana* 6, September 1938, 15–21.

25   Letter from Aldo Garosci to Fernando Schiavetti, 15 November [1938], in Marina Tesoro, 'Per una società liberalsocialista. Due lettere inedite di Aldo Garosci (ottobre-novembre 1938)', in Sandro Rogari (ed.), *Partiti e movimenti tra otto e novecento. Studi in onore di Luigi Lotti*, Florence: Centro editoriale toscano, 2004, 728.

and Friedmann's *De la Sainte Russie à l'URSS*. However, he ignored the Trotskyist writer Boris Souvarine's seminal biography of Stalin, published in 1935: it was probably considered excessively critical by those who wanted to understand how far rejection of the Soviet experiment could go without abandoning a socialist perspective altogether. In fact, 'the significant struggle of those of a communist faith to come to terms with the reality of Russia', which helped to redefine 'those theories and sentiments that had made them rebels or critics of the bourgeois world', led to a more general reflection on the theory and history of socialist and revolutionary movements. Like the Yugoslav politician and writer Ciliga, who had become an anti-Stalinist through his Gulag experience, Venturi opposed 'the increasing identification of the revolutionary idea with the party, with the state organization, with the apparatus of power' and rejected 'the idea of proletarian consciousness being represented by a single organization possessing the absolute, totalitarian truth'. Venturi, however, primarily shared the reflections of Yvon (Robert Guiheneuf), a former communist worker who had lived in the motherland of socialism for eleven years before publishing a rather negative account of the USSR in *La Révolution prolétarienne*, the revolutionary syndicalist magazine established by Pierre Monatte in 1925. Rereading Yvon, Venturi saw the Soviet experiment as more indebted to Enlightenment, Saint-Simonianism, and positivism than to Marxism. 'The present elite justifies itself not only as representing the consciousness of the proletariat, but also (and increasingly in recent years) as the technical leadership, the leadership of the "knowers" '. Despite Yvon's strong criticism of the Soviet experiment, Venturi explained, 'the problem of technology in power, of the negation of politics for economics' remained: on the one hand, politics was objectively subordinated to technology; on the other, it was reborn as a 'fundamental negation of politics' itself, not only within the party but also through social conflict.[26] This dilemma, in turn, pointed to the 'anti-historical, "totalitarian" (Élie Halévy would say "tyrannical") aspect of so much socialism'.[27]

The primacy of economics over politics was a distinctive feature of Stalinist totalitarianism, Venturi argued at the time. This conviction,

---

26 Gianfranchi [Franco Venturi], 'Tre libri . . . sull'U.R.S.S.', *GL*, 29 April 1938.
27 Gianfranchi [Franco Venturi], 'P. Leroux, socialista romantico', *GL*, 25 November 1938.

however, was at odds with a new leftist literature – from Trotsky to Victor Serge, from Bruno Rizzi to James Burnham – that emphasized the pathological dimension of the Soviet bureaucracy. From 1936 onward, Trotsky's *The Revolution Betrayed* provided the cue for criticizing the bureaucratic degeneration of the USSR, without thereby making the bureaucracy a class in its own right, the new social basis of Soviet power. The USSR remained a 'workers' state', albeit a 'degenerate' one. In a departure from Trotsky, other libertarian-inspired anti-Stalinists, drawing on the Leninist thesis of 'state capitalism', recognized the now complete autonomy of the bureaucratic class and its absolute rule over Soviet society. While this view questioned the possibility of a revolutionary transformation of Stalin's regime, the 'bureaucratic collectivist' nature of the Soviet Union, compared to other realities (from Hitler's Germany to Mussolini's Italy, from Kemal's Turkey to Roosevelt's America), ultimately embodied a global trend.[28] On the other hand, unorthodox Marxists like Otto Bauer, Rudolf Hilferding, Franz Borkenau, or Franz Neumann reflected on the new political phenomena of 'totalitarianism'. Starting from the categories of imperialism, Bonapartism, and fascism, they combined them with the theory of 'finance capital' (*Finanzkapitalismus*), pointed out by Hilferding, and the perspective of the 'primacy of the political', elaborated by the Frankfurt Institute for Social Research. Notably, in the late 1930s, the Austro-Marxist and German Social Democrat Hilferding moved beyond the 'state capitalism' thesis to assess the 'totalitarian' character of the Soviet system, in which the political elite used the bureaucracy to create 'a totalitarian state economy'. In Hilferding's mind, the 'unrestrained political absolutism' and the 'controlled character' of the economy established the 'unprecedented primacy' of politics in the Soviet Union, comparable to that of Fascist Italy or Nazi Germany.[29] Venturi thus did not abandon the critical engagement

---

28   Bruno Rizzi, *La bureaucratisation du monde*, Paris: Les presses modernes, 1939; James Burnham, *The Managerial Revolution, or, What Is Happening in the World Now*, New York: John Day Co., 1941. For a comprehensive and still valuable analysis see Alfredo Salsano, *Ingegneri e politici. Dalla razionalizzazione alla 'rivoluzione manageriale'*, Turin: Einaudi, 1987.

29   See in general William David Jones, *The Lost Debate: German Socialist Intellectuals and Totalitarianism*, Chicago: University of Illinois Press, 1999, and most recently Nicholas Devlin, 'Hannah Arendt and the Marxist Theories of Totalitarianism', *Modern Intellectual History* 20, 2023, 247–69. See also André

with 'Marxist' thought altogether, although he recognized its analytical and political limitations insofar as it was unable to understand the overall development of European history and to cope with its series of repeated, cataclysmic defeats – from 1848 to 1914, and from 1922 to 1933.[30]

The theoretical and historical problems of the unity of the international workers' movement and of the elaboration of a political culture capable of overcoming the previous rifts, were at the centre of Venturi and Garosci's discussion, from 1938 on, with Leo Weiczen (later Valiani), a militant, albeit heterodox, communist at the time. In his autobiographical account, *Tutte le strade conducono a Roma* (1947), Valiani had this to say: 'What fascinated me about "Giustizia e Libertà" was its intellectual audacity, its attempt to reconcile, in a superior synthesis, Marxism and the labour movement with the great liberal philosophy of the nineteenth century.'[31] In Paris, Garosci and Venturi discussed a manuscript on the history of Hungary that Weiczen was writing in 1939.[32] Weiczen was born in Fiume (then part of the Kingdom of Hungary) into a secularized German-speaking Jewish family from Brčko in Bosnia, with roots in the vast lands of the Austro-Hungarian Empire. His upbringing was shaped by the cosmopolitan and multicultural Upper Adriatic region in the early twentieth century. Young Leo consciously decided to become Italian, due to his early political interests developed in the 1920s. Weiczen's uncle, Wilhelm

---

Liebich, 'Marxism and Totalitarianism: Rudolf Hilferding and the Mensheviks', occasional paper presented at the George Kennan Institute for Advanced Russian Studies, 18 February 1986, Woodrow Wilson International Center for Scholars, 1987, wilsoncenter.org

30   Gianfranchi [Franco Venturi], 'Inventario marxista', *GL*, 21 April 1939. This was the review of Boris I. Nicolaevsky and Otto Maenchen-Helfen, *Karl Marx*, Paris: Gallimard, 1938; Lucien Laurat, *Le marxisme en faillite? Du marxisme de Marx au marxisme d'aujourd'hui*, Paris: Éditions Pierre Tisne, 1939; Victor Serge, 'Puissance et Limites du Marxisme', *Masses*, March 1939.

31   Leo Valiani, *Tutte le strade conducono a Roma*, Bologna: Il Mulino, 1995 (1947), 83.

32   Angelo Ara, 'Leo Valiani uomo della Mitteleuropa', in *Trieste, Austria, Impero*, Milan: Garzanti, 2009, 564–5. This history of Hungary has never been published as such, but was the basis for a major work published in 1966 (see the English translation: Leo Valiani, *The End of Austria-Hungary*, New York: Knopf, 1973, alongside Laurence Cole, 'L'opera di Leo Valiani *La dissoluzione dell'Austria-Ungheria* nel suo contesto storiografico', *Studi trentini. Storia* 96, no. 2, 2017, 489–508).

Ippen, an Austrian socialist living in Czernowitz in Bukovina (which fell to Romania in 1918–19), had undoubtedly exerted an important influence on the young man's socialist ideas. After joining the Communist Party, Weiczen was arrested in Fiume in 1928 and detained in the prisons of Civitavecchia and Lucca, where he received guidance from Pietro Secchia and Umberto Terracini. Following his release in 1936, he went to Paris and under the pseudonym Paul Chevalier he began to contribute clandestinely to the communist dissident magazines *Que faire?* and *Le drapeau rouge*. The former publication had been set up by André Ferrat, a former politburo member of the French Communist Party, from which he had just been expelled together with the Pole George Kagan, the Spaniard José A. Echeverría, who later died in combat in Madrid, and the Austrian Kurt Landau, murdered by the Stalinists in Barcelona as a 'Trotskyist'.[33] These milieus, which aspired to a revolutionary, anti-Stalinist, Marxist 'democratic' communism, shared certain similarities with the ideological views of GL, notwithstanding certain other profound differences. Nevertheless, Weiczen did not openly express any concerns and doubts regarding communism at that time.

Between 1937 and 1939, GL was also affected by a completely different and in many ways surprising line of thought that encouraged its members to criticize Marxism and liberalism, develop a comparative analysis of the new tyrannies, and ponder the connection between revolution and religion. Roger Caillois and Georges Bataille, together with Michel Leiris, founded an unusual institution called the Collège de Sociologie.[34] The initiative of these two surrealist writers, both of whom were students of the anthropologist Marcel Mauss, stood in stark contrast to Kojève's important series of lectures on Hegel's philosophy. Kojève questioned the meaning and purpose of history embodied in a universal, homogeneous state

---

33   See Leo Valiani, *Sessant'anni di avventure e battaglie. Riflessioni e ricordi raccolti da Massimo Pini*, Milan: Rizzoli, 1983, 52–69; Andrea Ricciardi, *Leo Valiani: gli anni della formazione: tra socialismo, comunismo e rivoluzione democratica*, Milan: Franco Angeli, 2007, alongside Guido Franzinetti, 'Leo Weiczen: Communist, Democratic Communist, Revolutionary Democrat', *Časopis za povijest Zapadne Hrvatske/West Croatian History Journal* 10, 2015, 39–53.

34   See Dennis Hollier (ed.), *The College of Sociology, 1937–1939*, Minneapolis: University of Minnesota Press, 1988.

implicitly identified with Stalin's Soviet Union.[35] The Collège meetings, held in the back room of a bookstore in the Latin Quarter, analysed and discussed the myths and rituals that totalitarian movements adopted in order to attach a new communal and religious meaning to a decayed, desacralized contemporary society. Some of those present, such as Walter Benjamin, accused the Collège discussions of clouding any judgement of the Fascist and Nazi experiments with a veil of ambiguity.[36] The issues raised by the Collège were central to the reflections of Carlo Levi, Caffi, and Chiaromonte, even though the three do not appear to have participated directly in its meetings. Carlo Levi wrote his essay *Fear of Freedom* between September and December 1939, on the Breton coast of La Baule, though it would not be published until after the war. In this work Levi shed unusual light on the 'Idol State', understood as a 'sign both of the need for true human relationships and of the inability to establish them freely – of the sacred nature of these relationships and of the inability to differentiate them without rendering them barren'.[37] Fear as the basis of the political sphere, and sanctity as the basis of authority, framed a reflection that had come to Levi's mind during his confinement in Southern Italy (Lucania). Between 1943 and 1944, he returned to Florence, 'closed in one room, in a world apart', and he wrote about 'that other world, hedged in by custom and sorrow, cut off from History and the State'. His well-known novel *Christ Stopped at Eboli* explores the conflict between the peasants and the so-called 'luigini', the latter being a literary and anthropological representation of the mysterious and overarching power of the state. The reflections on the 'Southern question' offered since the early 1920s by Salvemini, Guido Dorso, and Giustino Fortunato in Gobetti's milieu, led Carlo Levi

---

35   See Kojève, *Introduction to the Reading of Hegel*.

36   See Carlo Ginzburg, 'Mitologia germanica e nazismo. Su un vecchio libro di Georges Dumézil', in *Miti emblemi spie*, Turin: Einaudi, 1986, 210–38; Carlo Ginzburg, 'Sacred Sociology: A Few Reflections on the Collège de Sociologie', in *Secularism and Its Ambiguities: Four Case Studies*, New York: Central European University Press, 2023, 41–67; Michele Battini, 'L'assenza del Sacro come patologia', in Maria Donzelli and Regina Pozzi (eds), *Patologie della politica: crisi e critica della democrazia tra Otto e Novecento*, Rome: Donzelli, 2003, 381–90.

37   Carlo Levi, 'Paura della libertà', in *Scritti politici*, ed. David Bidussa, Turin: Einaudi, 2001, 137, with an introduction by David Bidussa, 'Prima di Eboli. La riflessione civile e politica di Carlo Levi negli anni del fascismo e dei totalitarismi', V–XXXIII.

to become a compassionate, impartial observer of the peasantry of southern Italy. He recalled how the peasants in that land lived 'without comfort or solace, where the peasant lives out his motionless civilization on barren ground in remote poverty, and in the presence of death'.[38] During his confinement in Lucania, Levi had mused on the simultaneous presence and contrast of the cyclical rhythms of rural life and the linear time of industrial society, the 'primitive mentality' of 'participatory logic' and the Western mentality of 'intellectual logic'.

Although using different styles and means, *Fear of Freedom* and *Christ Stopped at Eboli* both aimed to understand the sacred and sacrificial dimensions of power, politics, and the state. Carlo Levi engaged (mostly implicitly) with a polyphonic European culture of crisis comprising the works of Ortega y Gasset, Carl Gustav Jung, James G. Frazer, Lucien Lévy-Bruhl, Oswald Spengler, Johann Huizinga, Roger Caillois, and Georges Bataille. Even Levi, who, in his professed attachment to the Gobettian tradition, had cultivated a profound 'moralism' in contrast to the 'other Italy', that of Fascism, eventually developed a very different, inherently 'anti-moralist' awareness of the European crisis. Carlo Levi was in contact with Caffi and Chiaromonte, who between 1938 and 1939 had resumed their interaction with GL after this had been abruptly interrupted in 1936; and they had thus also rekindled relations with Garosci and Venturi. In a manifesto entitled 'Le vent d'hiver', published in the literary magazine *Nouvelle Revue Française* in July 1938, Caillois directly addressed the main themes dear to the Collège de Sociologie. Caillois wanted to restore the sacred and organic unity of society by creating secret sects, monastic orders of knights, and paramilitary forces based on the sociological model of the closed, disciplined, militant community.[39]

In an unpublished note, Caffi built on the dual dynamics of 'spiritual decomposition and technical reinforcement' ensuing from the European crisis of 1914–22. In his view, Caillois had taken the ambiguity of this context shaped by World War I and used it for the purposes of a planned authoritarian reorganization of social bonds. In this way, Caillois had

---

38   Carlo Levi, *Christ Stopped at Eboli: The Story of a Year*, New York: Time, 1964 (1945), 1.

39   R. C. [Roger Caillois], 'The Winter Wind', in Hollier, *The College of Sociology*, 32–42.

turned a legitimate rebellion against the existing order into the *raison d'être* of paramilitary forces designed to exercise sacral power over the masses 'along the lines of the Grand Inquisitor'. Caffi, by contrast, held that the fundamental agents of social renewal were small groups (intellectual circles, cultural associations, philosophical schools, religious orders, secret sects of initiates), and that these were very different from the *minorités agissantes* such as Fascism and Bolshevism. Caffi therefore warned against the temptation, still widespread among political revolutionary circles, to 'identify "intransigent" intellectual demands with an "intransigent" way of regulating interpersonal relations – or even of "organizing" society – and to unite the two forms of intransigence under the label of "orthodoxy" '.[40] No less critical of Caillois was Chiaromonte, who rejected the 'rather confusing image of "military" and monastic formations existing at one and the same time'. The idea of the restricted community, which Caillois saw as an instrument for the realization of a 'sacred sociology', was reminiscent of the revolutionary syndicalist vision of *minorités agissantes* and the Marxist-Leninist conception of the 'revolutionary vanguard', which Chiaromonte saw as leading, one and all, to 'political tyranny'. Nevertheless, Chiaromonte claimed that the revolutionary party was superior to the *minorités agissantes* for two reasons: first, because the revolutionary party had been – and, despite everything, still seemed to be – 'the only serious enterprise of social transformation in modern times'; second, because the revolutionary idea represented 'the most valid criterion for an "election of the best" – and thus for the formation of an aristocracy in the original sense of the word'.[41]

Caffi and Chiaromonte were attracted to Bataille and Caillois's idea of a 'sacred sociology', but they rejected its hierarchical, authoritarian tendencies, which echoed the legacy of the Great War and the Russian Revolutions. In a letter to Halévy following his lecture on the age of tyranny, Marcel Mauss, who had been Caillois and Bataille's mentor, drew on the study of ancient 'societies of men' to try and understand the *minorités agissantes*, and

---

40   Andrea Caffi, *À propos d'un 'Collège de Sociologie'* (*Nouvelle Revue Française, août 1938*), Fondo Andrea Caffi, Subfondo Carte Caffi provenienti dall'archivio di Nicola Chiaromonte, Serie I: manoscritti e appunti, Associazione Nazionale per gli Interessi nel Mezzogiorno d'Italia (Rome).

41   Nicola Chiaromonte, *Sur le 'fait social', le mythe et le sacré* [1938?], Box 5, Folder 204, Series II. Writings, Manuscripts, Chiaromonte Papers, Beinecke Library (New Haven, CT).

insisted on the 'fundamental fact of secrecy and conspiracy'. Mauss, an anthropologist with socialist sympathies, considered that a mysterious and archaic form of power manifested itself in Fascism and Bolshevism, and that this power was interlinked with certain long-standing social and cultural phenomena.[42] Raymond Aron, who had attended Halévy's lecture 'L'ère des tyrannies' and who, in turn, lectured on 'États démocratiques et États totalitaires' at the Société française de philosophie on 17 June 1939, reflected on the role that primitive elites play in the emergence of modern totalitarianisms, such as Fascism and National Socialism.[43] Aron supplemented Pareto's theoretical considerations with the historical analysis set out in *The Revolution of Nihilism* by Hermann Rauschning, published in German in 1938 and then in French in 1939. Rauschning, the Danzig senate president between 1933 and 1934, was a radical conservative politician, then close to Nazism but ultimately critical of Hitler's regime. The French philosopher and sociologist Aron, who had met Rosselli during a visit to Halévy's house in April 1937 and had been a guest of Rauschning in 1938–39, was already in contact with Chiaromonte and Venturi. Through them, his proposals for analysis and interpretation began to circulate among GL's circles, at a stage when the comparison between the two totalitarian regimes was discussed more openly than it had been in the Popular Front era.[44] Rauschning's work – which *GL* reviewed as being a 'profound, insightful and unsparing

---

42   Letter from Mauss to Halévy, in Halévy, *L'ère des tyrannies*, 230–1. See also Marcel Mauss, 'Appréciation sociologique du bolchévisme', *Revue de Metaphysique et de Morale* 31, 1924, 103–32. On the position of Mauss with respect to the Bolshevik experience and its connections with his reflection on the notion of gift, see Michele Battini, 'Gli studi del 1924–1925. Etica sociale e forme di scambio in società selvagge, arcaiche e nella società sovietica', in Riccardo Di Donato (ed.), *Gli uomini, le società, le civiltà. Uno studio intorno all'opera di Marcel Mauss*, Pisa: ETS, 1985, 61–82, and Carlo Ginzburg, 'Lectures de Mauss. L'essai sur le don', Conférence M. Bloch (juin 2010), *Annales* 65–6, November–December 2010, 1313–14.

43   Raymond Aron, 'L'ère des tyrannies d'Élie Halévy', *Revue de Métaphysique et de Morale* 46, April 1939, 283–307, and 'États démocratiques et États totalitaires', *Bulletin de la Société Française de Philosophie* 2, 1946, 41–2, in *Machiavel et les tyrannies modernes*, Paris: Éditions de Fallois, 1993, 165–83. For an analysis of Aron's antitotalitarian stance, see Iain Stewart, *Raymond Aron and Liberal Thought in the Twentieth Century*, Cambridge: Cambridge University Press, 2020.

44   Raymond Aron, *Le Spectateur engagé. Entretiens avec J.-L. Missika et D. Wolton*, Paris: Julliard, 1981, 59–60; Raymond Aron, *Mémoires*, Paris: Julliard, 1983, 147–8.

analysis' – illuminated the pathological, irrational, and destructive dynamics of National Socialism, led by a new and brutal elite that failed to follow
any logic of social class.[45] The Egyptian-born journalist and writer, Paolo
Vittorelli, a clandestine socialist activist who met Rosselli and Garosci in
Paris in 1937, was also engrossed by these considerations. He subsequently
established contacts mainly with Garosci and signed articles for GL, before
setting up a new branch of GL in Egypt in 1940. According to Vittorelli,
Chiaromonte, Garosci and Carlo Levi were often guests at Venturi's house in
Paris in the winter evenings of 1939–40, when their main topics of discus-
sion were Caillois and Rauschning.[46]

   This unique cultural constellation, which transcended the strict political
divide separating fascism from antifascism, confronted GL with the inherent
ambiguity and elusive ubiquity of the conflicts playing out in contemporary
Europe. In particular, the encounter with the Collège led GL to reflect on the
religious dimension that emanated from Durkheim's sociological school but
was expressed in politically ambivalent forms in the late 1930s. At the same
time, the Collège represented the most extreme variant of a broad tendency in
French 'non-conformist' culture, namely the attempt to face fascism on its
own ground and to defeat it with its own weapons. However, this attempt,
which was essentially based on mimetic strategies, fed a dangerous tendency
to identify with the enemy.[47] On the other hand, GL's members were clear who
the enemy was, and clearly distinguished themselves from it, even if they
deemed that much could be learned from that same enemy. Without relin-
quishing their concerns regarding the ethical and political options available to
antifascism, their readings and discussions recognized the extent to which
socialist perspectives or even revolutionary aspirations crossed the sharpest
ideological lines dividing the various regimes of Mussolini, Hitler, and Stalin.
Garosci, for example, unabashedly acknowledged the 'totalitarian element'
that appeared to be a constant in socialism, and was 'implicit in the modern
world'. Rather than being reduced to 'state capitalism', 'fascist socialism' in fact

   45   Fernando Schiavetti, 'Terrore dinanzi all'abisso', GL, 26 August 1939. For the
biography of Schiavetti, see Stéfanie Prezioso, Itinerario di un figlio del 1914: Fernando
Schiavetti dalla trincea all'antifascismo, Manduria: Lacaita, 2004.
   46   Paolo Vittorelli, L'età della tempesta, Milan: Rizzoli, 1981, 192–3.
   47   See Denis Hollier, 'Foreword: Collège', in Hollier, The College of Sociology,
VIII–XXIX; Denis Hollier, 'On Equivocation (Between Literature and Politics)',
October 55, Winter 1990, 3–22.

crystallized certain fundamental drives towards the disintegration of social strata marginalized by industrial development, towards the fragmentation of the global economy into autarchic, self-referential imperial spaces, and towards mass mobilization in vast organizational apparatuses aimed at conquering Europe and the world. Consequently, these changes in the relations between the state and civil society, between politics and economics, needed to be urgently combined with new forms of direct democracy. However, Garosci was now more aware than he had been, when first writing on socialism in 1934, that the myth of the workers' councils could imply a 'totalitarian', 'finalist and millenarian' character, and could reappear at any time and reinforce the political and social dynamics of tyrannies.[48]

The Ribbentrop–Molotov Pact, signed in August 1939, offered the clearest and most dramatic evidence of the convergence, indeed the interaction and superimposition, of Hitler and Stalin's totalitarian regimes. Venturi was then working on a history of communism and the Enlightenment, while waiting to have his dissertation on Francesco Dalmazzo Vasco evaluated, but, although this was scheduled for June 1940, due to the Nazi invasion it never happened. In addressing the historical problem of the 'vital core' of communism and its 'fundamental function' in the modern world, he developed a critique of the link between the labour movement and communism, while rejecting the Marxist distinction between utopian socialism and scientific socialism (or communism). Venturi saw nineteenth-century socialism as the 'shadow and negation' of the Enlightenment. According to Venturi, the political vocabulary of Rousseau (the 'social pact', the 'general will'), expressed in an 'absolute and totalitarian form' by the 'most characteristically communist' writers (such as Mably and Morelly), transformed the 'moralist revolt' of the Enlightenment into a 'new political morality based on democracy and justice'. On the basis of Halévy's research, or rather, on the basis of a specific rereading of this, Venturi concluded that 'democracy and communism' shared 'a common origin' in Enlightenment culture, which was also reflected 'in their further developments'.[49] In a gloomier, briefer comment

48   Magrini [Aldo Garosci], 'Socialismo e autonomismo', *GL*, 12 May 1939.
49   Franco Venturi, 'Manoscritto del 1939', in Manuela Albertone et al. (eds), *Franco Venturi. Comunismo e socialismo. Storia di un'idea*, Turin: University of Turin, 2014, 23–38.

in April 1940 concerning the 'origins and modern forces of totalitarianism', Venturi stated that communism, socialism, and anarchism were 'all different forms of the same force'. Fascism, which 'was established in opposition to them and developed like their shadow', had revealed the 'germ of totalitarianism' that these different forces contained.[50]

The reading and discussion of the works of Halévy, Mauss, Bataille, Caillois, Aron, and Rauschning brought about a significant change in Venturi and Garosci's viewpoint. The analysis of tyrannies made it possible to come to grips with Stalinist Communism, which, to their minds, differed from Soviet Socialism, and thus to affirm GL's revolutionary position. It helped frame the problem of Fascism and Nazism within a comprehensive view of the history of socialism and its transformations after the Great War and the Russian Revolutions. The perspective of the *minorités agissantes*, already outlined by Sorel, and subsequently expressed in various ways, indicated a means of social and political transformation linking the problem of tyranny to that of revolution. The interpretive scheme of the 'revolution of nihilism' made it possible to perceive the revolutionary character of National Socialism (and Fascism), and at the same time to recognize the radically destructive nature of this form of revolution compared to other, constructive revolutionary approaches, such as that of GL. GL's activists, far from being representatives of modern organized politics, oscillated between being attracted to, or repulsed by, politics. On the one hand, politics – in the specific dictatorial forms it took under the Fascist regime – represented the terrible obsession of that time. On the other hand, politics provided a set of tools for responding to the general crisis of Europe as encapsulated and exemplified by Fascism.

Nations, Europes, and Empires

The Italian war in Ethiopia (October 1935–May 1936), the German occupation of the Rhineland (March 1936) and the Spanish Civil War (1936–39) fractured and reconfigured the European political realm and the international balance of power, propagating ideas of revision of the

---

50   'Il nuovo quaderno di "Giustizia e Libertà". N. 1 – Serie di guerra', *GL*, 22 April 1940.

post-1919 order, deepening the threat of a new continental war, and push-ing Fascist Italy towards Nazi Germany. At the same time, the liberal and parliamentary institutions surviving in Western countries were subject to growing uncertainty and instability, furthering the perception of a 'crisis of democracy' despite the counterstrategies of the Popular Fronts, or perhaps because of their failures and contradictions.[51] The condition of exile allowed GL writers to closely observe this process of challenge to the democratic governments from within and from without. In general, Rosselli understood fascism as 'the most consistent and impressive effort ever made to transform a civil society into a warrior society'; he further noted that 'the necessities of war preparation' favoured the 'development of fascist germs' even under democratic conditions. 'One takes up arms to defend oneself against the fascist attack,' Rosselli wrote. 'But, by arming oneself, one becomes fascist.'[52] According to the GL leader, the looming 'totalitarian war' demanded the implementation of measures curtailing individual liberties, limiting opportunities for collective action, strength-ening the powers of the executive at the expense of the legislature, and expanding police powers. In a perverse cycle, the conditions for a totalitar-ian shift in democratic institutions were in turn created under the impetus of peace-threatening fascist movements and regimes. In Rosselli's view, an unconscious fascistization of Europe paradoxically might grow – and in some ways did grow – out of antifascism itself, which was in danger of becoming aligned with its declared enemy.

From July 1936 onwards, for more than a year, the fluctuating events of the Spanish Civil War had focused the attention of GL and European public opinion in general. At that stage, the polarizing force fields of fascism and antifascism revolved around the struggle between the Spanish Republican forces and the insurgents. Then, starting in mid-1937, with the political split of the Republican front and the apparent stabilization of the military conflict, the fierce passions that had initially flared up finally dissipated. The former GL activist Renzo Giua was still fighting in Spain,

---

51 See Marco Bresciani (ed.), *Conservatives and Right Radicals in Interwar Europe*, London: Routledge, 2021, and Kurt Weyland, *Assault on Democracy: Communism, Fascism, and Authoritarianism During the Interwar Years*, Cambridge: Cambridge University Press, 2021.

52 [Carlo Rosselli,] 'Pacifismo fautore di guerra', *GL*, 5 March 1937.

where he had rushed to the defence of the Republic and joined the anarchist column of Durruti in August 1936. Wounded in combat several times, he had been sent to the officers' school of the International Brigades in Albacete. In May 1937, he had been assigned to the Garibaldi battalion of the 12th International Brigade; in October he had been appointed captain and given command of the 3rd company of the Garibaldi Brigade. Shot during an offensive at Zalamea de la Serena on the Extremadura Front on 17 February 1938, Giua died one month later. In his obituary, Garosci recalled Giua's 'total faith in the value of one's deeds' and a 'heroism' that rose 'above politics, indeed above reality itself'.[53]

Over the course of 1938, the international political dynamics shifted from the Spanish peninsula, still racked by civil war, to Central Europe. Nazi Germany's diplomatic and military actions, designed to challenge the Versailles Treaty, led to the annexation of Austria in March 1938 and the annexation of the Sudetenland the following September. The Munich Agreement, signed with Hitler in September 1938 by the British and French governments thanks to Mussolini's mediation, prevented any general conflict for the time being, but also sanctioned the collapse of the Paris order. The conquest of Prague and the breakup of Czechoslovakia in March 1939 were the logical culmination of that process. In that context, GL saw Fascism and Nazism, unlike traditional dictatorships, as being constituted by activism and voluntarism: 'Fascisms act before they theorize; democracies persist in theorizing and refrain from action.'[54] The two regimes, 'animated by a frenetic dynamism of subversion', 'as a result of the twin blackmail threat of general conflagration and civil war', tended to accelerate the process of fascistization, not only in Europe but also at the global level.[55] GL wanted democracy to regain the 'faith' which ('though consisting of violence and the will to rule') had driven fascism, and which the French and British governments, with their readiness to disarm in the face of Hitler and Mussolini's aggression, had shown that they had lost.[56] As appeasement loomed, even before the Munich Agreement was signed,

53   Magrini [Aldo Garosci], 'Un eroe della nuova generazione: Renzo Giua. Ricordi', *GL*, 18 March 1938.

54   'L'"Aventino europeo"', *GL*, 7 January 1938.

55   'Le diplomazie e la realtà', *GL*, 11 February 1938.

56   'La nuova era di pace', *GL*, 4 November 1938.

the weekly *GL* denounced 'the moments of denials'. The gloomy prewar mood in Paris, darkened by the curfew, is reflected in Garosci's memoirs:

> Fear had made itself felt not only through distant wars (like that in Spain, which we had never before experienced in peacetime, whether taking part in it or not), but also through that which loomed over the city and civilization we knew, where darkness had ruled in the time of fear; and a kind of dark and distant solitude had returned, with the stars twinkling above the great dark canyons into which night had transformed the streets and avenues of Paris.[57]

This was a partially retrospective reconstruction. In Garosci's mind, however, it was clear that 'a conflict unleashed in Europe by the fascist desire for domination' would be 'a historic conflict, the greatest of all time', to which 'the destiny of world civilization' would be tied. Rather than a 'material' struggle between two imperialisms, such a war would constitute a 'moral' struggle between two civilizations, and as such would express 'the essence of an ideological conflict'. If Fascism had set in motion a civil war, it was in order to transform the Fascist war into a 'civil war of liberation'.[58] Garosci argued that the ideal of a 'United States of Europe' could only be achieved 'through revolution in the totalitarian countries'.[59] At that time, Caffi and Chiaromonte were associating above all with reformist socialists like Angelo Tasca, Giuseppe Faravelli, and Giuseppe Emanuele Modigliani. They pursued the reconciliation of antifascism and anti-communism and of Europeanism and pacifism, which in the spring of 1939 proved ever more arduous and ambiguous. In fact, Caffi believed that the imminent global war would unleash an 'orgy of destruction'.[60]

Calosso and Venturi shared the idea that an antifascist patriotism (a form of nationalism, indeed) was necessary to oppose Fascist and Nazi

---

57   Aldo Garosci, *Anni di Torino, anni di Parigi*, ed. Mariolina Bertini, Parma: Nuova Editrice Berti, 2019, 117.

58   'Guerra europea, rivoluzione italiana', *GL*, 31 March 1939.

59   Magrini [Aldo Garosci], 'Politica estera fascista e unità europea', *GL*, 10 February 1939.

60   [Andrea Caffi,] 'Notes', April 1939, Fondo Andrea Caffi, Subfondo Carte Caffi provenienti dall'archivio di N. Chiaromonte, Serie I: manoscritti e appunti, Associazione Nazionale per gli Interessi Mezzogiorno d'Italia (Rome).

imperialism: only a Europe of nations could fight and defeat the Europe of empires. An uncompromising antifascism must therefore appropriate the patriotic tradition of the Risorgimento, in stark contrast to projects for the imperial domination and violent disintegration of nations. This position, derived from reflections on the Fascist war in Ethiopia in 1935, became newly relevant in light of the real prospect of war on the European continent. Hitler's Germany, with its manipulation of German-speaking minorities in East-Central Europe, and Mussolini's Italy, with its forced fascistization of the Slovenian-speaking and Croatian-speaking communities in the northern Adriatic borderlands, constituted 'the decay of civilization'. Fascists aspired to building empires, turning every matter of justice into 'totalitarian violence' and trampling on the very principle of self-determination of the peoples they claimed to represent.[61] Between 1938 and 1939, the expansion of Nazism into Austria and Czechoslovakia led to the destruction of these two post-Habsburg states and subverted the Paris postwar order. It was at this point that Venturi addressed the problem of the 'violent reform of empires in Europe' and the 'return to the forefront of the problem of autonomous nations in a free Europe'. His analysis of this cycle of instability and conflict in Central and Eastern Europe pointed to the enduring impact of the ideas of Bakunin and Mazzini. From a historical perspective, Venturi emphasized the importance of the 'Slavic problem' and hence the role of 'Russia' in the 'great European revival'. Indeed, in Tsarist Russia, more than elsewhere, romanticism had become 'a reaction on the part of the country's traditions against French, revolutionary, and imperial cosmopolitanism'. From this point of view, Bakunin could be considered 'the Mazzini of Russia, the champion of the principle of Slav nationhood in the struggle against Tsarist rule and the Austrian Empire'.[62] Venturi recognized the need to include Bakunin and Mazzini in thinking about the 'European and revolutionary function of the Slavic nations' and considered the 'Slavs' national revolts as parallel and complementary to the Italian one': Mazzini had outlined a strategy in 1848 in which he

---

61   'L'impero antinazionale', *GL*, 9 December 1938. For the rise of the 'fascist empires', see Mark Mazower, *Dark Continent: Europe's Twentieth Century*, London: Allen Lane, 1998, 71–6.

62   Gianfranchi [Franco Venturi], 'Bakunin', *GL*, 24 March 1939. This was a review of Hans-Erich Kaminski, *Michel Bakounine: la vie d'un révolutionnaire*, Paris: Aubier, 1938.

recognized 'the importance of the intellectual and political uprisings that were maturing in Eastern Europe'. In 1939, Venturi denounced the now contradictory relationship between the Fascist (Italian) imperial project and the nationalist movements in Central and Eastern Europe.[63]

In a separate but complementary take, Calosso reiterated his commitment to the legacy of Giovine Italia and Mazzinian thought within a framework centred on the circulation of ideas between France and Italy in the first half of the nineteenth century. Mazzini's Partito d'Azione had been characterized by its emphasis on the role of youth, the importance of local initiatives, the call for unity, and the spontaneity of religious faith. In Calosso's view, GL needed to embrace this legacy of the Risorgimento and adapt it to the present, if it was to respond to the crisis of the nation-state brought about by Fascist imperialism. Strongly rejecting the 'scandal of the old democracy', Mazzini's Giovine Italia had established itself as a 'religious society' that had, via Saint-Simonianism, become the 'most extreme and modern aspect of European socialism'. Accordingly, Calosso believed that generational change – common to both the plan for national democratic emancipation and the design of revolutionary antifascist opposition – was channelled through the use of a symbolic language critical of the abstract and materialistic values of the Enlightenment and the French Revolution.[64]

Although their thinking tended to focus on Italy's relationship with Europe, east and west respectively, Venturi and Calosso sought to recover and appropriate the national-patriotic tradition in an anti-imperial, antifascist key. Both of them having recognized the links between imperialism and racism since 1936, they elaborated further on the subject after the Racial Laws were proclaimed in September 1938. Venturi denounced above all the structural weakness of the concept of the 'Italian race', for constant crossbreeding over the course of history negated the existence of any racial purity. Pointing to the multifaceted history of the Italian peninsula over the centuries – a history that had only recently seen the establishment of the Italian nation-state – Venturi strongly disputed the historical arguments of Fascist racism. The last thousand years of

---

63   G. [Franco Venturi], 'Valore delle nazioni nella lotta contro gli imperi', *GL*, 2 June 1939.

64   Subalpino [Umberto Calosso], 'Momentosa risposta di Mazzini al non intervento democratico', *GL*, 2 December 1938.

'Italian' history, which was primarily an urban history, had been marked
by the 'desire to constitute a civilization' and, since the Risorgimento, by
the 'desire to constitute a nation'. The origins of Italy, a nation more
complex and heterogeneous than any other in Europe, had 'nothing mythical' about them. According to Venturi, the Italian nation had emerged
from 'the desire and dreams of a few, the efforts of modern individuals
receptive to the needs of a modern Europe'. In this sense, any reduction of
Italian history to 'zoology' had to be rejected.[65]

At the same time as Fascist Italy's antisemitic turn, the Munich crisis
clearly indicated the democratic governments' submission to Nazi
Germany's aggression: hence the feeling that the communists and the
Soviet Union were now the only bulwark against complete domination
by the forces of fascism. Convinced of the urgent need to link thought
with action, GL's members intensified their contacts with the Italian
Communists and in particular with the Italian Popular Union, an organization founded in 1937 as part of the Popular Front.[66] However, news of
the pact between Hitler and Stalin, signed by Foreign Ministers
Ribbentrop and Molotov in Moscow on the night of 23 August 1939,
caused consternation and bewilderment among GL's membership. There
was a sense that a significant turning point was fast approaching, even if
the wider military and political consequences of the agreement between
Nazi Germany and the Soviet Union could not yet be foreseen. In
Toulouse, Trentin condemned the USSR for having 'rehabilitated the
worst methods of the old secret diplomacy', but hastened to add that he
did not consider 'legitimate' the 'reversal of the guidelines hitherto
adopted for the orientation of our struggle on the ideological plane'.[67] In
a letter to the committee, Cianca and Garosci stated that 'Russia's absten-
tion from the Antifascist Front' was 'the decay of an ideal' rather than 'a
diplomatic betrayal' which per se could be considered 'provisional'.[68] The

65   Gianfranchi [Franco Venturi], 'La razza italiana o l'italiano allo specchio',
GL, 22 July 1938.
66   See Eric Vial, *L'Union populaire italienne 1937–1940. Une organisation de
masse du Parti communiste italien en exil*, Rome: École Française de Rome, 2007.
67   Letter from Silvio Trentin to GL's central board, 23 August 1939, Fondo
Silvio Trentin, UA 10, scatola 3, cartella 8, Centro Studi Piero Gobetti (Turin).
68   Letter from Mag. [Aldo Garosci] and C. [Alberto Cianca], 28 August 1939,
in Archivio Giustizia e Libertà, Fondo Fernando Schiavetti, busta 4, fascicolo 6, 4/28,

letter's title and editorial line, which shifted the emphasis from Soviet responsibility in signing the pact to the consequences for the antifascist front, were ambivalent, reflecting the conflicting positions of the members of GL's editorial board. The severity with which the Munich Agreement had been denounced was only faintly echoed in the denunciation of the Moscow Pact: in this sense, the emphasis on the provisional nature of Soviet diplomatic decisions was as significant as ever. An anonymous communication of 1 September 1939, however, moved from the negative evaluation of Stalin's regime into a radical reassessment of the social and political character of the Soviet experiment. It argued that GL had 'always accounted for the October Revolution, defended the Soviet Republic, and accepted the Revolution despite all the errors made, from 1917 to 1939'. It now considered the USSR, which was 'complicit in the fascist aggression and the possible triumph of fascism in Europe and the world', to be a 'reactionary and nationalist regime': 'collectivism' had become nothing other than 'state capitalism'.[69]

The international communist world, which in antifascism had discovered an extraordinarily popular and passionate cause, obviously suffered the devastating effects of the Ribbentrop–Molotov Pact even more than GL did. In moving away from the strategies adopted by the Popular Front, which despite their tragic contradictions involved a commitment to isolating and resisting Hitler's Germany, many communists experienced a serious crisis of conscience.[70] For French Communists, as for the international communist émigrés in Paris, the traumatic news of the German–Soviet Pact was compounded by the drama of their banishment and persecution by the French police. Despite their profound disagreements, Leo Weiczen decided not to leave the Communist Party after it had been forced into clandestinity following the signing of the Pact: he wanted to avoid being accused of 'treason' by his fellow communists. Then, at the end of September, he was arrested, detained at Roland Garros stadium, and deported to the Le Vernet prison camp in the Pyrenees. There he met the

---

corrispondenza varia, Istituto Storico Toscano della Resistenza e dell'Età Contemporanea (Florence).

69   'La grande avventura', *GL*, 1 September 1939.

70   In general, see Silvio Pons, *The Global Revolution: A History of International Communism, 1917–1991*, New York: Oxford University Press, 2014, 91–101.

Hungarian-born writer Arthur Koestler, who was preparing to quit the German Communist Party after the Nazi–Soviet Pact, and to complete his literary masterpiece, *Darkness at Noon*, based on the Moscow Trials. Koestler's work, written between January and March 1941, dispelled all remaining illusions about Stalin's regime, and as such it left a lasting impression on Weiczen, who was the first person to read the original German manuscript of the novel.[71]

The summer of 1939, the last before the outbreak of war, was when Venturi realized that Fascism and Nazism were ushering in a new phase of colonization of the European continent, through the building of empires designed to rule over other European nation-states. He perceived the 'formation of totalitarian and tyrannical states in Europe', including Stalin's Soviet Union. According to Venturi, however, it was primarily the Hitler and Mussolini regimes – 'the principal drivers of European civil war' – that were working to destroy the idea of nationhood.[72] During those weeks, *GL*'s editorials described Fascist Italy's ever-dwindling sovereignty as a result of its alliance with Nazi Germany. Through their 'increasingly indis-soluble complicity', the 'two totalitarian polities in Europe' formed the 'anti-European camp': here lay the basis of the 'current European civil war'.[73] The meaning of this category had been inverted: while in 1933–34, faced with the continental spread of fascism, Rosselli had used it to trans-form national antifascism into a Europe-wide phenomenon, by 1939 Venturi believed that the national dimension of revolutionary antifascism needed to be recovered in the face of the European and imperial challenge posed by the alliance between Hitler's Germany and Mussolini's Italy.

In order to determine the roots of the 'contemporary political crisis', Trentin examined the long-term history of the modern state in an essay enti-tled 'Stato-Nazione-Federalismo', written between the autumn of 1939 and

---

71   See Leo Valiani, 'Koestler the Militant', *Encounter* 63, no. 2, July–August 1984, 68–72; Arthur Koestler, *Scum of the Earth*, London: Eland Publishing, 2007; and Michael Scammell, *Arthur Koestler: The Literary and Political Odyssey of a Twentieth-Century Skeptic*, New York: Random House, 2009, 173–202. The original version of Koestler's *Darkness at Noon* has recently been discovered. See Scammel, 'A Different "Darkness at Noon" ', *New York Review of Books* 63/5, 7 April 2016.

72   Gianfranchi [Franco Venturi], 'Emigrazione, problema rivoluzionario', *GL*, 14 July 1939.

73   'Hitler contro l'Italia! L'Italia contro Hitler!', *GL*, 22 April 1940.

the winter of 1940. His interpretation, inspired by Proudhon, saw the Great War as the culmination of the 'monocentric state'. A federalist revolution had to be started to overcome this historical process of the unification of society under state sovereignty, and to re-establish the self-government of individuals and social groups in Europe.[74] During that same period, Trentin wrote the essay 'L'abdicazione della Francia o la fine di un mondo. Note di un sopravvissuto'. These notes recorded at first hand the causes and consequences of the 'staggering catastrophe' that had befallen France in June 1940: they included 'the sophistry and superstition of "security"', 'the immobility of the anachronistic, blissful worship of the past', 'obstinate, contented blindness in the face of increasingly manifest and immediate danger', and 'naive faith in the thaumaturgical virtues of immortal princes'. Accordingly, the republican ruling class had been willing to establish 'a fascist order capable of collaborating with totalitarian regimes destined, in the event of victory, to dominate the continent and bury democracy in Europe'. Nevertheless, Trentin was quick to contrast the 'unitary, monocentric, oppressive state' that had led to Fascism and Nazism with 'the irrepressible need for autonomy as the reagent for dissolving the old state structure, and as the yeast fermenting a new form of collective life'. Trentin saw in the 'people' that refused to 'abdicate' 'the inexorable incubation of a process of French and European resurgence under the invader's lash'.[75]

Trentin's reflections combined a sharp analysis of the crisis of the French Third Republic with his utopian enthusiasm for a 'people' resisting the new totalitarian order and rebelling against Hitler and Mussolini's regimes. His results were mixed. On the one hand, the attribution of sole responsibility for the 1940 defeat to the political choices and cultural sensibilities of the ruling class amounted to the acquittal of French society as a whole. On the other hand, this notion of a 'people' ready to rise up in the name of antifascism contributed to legitimizing numerous, situationally-determined options and decisions for the Resistance – starting with Trentin's own.

---

74   Silvio Trentin, 'Stato-Nazione-Federalismo', in *Federalismo e libertà: scritti teorici, 1935–1943*, ed. Norberto Bobbio, Venice: Marsilio, 1987, 35–231.

75   Silvio Trentin, 'L'abdicazione della Francia o la fine di un mondo. Note di un sopravvissuto', in *Scritti inediti: testimonianze, studi*, ed. Paolo Gobetti, Parma: Guanda, 1972, 107–86 (the manuscript dated back to October 1940).

Exploring the World (from a Prison Cell in Rome)

The Fourth Wing of Rome's Regina Coeli Prison held 'GL's collective group' (as GL itself referred to it), comprising Rossi and Bauer (imprisoned since 1931), and Foa, Mila, and Monti (sentenced in July 1935). During the period from mid-1935 to mid-1939, this group often lived together in the same cell, taking the same hour of exercise, sharing food packages sent by their families, and playing chess together. The prison's detainees continued to feel part of the same group, and their political education and worldview progressed under the harsh conditions of Fascist incarceration. In this sense, the story of Regina Coeli Prison's Fourth Wing constitutes another chapter in the history of GL, even though the prisoners in question were no longer politically active. This story is recounted mainly through the letters sent to family members – subject though they were to censorship and self-censorship – in which their daily chronicles of prison life were characterized by a steadfast resistance to abuses by the authorities (albeit with the occasional capitulation) and by the solidarity of fellow prisoners (despite certain tensions among them). The restless endeavour to escape the watchful eyes of the prison warden and the Ministry of the Interior was accompanied by a no less obsessive desire to reassure relatives on the outside, intensified by the repeated psychological setbacks. Among the many additional problems arising from prison regulations and their strict interpretation by the wardens, which imposed degrading conditions on inmates, the delays in receiving and sending mail were among the most unbearable.

The experience of prison and confinement under Mussolini's regime proved quite different from that of the concentration or labour camps in Hitler's Germany and Stalin's Soviet Union. Alongside arbitrary deprivations and intimidations, prisoners often experienced severe, though not complete, isolation. In his memoirs, chemistry professor Michele Giua, a GL activist incarcerated first in Rome and then in Castelfranco Emilia, recalled that fragmented international news found its way in, so that 'there was discussion of political events' such as the Ethiopian War, the Spanish Civil War, or the outbreak of World War II.[76] News of the Rossellis' murder

---

76 Michele Giua, *Ricordi di un ex-detenuto politico, 1935–1943*, Turin: Chiantore, 1945.

reached their cell in June 1937, and the prisoners from GL responded by sending a message of solidarity to their militant Parisian comrades, which was secretly relayed through Rossi's mother. Contrary to the prisoners' expectations, however, the letter was not published in the weekly *GL* so as not to put them into further danger.[77] The painful experience of prison is conveyed in a poignant letter that Rossi wrote to Salvemini:

> I have been alone in my cell for so many months without exchanging more than ten words with the warden looking through the flap. I have spent so many years without seeing a flower, a tree, a colour to break the monotony of the prison walls, without running my hand across the velvety fur of a cat, or through the soft hair of a child, without hearing the laughter of a young girl, the sound of the wind in the forest, that I seem to have shrivelled up like a dry leaf between the pages of a book, as parched as a pumice stone. Books, books, and only books.[78]

In fact, Rossi, Bauer, Foa, and Mila read a lot during those years, both individually and collectively, borrowing books from the prison library or from other libraries with the permission of the prison management. Letters from prison were often valuable means in themselves of requesting books, discussing readings, taking notes and recording thoughts. Books permitted one to 'explore the world so as to prepare for the future', in Foa's words.[79] Paradoxically, this place of Fascist oppression thus became a training ground for the new antifascist leadership.

The central problem in the reflections of, and the discussions involving, Foa, Mila, Rossi, and Bauer during their imprisonment concerned the construction of the state and the various meanings of liberalism, understood as both an institutional form and a political culture. Croce's idealism was the favourite target of the ironic (sometimes sarcastic) arguments put forward by Ernesto Rossi, with his sound positivist background enriched

---

77   Ernesto Rossi, 'In morte dei fratelli Rosselli', in Giuseppe Armani (ed.), *Ernesto Rossi. Un democratico ribelle*, Parma: Guanda, 1975, 150–4.

78   Ernesto Rossi and Gaetano Salvemini, *Dall'esilio alla Repubblica: lettere 1944–1957*, ed. Mimmo Franzinelli, Turin: Bollati Boringhieri, 2004, 5.

79   Vittorio Foa, 'In carcere con Ernesto Rossi', in Ernesto Rossi, *'Nove anni sono molti'. Lettere dal carcere 1930–39*, ed. Mimmo Franzinelli, Turin: Bollati Boringhieri, 2001, X.

by the study of economics and law. His reading of Croce's *History of Europe* revealed both similarities and differences in their respective conceptions of liberal philosophy. He rejected the contrast between liberal and democratic ideals as set forth in the chapter titled 'Opposing Religious Faiths'. Rossi pointed to said ideals' 'common pursuit of individual liberty, civil and political equality, and popular sovereignty'. Democracy, he said, was 'the only form of political organization through which that part of the liberal ideal can be realized which can function under the concrete conditions of society': insightfully, he argued that it was therefore conceivable to have 'illiberal democracy, but not liberalism without democracy'.[80] Consequently, Rossi, Foa, Mila, and Bauer tried to understand the structural changes in the state–economy relationship triggered by World War I and reinforced by the 1929 economic crisis. From their cell in Regina Coeli, GL's members were able to follow the European debates conducted during the interwar period, which analysed the various techniques of political intervention in production systems and the methods used by the state to redistribute wealth: one of the focal points of these debates was the severe criticism of the Soviet model of planning. Not surprisingly, confronted with the efforts being made to construct the ideological and legal framework of the Fascist corporate system, Rossi, Foa, Mila, and Bauer followed the line of the liberal critique of etatism. At the centre of these debates were works such as *Collectivist Economic Planning: Critical Studies on the Possibilities of Socialism*, which was edited by Friedrich Hayek, published in 1935 and included a contribution by Ludwig von Mises. This multi-authored work rejected the public sector's attempts to dominate and control all economic resources. An inveterate opponent of communism on both ethical and philosophical grounds, Rossi was particularly intrigued by the reformist line that emerged from Philip H. Wicksteed's 'common sense political economy' and Arthur C. Pigou's 'welfare economics'. Basing himself on the same reading, Foa focused on the historical and theoretical problem of a liberalism that moved beyond Croce's categories and a unionism that overcame Sorel's militant conception of the myth of the general strike. Following up on his reflections on Fascist corporatism set out in the *Quaderni di GL* of 1933–34, Foa argued

---

80   Letter of Ernesto Rossi, 4 March 1932, in Ernesto Rossi, *Elogio della galera: lettere, 1930–1943*, Bari: Laterza, 1968, 109.

that revolutionary syndicalism and its guild and corporatist heritage were now redundant.

Although aware of the nervous, increasingly tumultuous rhythms with which European crises had developed beyond the walls of Regina Coeli, the incarcerated members of GL loved to escape into the lengthy, slower rhythms of history. What fascinated them first and foremost was the Risorgimento: a 'history, you might say, made up exclusively of trials, banishments, policemen, and censorship. How many people were just like us!' Mila observed.[81] He then compared his experiences to those of 'the many distinguished minds who over the centuries have built up Italy's greatness from the depths of its prisons' and recognized 'the historical continuity of this great tradition'.[82] However, the analogy between the prisoners of the Habsburg Empire and those of the Fascist regime was merely evocative: the members of GL were highly conscious of the limitations of this self-representation. They read, among other things, Silvio Pellico's *Le mie prigioni* or Luigi Settembrini's *Ricordanze della mia vita* – the latter's recollections would be, according to Foa, 'incomprehensible to a twentieth-century political prisoner', with their 'mystical impurities'.[83]

It is unlikely that the dispute over the Risorgimento, which had split GL's Paris group in the spring of 1935, reached Regina Coeli Prison's inmates. Nevertheless, for them too, the reference to nineteenth-century Italy was part of an ongoing reflection on the moral significance of the nation and the historical construction of the nation-state. In arguing against Gioacchino Volpe's *Italia in cammino*, Mila explained that the Risorgimento, though 'the work of a minority and of bourgeois elites', nevertheless created the conditions for the 'rise' of the 'lower classes': 'After all, what great historical movement has not been accomplished by elites?' Mila quizzed.[84] Foa, meanwhile, was more critical of the 'rhetorical and

---

81   Letter of Massimo Mila, 3 July 1936, in Massimo Mila, *Argomenti strettamente famigliari. Lettere dal carcere 1935–1940*, ed. Paolo Soddu, Turin: Einaudi, 1999, 220.

82   Letter of Massimo Mila, 6 March 1936, in Mila, *Argomenti strettamente famigliari*, 183.

83   Letter of Vittorio Foa, 10 September 1937, in Vittorio Foa, *Lettere della giovinezza. Dal carcere (1935–1943)*, Turin: Einaudi 1998, 282.

84   Letter of Massimo Mila, 21 January 1938, in Mila, *Argomenti strettamente famigliari*, 428.

emotional background' of the Risorgimento, which led to 'comforting actions' due to an 'only apparent analogy' with the present. In fact, the ideals of the Risorgimento had recently undergone a profound transformation: 'The same terms are used to express very different things today.'[85]

The meaning and implications of 'nation' had changed more than anything else, and accordingly the legacy of the Risorgimento had to be reconsidered against the backdrop of imperial and ideological conflicts during the latter half of the 1930s. Both Rossi and Foa, who had maintained a strictly anti-Habsburg, Mazzinian stance towards the Risorgimento, changed their views to some extent. At a time when German-speaking writers born in Austria–Hungary were elaborating the posthumous myth of the Habsburg Empire, Rossi and Foa were engaged in reading Franz Werfel's *Twilight of a World* (1936). This and other works by Werfel, by Stefan Zweig and Joseph Roth, enabled GL's activists to identify a complacent, decadent attitude from the critical perspective that such writers harboured towards Europe as it emerged from the collapse of the continental empires following the Great War.[86] Ernesto Rossi had fought against the Austro-Hungarian monarchy and had been on the winning side in the war. During his first years in prison, memories of life in the trenches and the reasons for his idealistic volunteering had resurfaced. However, his encounter with Salvemini (and others) liberated his Mazzinian beliefs from such 'sentimental and non-logical dross'.[87] Despite having distanced himself from Werfel's lyrical (indeed, at times elegiac) tones, he now recognized that the Habsburg Empire had represented 'the necessary means by which different peoples could together pursue a common civilizing purpose, against disruptive materialistic forces deriving from a shared race, language, and economic interests'. Rossi continued:

> The endeavours of the Austro-Hungarian Empire in the last war showed how wrong were the diagnoses of those who saw that state as a grotesque jumble of different peoples oppressed by a common tyrannical power,

---

85   Letter of Vittorio Foa, 16 August 1938, in Foa, *Lettere della giovinezza*, 461.

86   For a still-fascinating analysis of the Habsburg myth in interwar Europe, see Claudio Magris, *Il mito absburgico nella letteratura austriaca moderna*, Turin: Einaudi, 2009 (1963).

87   Letter of Ernesto Rossi, 23 July 1937, in Rossi, *Elogio della galera*, 382.

and who predicted that it would fall to pieces at the first hurdle. And the heirs to the Empire are such that one can only pity this great defunct entity. So much for Mazzini's ideal of the liberation of the peoples! The few to whom the dignity of man still means something cannot help but feel disgust and horror at the insane and bloodthirsty furies originating from those nationalistic ideas which last century appeared a fundamental prerequisite for all political liberties and the cooperation of diverse peoples.[88]

Foa's reading of Werfel was stricter and more prudent than Rossi's. While welcoming Werfel's 'humanitarian attitude', Foa also noted that 'nostalgic and aesthetic aspects' outweighed 'genuinely critical and political' ones. In his view, the 'striving for a supranational ideal', far removed from the existing model of the state, could not boil down to having 'regrets about the past'.[89] Although he had been educated as a patriot, Foa wondered with growing unease whether the concept of 'national democracy' was not in fact an oxymoron. In his view, it was time to historicize the construction of the nation-state and to separate the principle of national independence, which to Mazzini was 'a necessary condition for freedom and cooperation among peoples', from the principle of absolute state sovereignty, which had fuelled the most aggressive forms of nationalism. A democratic constitution that institutionalized federal ties between states of varying degrees of civilization and strength would ensure a fair redistribution of benefits.[90]

Together with a radical rejection of nationalism, the challenge to absolute state sovereignty and its connection to war thus stimulated the reflections of GL's imprisoned activists. Ever since 1918, the economist Luigi Einaudi had been sharply critical of the League of Nations. He believed that, instead of fundamentally changing the notion of state sovereignty, it continued to rest on the division of the international order into nation-states and postponed the striving for a European federation indefinitely. Reading the British federalists showed the way to Rossi and his cellmates, as did the at-a-distance conversation with Luigi Einaudi. From the

---

88 Letter of Ernesto Rossi, 19 February 1939, in Rossi, 'Nove anni sono molti', 769.

89 Letter of Vittorio Foa, 2 July 1939, in Foa, Lettere della giovinezza, 646.

90 Letter of Vittorio Foa, 30 April 1937, in Foa, Lettere della giovinezza, 572–3.

mid-1930s on, Lord Lothian and Lionel Robbins analysed the crisis of the
European state-system, the resulting international anarchy, and the likeli-
hood of a new global war. Rossi and Foa's views, which were inspired by
Kant and Hamilton, drew mainly on the work of Robbins.[91]

In the late summer of 1939, news of the outbreak of war suddenly
disrupted the prisoners' meditations and discussions, not always centred
on current affairs. At the same time, it was a common belief that war was
an inescapable, albeit tragic, step to be taken towards defeating Fascism.
However, both Foa and Mila immediately realized the civil, fratricidal
nature of a conflict tearing apart European societies. From his cell in
Regina Coeli, Foa continued to hope it were possible to 'abolish, not all
wars in all possible forms, but the wars of the European nations, the "civil
wars" of Europe'.[92] Even in the next spring of 1940, in the face of the enormous expansion of Nazi Germany in Europe, Foa would not be discour-
aged: 'I know very well that even when all the institutions on which we
base our faith in a tolerable future have fallen in Europe, nothing is yet lost
if they remain alive in the minds of a few thousand Europeans; and against
this spiritual tension Germany's army can have little influence.'[93] On a
slightly more pessimistic note, when war broke out, Mila confided to his
mother that it was a 'very difficult time, one of great upheavals and essentially religious struggles'. However, he believed that 'apart from the obvious
moral considerations', it was necessary to 'master it, indeed everything,
with an intelligent mind'. In this respect Mila and his fellow prisoners, who
'lived in times made disastrous by the struggle between opposing views',
were apt to compare themselves to the reformers of the sixteenth
century.[94]

This analogy, which was central to GL's self-representation, reveals a
deeper layer of their culture that has been repeatedly touched upon, but
still needs to be properly explored.

---

91   See John Pinder, 'Federalism in Britain and Italy: Radicals and the English
Liberal Tradition', in Peter M. R. Stirk, *European Unity in Context: The Interwar
Period*, London: Pinter Publishers, 1989, 201–22.

92   Letter of Vittorio Foa, 10 September 1939, in Foa, *Lettere della giovinezza*,
676–7.

93   Letter of Vittorio Foa, 19 May 1940, in Foa, *Lettere della giovinezza*, 825.

94   Letter of Massimo Mila, 10 September 1939, in Mila, *Argomenti strettamente
famigliari*, 680.

In the Footsteps of Heretics and Utopians

The signing of the Lateran Treaties in February 1929 not only put an end to the political and religious conflict between the Italian state and the Roman Catholic Church that had been ongoing since 1870; it also opened up an unprecedented, immense cultural space for Fascism and Catholicism to interact and intertwine (but also to compete and conflict) in Italy's nation-building process. In a speech delivered to the Senate on 24 May 1929, Benedetto Croce recalled that the first seeds of 'secular thought and institutions towards the Church' dated back to the beginnings of the Risorgimento. However, during the protracted process of estrangement between liberalism and Catholicism, the 'protomartyr' had been Pietro Giannone, an eighteenth-century representative of a secular culture combating institutionalized religion. In *Politics and Morals* (1931), Croce set out the theoretical premises of his reflections on the decline of traditional religions and the meaning of the recent confrontation between liberalism and authoritarianism. However, it was above all his work *History of Europe in the Nineteenth Century* (1932) that conveyed to GL the need for an extraordinary relaxation of intellectual boundaries, by projecting the question of Fascism far beyond the national context. The concept of the 'religion of liberty', which summed up the logic inherent in the historical process witnessed between the Restoration and the Great War, summarized Croce's reflections on the 'meta-political' foundations of liberalism, set against the background of the 1930s European crisis.

Up until the mid-1930s, GL had adopted a bitter anticlerical argument and a strictly liberal position regarding the separation of the state and the Church. However, the Church's open and convinced participation in the Ethiopian War in the name of a Christian civilizing campaign marked a turning point. Accordingly, GL radicalized its anticlerical orientation, and by the mid-1930s it began to put forward anti-Catholic, if not decidedly atheistic, arguments.[95] The 'task of the revolutionaries' was to 'take an axe to the root of the trees': this is how Rosselli and Calosso summed up the meaning of the 'Manifesto agli Italiani' published in September 1935.[96]

---

95 For a more detailed analysis, see Marco Bresciani, 'Giellisti come utopisti ed eretici', *Contemporanea* 1, January–March 2017, 31–62.

96 [Carlo Rosselli,] 'Che cosa è stato il convegno di "Giustizia e Libertà" ', *GL*, 20 September 1935.

This metaphor already appeared in a short note that Calosso wrote in *GL* a few days prior to the publication of the 'Manifesto'. In his view, the crisis of the modern world was unmistakeably a 'religious crisis', comparable to that of the 'decaying pagan world'. The antifascists could thus be the 'heirs to Christianity', 'but only on condition that they first supersede and bury it with that piety which sons owe to their fathers'. In Calosso's opinion: 'One does not put new wine into old casks. The axe is at the root of the trees. Our religion is atheistic, immanentist, humanistic: anti-Catholic, anti-Christian, anti-theistic'.[97] Despite their friendship, Croce and Calosso's positions increasingly diverged: the latter distanced himself from the former's notion of 'the religion of liberty' and embraced the heretical and rebellious ideas that had led, by subterranean routes, to the emergence of socialism and communism. Calosso benefited from the religious studies that had recently flourished on the ground of the 'immanentist orientations of contemporary Italian philosophy'. Given the increasingly close relationship between the Fascist regime and Catholicism, which had marginalized Gentile and actualism, Calosso prioritized the prospect of religious revolution over the liberal solution to the relationship between Church and state. In his view, Fascism represented the denunciation of the 'real vacuum' present in socialist culture, thus raising a 'religious problem'. Accordingly, an antifascist revolution 'in these hard and surprising times' could be nothing other than a 'radical religious revolution'.[98] Since 'Marxist politics' had not been able to recognize the novel nature of post-1914 Europe, in which the war between nations had turned into a 'religious war', opposition to Fascism had to stand 'on its own ground'.[99] From this point of view, Calosso intertwined Mazzini's national revolutionary legacy with the need for the religious renewal of socialism. However, only a recourse to the irrational, mythical, and symbolic dimension of the Risorgimento could allow the uncompromising antifascism of GL to compete with Fascism with regard to mass mobilization.

GL's radical shift towards the Catholic standpoint in 1935 contributed to inflaming the argument between Rosselli and Salvemini: while the latter

---

97   C. [Umberto Calosso], note to Angelo Crespi, 'Polemica sulla Chiesa', *GL*, 13 September 1935.

98   Umberto Calosso, 'Rivoluzione antisacerdotale', *GL*, 21 February 1936.

99   C. [Umberto Calosso], 'Gli "idoli gialli" ', *GL*, 29 May 1936.

distinguished between ecclesiastical institutions and the community of believers, and sought to salvage a popular form of Catholicism, the former insisted on the need for liberal anticlericalism, although he rejected the harsher currents of anti-Catholicism. In a letter to Rosselli, Salvemini argued that the positions of the Vatican and the wider Catholic community regarding the Abyssinian conflict should be distinguished, for reasons of propaganda as well as truth. The leader of GL accepted Salvemini's advice; however, while, for Salvemini, this was a distinction 'on principle', for Rosselli, it was a distinction 'only for the purposes of expediency'.[100] Garosci, more attentive to the political and legal aspects of religious questions, explained his own position in a lecture delivered at the Salle de la Mutualité in Paris in January 1936. Since the Reformation, he said, the Church, a 'reactionary force in modern society', had striven to prevent the 'liberation of Man'; it had contributed to the establishment of state sovereignty because this was based on a direct relationship with the source of divine legitimacy. While the antifascist revolution had to attempt to destroy both state and Church, it also had to 'develop in Man an awareness of human values, a sense of his own dignity and abilities', and to 'transfer religious feeling from the transcendent God to humanity'. In a departure from his initial acceptance of liberal separatism, Garosci espoused a jurisdictionalist, state-led reform perspective during the transitional phase before the new social and religious bonds unfolded.[101]

These reflections derived from Garosci's historical research into the political thought of Jean Bodin and the theory of national interest, built principally on the works of the philosopher of law Gioele Solari and of the historian Frederick Meinecke. Garosci's reflections were formulated against a backdrop of intense debate going back to the 'circulation of Italian thought in Europe at the end of Renaissance philosophy'.[102] Garosci's study of the origins of modern state sovereignty drew on the thinking of Francesco Ruffini, a professor at the University of Turin who lost his job when he refused to swear an oath to the Fascist regime in 1931. Garosci

---

100   Curzio [Carlo Rosselli], 'Pio XI o Chiesa cattolica?', *GL*, 15 August 1935.

101   Magrini [Aldo Garosci], 'La Chiesa in Italia e i problemi della rivoluzione', *GL*, 24 January 1936.

102   Aldo Garosci, *Jean Bodin. Politica e diritto nel Rinascimento francese*, Milan: Corticelli, 1934, 7.

recognized the value of Ruffini's teaching, which was grounded in a 'belief in liberty' dating back to before the World War I, and strengthened by his friendship with Gobetti and with the journal *La Rivoluzione Liberale*. Ruffini's studies had focused on Matteo Gribaldi Mofa, Celio Secondo Curione, Bernardino Ochino, Fausto and Lelio Socino, all 'Italian Protestants who, during the Reformation, represented the proliferation of democracy and freedom, and were the first to spread the idea of tolerance'.[103] Following this inspiration, a profound correlation emerged between the GL exiles' self-representation and their analysis of the heretical experience of the sixteenth century, in Franco Venturi's 1935 review of Frederic Church's book, *The Italian Reformers, 1534–1564*. According to Venturi, this study of 'the first significant wave of Italian exiles' collected 'the memories of the restles force that Protestant exiles had acquired as a result of their constant rebellion against the world of the Inquisition'.[104] The gist of Venturi's review chimed with Delio Cantimori's introduction, which claimed that Frederic Church had overlooked the irregulars and heretics, no less despised and repressed by the Roman Catholic Church than they were by the Geneva and Württemberg churches.[105] Tellingly, Cantimori considered the Italian exponents of the Reformation to have been 'the first émigrés [*fuoriusciti*] as a result of their ideas, in the history of modern Europe', in a context where this term applied to the exiled antifascists.[106]

At that time, Venturi began to study the Enlightenment *philosophes* by focusing on the writings of Denis Diderot. He turned to the eighteenth century at a moment when the communists, having introduced the Popular Front policy, were trying to appropriate eighteenth-century French culture by proposing a materialist, anti-bourgeois reading of Diderot. Commenting on one of Diderot's dictums ('The day will be hard'), Venturi shared the eighteenth-century revolutionary perspective: 'To give

---

103   A. Magrini [Aldo Garosci], 'Francesco Ruffini. Ricordi di un suo allievo', *La Libertà*, 5 April 1934.

104   Gianfranchi [Franco Venturi], 'Una storia di fuoriusciti', *GL*, 13 December 1935, review of Frederic Church, *I Riformatori italiani*, Florence: Sansoni, 1935 (1932).

105   Delio Cantimori, 'Prefazione del traduttore', in Church, *I Riformatori italiani*, 16.

106   Delio Cantimori, 'Recenti studi intorno alla Riforma in Italia e ai riformatori italiani all'estero (1924–34)', *Rivista Storica Italiana*, 1936, fasc. 3, in Cantimori, *Storici e storia*, Turin: Einaudi, 1971, 468, 480.

morals to people means increasing their energy, for good and for ill; it encourages them to commit great crimes and to display great virtues, if you will.'[107] When he visited Leningrad between December 1936 and January 1937, he was able to see the extent of the crimes and the virtues of the Soviet experiment first-hand: his desire to study works from Diderot's archives gave him the opportunity to get an insider's view of the Soviet society that so fascinated him. Accordingly, in his 'Note dalla Russia' published in January–February 1937, he drew a 'parallel between the eighteenth century and certain aspects of communist civilization', although he made no mention of Stalin's Great Terror.[108]

Many intellectuals saw communism as a response to the 'need to resume and develop the movement of "Enlightenment" ', as the sociologist Georges Friedmann, a friend of Venturi's, put it.[109] Unlike the Marxists, who sought to reconcile the Enlightenment and historical materialism, Venturi established a far-reaching correlation between the claim to a heretical heritage, the passion for republican and democratic utopias, and the pursuit of a 'different' communism.[110] He brought together the various aspects of the national, social, and religious questions, and examined the future prospects for socialism and communism, while at the same time remaining critical of the Marxist tradition. As early as 1937 Venturi took an interest in Filippo Buonarroti, the Pisan revolutionary who one hundred years after his death was remembered as the main player of the Babeuf Conspiracy – 'the first great attempt to put into practice the dreams of civil and economic equality held by so many men of the eighteenth century,

107   Gianfranchi [Franco Venturi], 'Lettere di Diderot', *GL*, 29 March 1935.
108   Gianfranchi [Franco Venturi], 'Le strade di Leningrado', *GL*, 15 January 1937.
109   Georges Friedmann, *Journal de guerre, 1939–1940*, Paris: Gallimard, 1987, 142–3 (10 January 1940), but also Franco Venturi, *Utopia and Reform in the Enlightenment*, Cambridge: Cambridge University Press, 1971 (1970), 1–17.
110   Edoardo Tortarolo, 'La rivolta e le riforme. Appunti per una biografia intellettuale di Franco Venturi (1914–1994)', *Studi settecenteschi*, XV, 1995, 9–38; Edoardo Tortarolo, 'L'esilio della libertà. Franco Venturi e la cultura europea degli anni Trenta', in Luciano Guerci and Giuseppe Ricuperati (eds), *Il coraggio della ragione. Franco Venturi intellettuale e storico cosmopolita*, Turin: Fondazione Einaudi, 1998, 89–114; Bronisław Baczko, 'Curiosità storica e passioni repubblicane', in Franco Venturi, *Pagine repubblicane*, ed. Manuela Albertone, Turin: Einaudi, 2004, VII–XXXI.

and the last attempt to revive, in a reactionary climate, the true spirit of the French Revolution.[111]

Meanwhile, Venturi continued his original research into minor Enlightenment figures such as the Benedictine monk Dom Deschamps, the engineer and philosopher Nicolas-Antoine Boulanger, and the economist Count Francesco Dalmazzo Vasco. His doctoral dissertation on the adventures and thoughts of a 'Piedmontese ideologue' like Vasco led him to raise two fundamental questions that also bore on Italy's historical development: the need for an 'enlightened' ruling class and the prospect of social equality based on natural law. Venturi thus assimilated the suggestion of Gobetti, who had sought 'the origins of a free Italy' in eighteenth-century Piedmont. Compared to the 1935 argument with Caffi and Chiaromonte, Venturi's assessment of national revolutionary tradition had taken on a more critical tone, while his judgement of Gobetti's *Risorgimento senza eroi* (1926) had now become decidedly positive.[112] However, it was in following Diderot that Venturi more closely interrelated history and politics: his *Jeunesse de Diderot*, published in Paris in 1939, was dedicated to the memory of Carlo Rosselli. For Venturi, Diderot had been able to 'give political meaning to the French Enlightenment' by expressing through the *Encyclopédie* 'an enthusiasm, an energy, and a form that made France the centre of Enlightened Europe'. This corresponded to the 'partial realization of his dream of a group of free people who, like a leaven, a "levain précieux, changeraient toute la masse" '.[113] Garosci sympathized with Venturi's attempt to situate Diderot in the field of politics – politics 'of course in the broad sense, that is, the creation and establishment of those sentiments, those general values, that are the true political institutions, and that transcend the struggle for direct power, for politics in the narrow sense'.[114]

The thorny question of politics and its ambivalent meaning, characteristic of so much of GL's reflections, resurfaced once again. Despite their close relationship, however, the rapprochement between Garosci and

111   Gianfranchi [Franco Venturi], 'Filippo Buonarroti, primo egualitario (1837–1937)', *GL*, 13 August 1937.

112   See Franco Venturi, *Francesco Dalmazzo Vasco (1732–1794)*, Paris: Librairie E. Droz, 1940, 8.

113   Franco Venturi, *Giovinezza di Diderot (1713–1753)*, Palermo: Sellerio editore, 1988 (1939), 22–3, 269.

114   Magrini [Aldo Garosci], 'Diderot politico', *GL*, 28 July 1939.

Venturi was only of a partial nature. In the latter half of the 1930s, Garosci began to reassess his own revolutionary position at the time of the Popular Front and the Spanish Civil War, by engaging with early nineteenth-century liberalism through Edgar Quinet, Benjamin Constant, and Madame de Staël. However, his most decisive reading in 1938 was that of Aldo Capitini's *Elementi di un'esperienza religiosa* (1937). Capitini, together with Guido Calogero, was the founder of the liberal-socialist movement that developed in the late 1930s in Pisa and Perugia. Capitini cultivated an antifascism that was sceptical of any militant and totalizing conception of politics. His original syncretism, which started from the crisis of Gentile's idealism and engaged with Kant and Gandhi, formed the philosophical and religious foundation of his theory of persuasion and non-violence.

Unlike Venturi and Garosci, Calosso rejected the definition of 'politics' as applied to Diderot's thoughts and actions, recalling how the watchword *politique d'abord*, coined by eighteenth-century revolutionary radicals, had been adopted by the founder and leader of Action française, Charles Maurras. According to Calosso, it was thus necessary to touch on 'something deeper and more secret' than the 'grandiose diplomatic breakthrough of global antifascism' – namely, 'the religious essence of the Italian antifascist experience'.[115] In his *Colloqui col Manzoni* (1940), a book devoted to the Catholic author of the famous novel *The Betrothed*, Calosso established a surprising convergence between the rejection of the Fascist imperial project, the socialist renewal of nationalism, and the adoption of a personalized form of Catholicism. He recognized the connection between Mazzini and Manzoni 'on a level other than that of politics'. Regardless of the primacy of national unity or of local actions over international initiatives, this connection mainly lay in the 'call for a moral conscience', transforming the Risorgimento into 'an attempt at an Italian religious revolution, albeit a rather ragged and unfinished one'.[116] From this point of view, the recurring topos of the 'failed Reformation' took on a new and original character that combined an anti-classical, anti-rhetorical, modern version of Christian Romanticism, a rejection of Alfieri and Leopardi's pessimism, and an affinity with Kant's moral assertions. While the concept of religion formulated

---

115   Umberto Calosso, Postcard, 5 [August?] [19]39, Family Archive Franco Venturi (Turin).

116   Umberto Calosso, *Colloqui col Manzoni*, Bari: Laterza, 1948 (Malta: 1940), 35.

by Calosso was permeated by irrational and romantic elements, Venturi knitted together the various threads of a complex historical plot that originated with the Italian philosopher Tommaso Campanella, 'so modernly natural, rational and enlightened'. Campanella's major work, *The City of the Sun* (1602), actually contained the initial seed of 'modern political religion' – that is, of communism.[117] Inspired by Croce's youthful essay on Campanella's communism, however, Venturi believed that the requirements of reason and nature that had helped define the new category of 'praxis' had been primarily affirmed during the Enlightenment. Garosci, in turn, recognized in Campanella an 'unshakable force' in intellectual and political terms. His 'prophetic' greatness lay not so much in his ability to affect reality in the short term, but in his capacity to rouse the long-term transformative potentials to be found in the depths of society. The myth of a natural religion, on which Campanella's idea of a communist society was based, had paved the way for the utopias of the eighteenth century. In *The City of the Sun*, Garosci singled out the source of the 'rationalist communist myths' that persisted as an 'extremely solid and unassailable substratum' in the modern socialist movement.[118]

GL thus worked to restore the 'religious' dimension of modern forms of socialism and communism through its research into, and discussions of, the seventeenth-century heretical legacy, an Enlightened critique of utopian literature, and the elaboration of a new category of justice. Benedetto Croce drew people's attention to the emergence of a rational, positive, natural religion established by the 'Italian reformers' who had come to the rationalism of Bruno, Campanella, Vico, and Giannone against the background of the sixteenth-century crisis. Unlike Gentile, Croce downplayed the idea of a 'failed Reformation' resulting in national decadence, and instead knit together the deep-rooted threads linking the Renaissance and the Risorgimento via the Baroque age.[119]

These historical and philosophical discussions reverberated around the walls of Regina Coeli Prison, where the inmates Rossi, Mila, Bauer,

---

117   Gianfranchi [Franco Venturi], 'Centenario di Campanella: uomo e natura', *GL*, 30 June 1939.

118   Magrini [Aldo Garosci], 'Ragione e eguaglianza solare', *GL*, 30 June 1939.

119   Benedetto Croce, 'La crisi italiana del Cinquecento e il legame del Rinascimento col Risorgimento', *La Critica*, November 1939, 401–11.

and Foa were anything but insensitive to the question of religious freedom and its distant roots in Humanism, the Renaissance, and the Baroque
age. In 1932, Croce's theory was that 'spiritual upheavals' occurred 'from
the top down'; he declared himself in favour of the Calvinist suppression
of anti-Trinitarians and Anabaptists in mid-sixteenth-century Geneva. In
his view, the latter's beliefs led to 'extreme democratism and communism'
through the cultivation of 'intellectualist radicalism and egalitarianism'.[120]
Cantimori argued fiercely against the Neapolitan philosopher and his
'distrust of any extremist radicalism' that led him to accept the necessity
of authoritarianism to strengthen tolerance and religious freedom.[121] In
contrast to Croce and in agreement with Cantimori, Mila sympathized
with the 'Italian reformers' (especially the Socinians) and acknowledged
their role in the formation of a 'modern secular and democratic religiosity'. As opposed to Ruffini and his 'somewhat rhetorical consideration of
these heretics as mere precursors of the modern doctrines of tolerance',
Foa shared the perspective of Cantimori's book, *Eretici italiani del
Cinquecento* (1939), whereby the religious radicalism of the sixteenth-
century heretics was 'a genuine expression of the Italian Renaissance'.
Taking up Cantimori's attack on Croce, he dismissed 'the abstractionism
and utopianism that idealist historians tended to attribute to the heretical
movement'. Finally, in linking his passion for the Risorgimento with that
for the Renaissance, he sketched a form of self-representation by the 'GL
collective' that referred to the history of the 'heretics of Italy' and to a
national tradition based on 'a rebellious, subversive spirit, intolerant of all
authority and hierarchy, an uncompromising champion of the freedom of
conscience'.[122]

Ever responsive to the feverish, short-term actions of the political struggle, GL also engaged in a patient, long-term contest with Fascism over Italy's
cultural traditions. It revived the circulation of ideas between the Humanist
age and the Renaissance, and reconsidered their relationship with the
Risorgimento: it thus appropriated the deep-lying, stratified heretical ideas

120 Benedetto Croce, 'Il marchese di Vico Galeazzo Caracciolo' (1932) in *Vite
di avventure di fede e di passione*, Milan: Adelphi, 1989, 208, 265.
121 Delio Cantimori, 'Recenti studi intorno alla Riforma in Italia e ai riformatori italiani all'estero (1924–34)', *Rivista Storica Italiana*, 1936, fasc. 3, in *Storici e
storia*, Turin: Einaudi, 1971, 468, 480.
122 Letter of Vittorio Foa, 5 May 1940, in Foa, *Lettere della giovinezza*, 820–1.

that were also claimed by certain marginal sectors of radical Fascism. Moreover, it critically engaged with the cultures of the Enlightenment and Romanticism, which the Stalinist and Fascist tyrannies had respectively appealed to. Accordingly, by appropriating and reinterpreting the legacies of heretics and utopians, GL invented an unprecedented genealogy of liberalism and democracy, socialism and communism, while also contemplating their contradictions and ambivalences. In its pursuit of a new politics during the maelstrom of the European crisis, GL thus succeeded in anchoring the group's project for complete emancipation to the most solid and profound stratum of Italian national culture – that of religion.

5

A Posthumous (and Hidden) Vitality

From the Fall of Paris to the Resistance

Carlo Rosselli had been predicting war since the autumn of 1933. It eventually broke out in the late summer of 1939, but took unexpected forms following the pact between Hitler and Stalin and the Nazi–Soviet occupation of Poland. France was attacked and conquered by Germany between May and June, 1940: the democratic institutions of the Third Republic collapsed, leading to the establishment of the collaborationist Vichy regime. As a result, the lively world of exiles, rebels and persecuted intellectuals (including Hannah Arendt, Walter Benjamin, Rudolf Hilferding, and François Fejtö), all of whom had gathered in Paris in the 1920s and 1930s and were now forced to make a hasty flight southward, fell apart. This fate also befell the political parties and the representatives of Italian antifascism: the activists of GL disbanded when the German troops marched into the French capital. For those opposing Hitler and Mussolini, the fall of Paris was charged with an ambivalent meaning: on the one hand, it represented the 'end of a world', that of 'French democracy', which had been the outermost bulwark against Nazi and Fascist 'barbarism'; on the other hand, it meant the beginning of that longed-for war that alone could destroy Hitler and Mussolini's dictatorships. Garosci remained optimistic, despite 'the catastrophes that have occurred, the movements of crowds in the streets, phenomena that always have something of the primitive, telluric turmoil about them'. As he observed: 'The strange feeling is that of the world collapsing and yet at the same time everything appears to go on as before.'[1]

On closer examination, the 'strange defeat' of the French army in June 1940 actually marked the end of GL's existence as an organized group. It is not possible here to reconstruct the variety and complexity of the paths that the different members of GL took following the occupation of France, the next decisive step towards the establishment of the New Nazi Order in Europe. Many of them tried to cross the Atlantic, and quite a few succeeded. In the autumn of 1941, Chiaromonte, Cianca, and Garosci sought refuge in New York (where Salvemini, Bruno Zevi, and Lionello Venturi were already staying), while Valiani got to Mexico City where he met with anti-Stalinist dissidents such as Victor Serge and Julian Gorkin. In the meantime, between the winter of 1939 and the summer of 1940, some émigrés to America, like former GL members Salvemini, Ascoli, Tarchiani, Lionello Venturi, and later Garosci and Cianca, established the Mazzini Society. This association, led by the liberal Carlo Sforza, had two goals: to combat Fascist propaganda in the United States and to promote American intervention in the war, in order to found a democratic state in Italy. For their part, Mario Levi, Caffi, and Trentin fled in semi-clandestine fashion to Toulouse, where they cooperated in various ways with the French Resistance. Together with the American journalist Varian Fry and the German economist Albert O. Hirschman, Lussu helped refugees escape Marseille to Casablanca or Lisbon and then reach the US or Latin America.[2] Franco Venturi, for his part, was captured while crossing the Pyrenees and subsequently imprisoned in Spain (at Figueras), before being extradited to Italy and imprisoned in Avigliano (in Lucania). After moving to Brittany between 1939 and 1940, Carlo Levi returned to Florence, where he lived in semi-clandestinity. With Italy's entry into the war in June 1940, the Fascist

---

1   Letter from Aldo Garosci to his family, Lyon, 18 November 1940, in Ministero degli Interni, Direzione Generale Pubblica Sicurezza, Divisione Polizia Politica, fascicolo personale Aldo Garosci, busta 562, Archivio Centrale dello Stato (Rome).

2   For Lussu's involvement in this aid network for refugees in Marseille, see Varian Fry, *Surrender on Demand*, Boulder, CO: Johnson Books, 1997.

policy of repression intensified throughout the country. Regina Coeli Prison became less important than it had been in the 1930s, while the island of Ventotene became the confinement capital of Italy, and it was here that allegedly dangerous captives were sent, including GL members Rossi and Bauer. Foa was transferred to prisons farther away, first Civitavecchia and then Castelfranco Emilia. Ginzburg, as a 'foreign Jew', was deported, and then joined by his wife Natalia and children, in the village of Pizzoli in the Abruzzo Mountains.[3]

The Axis war and the construction of the New European Order entailed the fragmentation or destruction of national sovereignties. Resistance fighters throughout Europe stood up against Hitler and Mussolini's regimes, their occupations of other countries, and their multitude of collaborators, in the name of a patriotism that combined the pursuit of national liberation with various (liberal democratic, socialist, and communist) political projects for the reconstruction of their respective states after the end of the war. Meanwhile, scattered antifascist minorities reconsidered the federalist thinking that had emerged in the 1930s, adapting it to meet the urgent need for a comprehensive reorganization of post-Fascist, post-Nazi Europe.[4] Caffi and Valiani were more interested than Venturi and Chiaromonte in the prospect of a federal reordering of Europe, while Foa, Lussu, Ginzburg, and Levi favoured federalism as the key to the renewal of the nation-state. Federalist Europeanism found its highest, organic expression in *Per un'Europa libera e unita. Progetto di un manifesto*, the so-called Ventotene Manifesto, written during the winter of 1941 and the spring of 1942 by Ernesto Rossi and Eugenio Colorni together with the ex-communist Altiero Spinelli during their confinement on the island. Spinelli was inspired by British federalists such as Lothian and Robbins, while distancing himself from Proudhonian-style social federalism and ultimately advocating a radical abolition of state and national

---

3   A wonderful account of Leone Ginzburg's everyday life in internal exile at Pizzoli can be read in Natalia Ginzburg, 'Winter in the Abruzzi', in *The Little Virtues*, New York: Arcade Publishing, 1989.

4   In general, see Mark Mazower, *Hitler's Empire: How the Nazis Ruled Europe*, London: Penguin, 2008, and István Deák, *Europe on Trial: The Story of Collaboration, Resistance, and Retribution during World War Two*, London: Routledge, 2018; for the complexities of the Italian 1943–45 experience, see Claudio Pavone, *A Civil War: A History of Italian Resistance*, London: Verso, 2014 (1991).

sovereignty. A clandestine edition of the manifesto was circulated in Rome by Colorni in 1944.[5]

The German attack on the Soviet Union in the summer of 1941 marked a clear turning point in the war and, together with American intervention the following winter, helped create the conditions for a broad antifascist alliance. The former members of GL tried to come to terms with this breakthrough, but, at the same time, felt compelled to reframe earlier political analyses and discourses. Although the Pd'A was quite different from (and in some respects unrelated to) GL, some of the threads of GL's reflections and conversations during the period from 1941 to 1945, which were interwoven with those of 1938–41, should be considered here. A critical, comparative assessment of Soviet Communism and its convergences with Fascism and Nazism, as part of an overall view of the European crisis, had been carried out prior to the Hitler–Stalin pact. Despite the Soviet Union's subsequent participation in the war against the Axis powers, former members of GL like Venturi, Garosci, and Valiani continued their search (each in his own way) for a socialism that was 'different' from the existing one. Nevertheless, the experience of wartime exile in the US was highly influential in terms of a critical reassessment of socialism, communism, and Marxism through the prism of totalitarianism. Notably, Chiaromonte hooked up with the intellectual networks around the magazines *politics* and *Partisan Review*, in conversation with the radical, pacifist, and anti-communist figures of New York culture (such as Dwight Macdonald, Philip Rahv, Mary McCarthy, and Lionel Abel) as well as with German exiles like Hannah Arendt.[6]

Between late 1942 and early 1943, the tide of world conflict turned: from North Africa to the Soviet Union, the advance of the antifascist coalition forced the Axis powers onto the defensive. This enabled the former members of GL to return to Italy from exile or leave their prisons or places of confinement after 25 July 1943, the day Mussolini's regime fell. Only then did many of them join the Pd'A, which had been constituted during a secret meeting held on 4 June 1942. Its programme consisted of seven points,

---

5   Altiero Spinelli and Ernesto Rossi, *Il Manifesto di Ventotene*, Milan: Mondadori, 2006.

6   See Gregory D. Sumner, *Dwight Macdonald and the Politics Circle*, Ithaca, NY: Cornell University Press, 1996.

which included a parliamentary, federal republic, the establishment of a two-sector economy, agrarian reform, the separation of civil and religious powers, and the setting up of a European federation of democratic states. On 27 August 1943, Venturi, Ginzburg, Foa, and Rossi attended the founding meeting of the European Federalist Movement in Milan. The first Congress of the Pd'A was held in Florence, from 5 to 7 September.

That same September, the Nazi occupation of large parts of Italy, together with the advance of the Allies from south to north, led to the state's collapse, the establishment of the Republic of Salò and the formation of the first armed bands of resistance fighters. This triggered one of the numerous civil wars that accompanied the new Nazi order, resulting in the erosion and destruction of more or less recent state sovereignties. The Pd'A constituted partisan units that were given the name 'Giustizia e Libertà', as a kind of retrospective homage to GL. More than a decade of reflection on the crisis and transformation of the nation-state and on the prospect of civil war, along with their critical rethinking of the Risorgimento tradition and search for a new hybridization of socialism and nationalism, helped former members of GL to deal with a scenario that was not totally unexpected. Whether in the Piedmont valleys or in the Roman, Florentine, Milanese, or Torinese underground, they managed to combine their profound bond with the partisan struggle with a very comprehensive understanding of the European crisis, which they perceived as a 'European civil war'. For Venturi, as for Valiani, it was clear that a civil war was underway in the central and northern regions of Italy, one that would soon reveal its appalling fallouts. Leone Ginzburg was arrested on 20 November 1943 and on 5 February 1944; he was tortured and killed by the Nazis in the infirmary at Regina Coeli. A few weeks later, on 12 March, Trentin died in a clinic near Treviso, exhausted from his arrest and brutal detention in Padua since the previous November. Colorni was shot dead in Rome by militiamen from the Koch gang, on 28 May, when the city was on the brink of liberation. The contribution in blood of former GL members who perished during the course of the 1943–45 Italian civil war was extremely high.[7]

---

7 For an overall history of Pd'A, see Giovanni De Luna, *Storia del Partito d'Azione, 1942-1947*, Rome: Editori Riuniti, 1997 (1982); for a focus on the intellectuals in the 1943–45 civil war, see Marco Bresciani and Domenico Scarpa, 'Gli intellettuali italiani e la guerra civile (1943-1945)', in Sergio Luzzatto, Gabriele Pedullà, and Domenico

Between 1945 and 1946, the end of the civil war and the advent of the parliamentary Republic marked the culmination and conclusion of the previous phase of active politics, leaving a trail of disillusionment and bitterness for the former members of GL and Pd'A. At the same time, the coordinates within which ex-GL members had conceived the relationship between politics and culture under the Fascist regime, in exile as well as in hiding, and during the civil war, changed radically. It was no longer a matter of fighting the enemy with weapons, but of participating in public debates, electoral campaigns, parliamentary negotiations, social movements and collective actions. It was no longer possible to envision politics for small militant groups; it was necessary to mobilize for the organization of the masses. In that chaotic and brutal postwar period, the ex-militants of the Resistance presented (and felt) themselves more like losers than winners. Comparing their idealistic expectations with the actual political-institutional achievements, the gulf appeared unbridgeable – all the more so in light of the short-lived and unhappy electoral experience of the Pd'A. Torn by the discord between liberal and socialist camps, the Pd'A proved utterly inadequate to cope with the demands and imperatives of the mass politics that was already looming in the immediate postwar period, dominated by the Socialist, Communist and Christian Democrat parties. At the elections for the Constituent Assembly in June 1946, it suffered a thorough defeat; the following March, the Congress of Rome declared its dissolution.

The Knight and the Castle

In retrospect, it is clear that GL's political commitment depended on the changing nature and dynamics of Fascism from the 1920s to the 1940s. Carlo Rosselli and the other GL members moved within political, cultural, and social spheres that were increasingly constrained, conditioned and shaped by Mussolini's regime and its international reach. During the course of their political travails, which were often marked by uncertainty, fluctuation, and ambivalence, they tried to build an alternative to Fascism for both the present and the future, based on a definition of antifascism

---

Scarpa (eds), *Atlante storico della letteratura italiana*, vol. 3, *Dal Romanticismo a oggi*, Turin: Einaudi, 2012, 703–17.

that was understood differently depending on each one's education, culture, political practices, and perceptions, but which, in each case, served to legitimize their own claim to represent the nation. At the same time, following the rise of Hitler's regime from 1933 onwards, GL members were faced with numerous problems as well as opportunities for action, which assumed continental proportions and required a transnational European political and intellectual network. Even when they encountered opposition, objections, and contradictions, they were convinced that the alternative would be all the more credible and effective if it was measured against the profound changes that fascism had produced in Italian and European society, and that the solution to the Italian crisis had to be found within a European framework. All of them (in different ways) suspected or feared that antifascism (especially in its communist version) could be – or could become – the mere negation of fascism, or, indeed, a form of inverted fascism. While competing with other political organizations and ideologies, Rosselli and his comrades-in-arms laid claim to, and blended, different political traditions and cultures, and thus converted a merely negative understanding of antifascism into a new, positive one, that indeed moved beyond fascism itself. They went so far as to imagine in what ways the dichotomy between fascism and antifascism could be superseded, and tried to project themselves into a post-fascist era. This strategy was obviously not unique to GL and Rosselli in the variegated intellectual constellation of interwar Europe. For instance, George Orwell, the writer and libertarian socialist activist who also took part in the Spanish Civil War and denounced the crimes of Stalinism, wrote in 1940: 'We cannot struggle against fascism unless we are willing to understand it, a thing which both left-wingers and right-wingers have conspicuously failed to do – basically, of course, because they dared not.'[8]

A close analysis of the experience of GL shows how revolutionary antifascism could counter Fascism by appropriating and reversing certain aspects of its practice and culture. Reflecting on the meanings and implications of the socialist defeat in 1919–22 led GL's members to embrace

---

8 George Orwell, review of Franz Borkenau, *The Totalitarian Enemy*, London: Faber & Faber, 1940 (*Time and Tide*, 4 May 1940), in Sonia Orwell and Ian Angus (eds), *The Complete Essays, Journalism and Letters of George Orwell*, Boston: D. R. Godine, 1968, vol. 2, 25–6.

ideas of nationhood and revolution that were consistent with republican tradition, to reject any sort of determinism in their understanding of historical process and political struggle, and to elaborate original views of a constitutional democracy based on individual and collective rights. Accordingly, calls for mass mobilization conveyed through propaganda were inspired, if not shaped, by the experience and study of totalitarian movements and regimes in Fascist Italy and Nazi Germany, as well as in the Soviet Union. State intervention in the economy, state organization of the production and redistribution systems, and partial forms of planning and nationalization were often embraced by GL's members as part of their reflection on the social and political consequences of the 1929 Great Depression, with special attention to the middle classes. Not least in their close, dynamic engagement with a range of authoritarian and totalitarian right-wing parties, movements, governments, and regimes during the interwar period, GL's antifascists grappled with the problem of 'democracy' by critically assessing mass politics and seeking to go beyond nineteenth-century liberal systems. If in the aftermath of the fascist defeats and wartime catastrophes democracy unexpectedly flourished in post-1945 Western Europe, all these post-1929 political and economic cultures processed by GL certainly contributed to the constitutional and parliamentary institutions' legitimation, by transferring important political and social ideas from the interwar period to the postwar period and reshaping them in antifascist terms.

At the same time, GL's members had in mind the potential connections and oppositions between nation-state, empire, and Europe – issues highlighted by the Great War and the Russian Revolutions, the collapse of the continental empires, and the attempted construction of a New European Order and a New Mediterranean Order by Nazi Germany and Fascist Italy. On the one hand, the fascist conceptions of Europe and empire led GL to consider different ways of understanding antifascist nationalism (as opposed to Nazi and Fascist expansionism) and of reconfiguring the nation-state through various models of federalism. These discussions, preoccupying and often dividing GL as of the early 1930s, indirectly contributed to the post-1945 propensity to query absolute national sovereignty and legitimize the coordination and integration of (Western) European nation-states within supranational economic and political institutions. On the other hand, GL discussions, provoked by the Fascist war in

Ethiopia, around nation and empire as well as fascism and imperialism, laid the groundwork for an original and varied interweaving of antifascism and anti-imperialism. These ideological combinations then developed in the era of decolonization, denouncing the ambiguities between democracy and imperialism and endorsing anti-colonial struggles for emancipation from the great Western empires.[9] In all these respects it is impossible to account for the 'Trente Glorieuses' (the boom years of 1945–75) without understanding the crucial input of the interwar political and intellectual experiences of exiles in general, and of GL in particular.

Some former GL members, then members of Pd'A, played a crucial role in the building of constitutional democracy through the government of Ferruccio Parri (April–November 1945) and their participation in the Constituent Assembly (June 1946–December 1947). Notably, Foa, Lussu, and Carlo Levi remained on the terrain of active politics. Foa and Lussu joined the Socialist Party, while Levi was elected as an independent on the lists of the Italian Communist Party. Foa also played an influential political role as deputy secretary of the pro-communist trade unions, the Confederazione Generale Italiana del Lavoro (CGIL). At the same time, GL's legacy, strongly identified with the memory of Carlo Rosselli, became part of broader public memory within the parliamentary Republic founded in 1946. The GL leader's heroic sacrifice was hailed as a decisive step towards the building of the antifascist nation, and his name still graces street signs in many Italian towns. However, a pessimistic appraisal of the new post-liberal constitutional order quite soon emerged, despite significant democratic progress.[10] Foa, Lussu, and Carlo Levi combined the demand for a clear-cut break with the awareness of a deeper continuity, voicing the need for more radical, bottom-up forms of 'democracy' while,

---

9 Mark Mazower, 'Democracy Transformed: Western Europe, 1950–1970', in *Dark Continent: Europe's Twentieth Century*, London: Allen Lane, 1998, 290–331; Tony Judt, *Postwar: A History of Europe Since 1945*, London: Heinemann, 2005; and Martin Conway, *Western Europe's Democratic Age, 1945–1968*, Princeton, NJ: Princeton University Press, 2020.

10 On the 'cognitive dissonance' characterizing the relation between politics and culture in the post-1945 democratic transformation of Western Europe, see Mark Lilla, 'The Other Velvet Revolution: Continental Liberalism and Its Discontents', *Daedalus* 123, no. 2, Spring 1994, 129–57 (with specific references to GL and Pd'A, 136–7).

at the same time, expressing their fears of a return of 'Fascism' in clerical disguise.[11]

The experiences of GL and Pd'A spawned a dense, lively network of journals and associations offering a space for conversation between politics and culture. The need to renew the ruling class and to elaborate a new culture aimed at building democratic institutions on antifascist foundations marked all the trajectories of the ex-GL members, and at the same time opened up a range of various, differentiated, individual paths. The Florentine magazine *Il Ponte*, founded in 1945 and directed by Piero Calamandrei, lay at the centre of this cultural geography. The Giustizia e Libertà Association was constituted in Florence; its official organ was *Italia libera*, then *Italia socialista* under the direction of Garosci. In 1949, Mario Pannunzio founded the weekly magazine *Il Mondo*, the vehicle of a left-liberal line that included ex-GL members like Salvemini and Ernesto Rossi and took up the cudgels against both Christian Democracy and the Communist Party. In 1955, Rossi and Pannunzio, together with Valiani and Chiaromonte, founded the Radical Party, which drew on the libertarian, free-market, liberal vein of this political tradition. The Turin-based monthly magazine *Resistenza. Giustizia e Libertà*, featuring the collaborations of Garosci himself, Bobbio, Venturi, Alessandro Galante Garrone, Franco Antonicelli, and Giorgio Agosti, tried to revive GL's antifascist tradition, increasingly accentuating its anti-imperialistic tone over the 1960s and 70s. The periodical *Italia socialista* edited by Garosci, together with Paolo Vittorelli and Altiero Spinelli, expressed an anti-totalitarian socialist and European-federalist orientation. In turn, it forged relations with Ignazio Silone's *Europa Socialista*. In 1955, Silone and Chiaromonte formed the Association for the Freedom of Culture, opening up a new, albeit isolated, space for conversation that was decidedly critical of communism.

To be sure, all the former GL members rejected the possibility of adopting the Soviet Communist model in a democratic system, but most of them still cleaved to the Soviet myth and remained open to dialogue with the Italian Communist Party. In the polarizing context of the Cold War, their paths were seen as part of a 'third way' between East and West, communism and capitalism, the Soviet Union and the United States;

11   See Luca Polese Remaggi, *La democrazia divisa. Cultura e politica della sinistra democratica dal dopoguerra alle origini del centro-sinistra*, Milan: Unicopli, 2011.

however, their understanding of these terms was asymmetrical. Far from holding positive, consistent positions concerning this alleged 'third way', their critical attitudes implicitly or explicitly *assumed* the existence of Western democratic institutions and free public opinion. Notably, Garosci, Venturi, and Valiani drew on research from the late 1930s and early 1940s to propose increasingly critical visions of the Soviet experiment, in which criticism was mainly aimed at Stalin's totalitarian system so as to preserve the authors' links with the European revolutionary tradition. In following this trajectory, they engaged with different representatives of 'Cold War liberalism' such as Raymond Aron or Isaiah Berlin.[12] Based on his critical reassessment of his experiences in GL, Chiaromonte himself became one of the most original interpreters of Cold War liberalism. However, unlike Arthur Koestler, Aron, and Berlin, who yoked the defence of individual freedoms to political realism, he continued to search for a new sense of politics based on a minimal, personalized understanding of utopia as a foundation of liberal democracy. The magazine directed by Chiaromonte together with Silone, *Tempo presente*, belonged to a series of publishing and cultural ventures close to the Congress for the Freedom of Culture, such as *Preuves*, *Encounter*, or *Kultura*, that attracted the contribution of European intellectuals such as Albert Camus, Czesław Miłosz, Gustaw Herling-Grudziński, Jerzy Giedroyc, and Alexander Wat.

Despite mounting divergences during World War II, and especially the Cold War, all the paths of the former GL members were deeply shaped by the experiences and legacies of the 1930s. Revolutionary antifascism formed the indispensable ideological premise of Rosselli's group; but the great originality of GL's experiment stemmed from an unusual willingness to learn from fascism in order to better confront it. This approach, a combination of the practical and the theoretical, was the most distinctive

---

12 See Jan-Werner Müller, 'Fear and Freedom. On "Cold War Liberalism" ', *European Journal of Political Theory* 7, no. 1, 2008, 45–64; Jan-Werner Müller, *Isaiah Berlin and Cold War Liberalism*, Basingstoke: Palgrave Macmillan, 2019. For a different take, see Joshua L. Cherniss, *Liberalism in Dark Times: The Liberal Ethos in the Twentieth Century*, Princeton, NJ: Princeton University Press, 2021, including analyses of Albert Camus, Raymond Aron, and Isaiah Berlin. For a most recent, very critical take on 'Cold War liberalism', see Samuel Moyn, *Liberalism Against Itself: Cold War Intellectuals and the Making of Our Time*, New Haven, CT: Yale University Press, 2023.

feature of GL's activists, constantly oscillating between moralism and anti-moralism, ideology and anti-ideology, rhetoric and anti-rhetoric. In the midst of the antifascist struggle, GL's fundamental ethical and intellectual common denominator emerged as a range of concrete attitudes: intransigence towards oneself and forbearance towards others; anti-dogmatic experimentation in the present and a capacity for openness to the future; the need to take the enemy seriously and, in the face of its challenges, the willingness to self-correct (or to 'self-subvert', as Albert O. Hirschman put it) one's beliefs and behaviour.[13] This lesson, summarized by Carlo Ginzburg in the formula 'learning from the enemy', was already present in Croce's reflections on the *History of Europe* as well as in Foa's letter from prison, mentioned at p. 19 of this book: Croce's rereading of a page of Vico's *New Science*, concerning 'untoward events' recast as 'opportunities', formed the deepest root of this attitude. Following a similar inspiration, Foa again proposed the metaphor of the Knight and the Castle. These were understood as 'two models of action, in politics as in life in general': 'the model of the Castle that moves in straight lines, confronting and clashing on a given, inescapable ground; and that of the Knight that jumps sideways as it searches for different grounds and levels'.[14]

This metaphor was closely related to the history of GL. In the 1930s, Carlo Rosselli and his comrades-in-arms combined the two moves, that of the Knight and that of the Castle, one in relation to the other: in other words, they saw the uncompromising need to confront the enemy, together with an astounding willingness to move sideways and to go beyond it.

The game is constantly different, and always open.

---

13   The economist Albert Hirschman encountered GL's thinking thanks to his friendship with Eugenio Colorni, during his stay in Trieste between 1936 and 1938: see Albert O. Hirschman, *A Propensity to Self-Subversion*, Cambridge, MA: Harvard University Press, 1995, and Jeremy Adelman, *Worldly Philosopher: The Odyssey of Albert Hirschman*, Princeton, NJ: Princeton University Press, 2013.

14   Vittorio Foa, *Il cavallo e la torre. Riflessioni su una vita*, Turin: Einaudi, 1991, VII.

Index